W9-AXH-877

Teachers, Discourses, and Authority
in the
Postmodern Composition Classroom

FOR MY HUSBAND, FRED, WITH LOVE

Teachers, Discourses, and Authority in the Postmodern Composition Classroom

Xin Liu Gale

PE
1404
.G35
1996

State University of New York Press

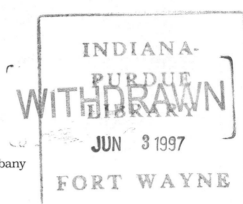

INDIANA-
PURDUE
LIBRARY
WITHDRAWN
JUN 3 1997
FORT WAYNE

Published by
State University of New York Press, Albany

© 1996 State University of New York

All rights reserved

Printed in the United States of America

No part of this book may be used or reproduced in any manner
whatsoever without written permission. No part of this book may be
stored in a retrieval system or transmitted in any form by any means
including electronic, electrostatic, magnetic tape, mechanical,
photocopying, recording, or otherwise without the prior permission in
writing of the publisher.

For information, address the State University of New York Press,
State University Plaza, Albany, NY 12246

Production by Christine Lynch
Marketing by Bernadette LaManna

Library of Congress Cataloging-in-Publication Data

Gale, Xin Liu, 1952–
    Teachers, discourses, and authority in the postmodern composition
classroom / Xin Liu Gale.
        p.   cm.
    Includes bibliographical references and index.
    ISBN 0-7914-2765-X (cloth : acid-free paper). — ISBN
0-7914-2766-8 (pbk. : acid-free paper)
    1. English language—Rhetoric—Study and teaching. 2. English
language—Discourse analysis. 3. English teachers—Training of.
4. Postmodernism. 5. Authority. I. Title.
PE1404.G35 1996
808'.042'07—dc 20   95-10268
                                                            CIP

10 9 8 7 6 5 4 3 2 1

AJE 8751

Contents

Foreword

Especially since the publication in 1969 of Paulo Freire's *Pedagogy of the Oppressed*, scholars in literacy studies and in rhetoric and composition have recognized that traditional power arrangements in the classroom are counterproductive and that learning is much more likely to occur when students are active participants in their own education—that is, when a significant portion of the teacher's "authority" is transferred to the students themselves. Xin Liu Gale's *Teachers, Discourses, and Authority in the Postmodern Composition Classroom* is a thorough examination of the role of teacher authority in the college composition classroom. Drawing on her years of experience as an English teacher both in China and in the United States, Gale attempts to mediate between two extreme positions: the traditional presentational model (Freire's "banking education") and the "radical" or "liberatory" position that attempts to redistribute authority in the classroom, especially by employing dialogic pedagogies and by teaching alternatives to the dominant discourse.

To some extent, most of us in rhetoric and composition, despite our ideological orientations, have, in one way or another, been interested lately in diminishing the teacher's classroom authority. As Gale points out, the cognitivists have placed distance between student performance and teacher expectation—though, as countless critiques have suggested, they ignore the social and political forces at play both in writing and in the classroom. The expressivists have made overt attempts to challenge teacher authority, perceiving teachers and discourse conventions as potentially damaging to students' ability to write and think with authenticity. And the social constructionists have been particularly eager, especially through their championing of collaborative learning, to devise ways to democratize the classroom, but their general belief that the task of the composition instructor is to help students enter a privileged academic discourse community undermines such attempts, since implicit in this scenario is the very same teacher-student hierarchy they ostensibly wish to subvert.

Of course, the most consistent and persistent effort to rearrange power hierarchies in the classroom derives from a group of

Freire-inspired scholar/teachers whom we associate with the terms "radical pedagogy" or "liberatory learning" and whom Gale terms "radical educationists." Such scholars perceive the traditional classroom as a site for the reproduction of dominant ideology and social inequality and attempt to, in Gale's words, "change teachers from oppressive figures working for the maintenance of the status quo into critical intellectuals struggling to make society more equal and democratic." However, even the radical educationists, those who are most associated with diminishing teacher authority, are, in Gale's analysis, potentially guilty of imposing a new and equally oppressive authority on students through their insistence on substituting the teaching of alternative discourses for the dominant discourse and through their "implicit conviction that radical theories are morally superior."

Although Gale generally supports the agenda of the radical educationists, she disagrees that the effort to replace the teaching of the dominant discourse with that of other discourses will ultimately result in change in either the traditional classroom or in the power and influence of the teacher's authority. In other words, all previous attempts to democratize the classroom, despite the source of these attempts, have on some level failed to account fully for the extent and pervasiveness of the teacher's authority and discourse and their effects on students. The teacher's discourse—that is, ideology (and dominant ideology, at that)—can never be separated from academic power and authority; a power relationship will always exist.

Influenced by the work of Mikhail Bakhtin, Pierre Bourdieu and Jean-Claude Passeron, Paulo Freire, Richard Rorty, and various poststructuralist theorists, Gale explores hitherto unexamined aspects of teacher-student power dynamics. Especially original is Gale's articulation of Rorty's distinction between normal and abnormal discourses. For Rorty, normal discourse constitutes the conventions, assumptions, values, and beliefs generally assumed by a discourse community. While Rorty himself defines abnormal discourse as both that discourse which challenges or subverts normal discourse as well as that which is ignorant or incognizant of the normal discourse, it is the former that most scholars in and out of composition have focused on. Gale reminds us that there are, in effect, *two* kinds of abnormal discourse (she terms them "responsive" and "nonresponsive" abnormal discourse), and she uses this distinction along with the notion of normal discourse as an analytical framework for exploring the role of teacher authority. To help accomplish this task, she borrows Rorty's concept of "edifying philosophers" and coins the term "edifying teachers": those who, while maintaining critical distance both from dominant culture and normal discourse, nevertheless "accommodate normal and abnormal discourses in teaching in such a way that the tension between the different, very often conflicting, discourses provides a space, or a context, for students to develop their own discourse." The resulting discussion is a sophisticated analysis of the role and effects of teacher authority and a thoughtful exploration of what we as teachers and scholars can do to work within the ever-present confines of a pedagogical hierarchy while still finding ways to empower students.

Perhaps what readers will find most interesting and revealing about *Teachers, Discourses, and Authority in the Postmodern Composition Classroom* is that the author uses her personal experience as an English teacher in China and her extensive knowledge of educational movements during the Cultural Revolution to support her theoretical, philosophical discussions. This personal dimension adds flesh and blood to an already insightful, intelligent, and revealing analysis. The work represents composition scholarship at its most mature and sophisticated and is a must for all serious scholars and teachers of literacy. It is a significant contribution to one of the most important scholarly conversations in literacy studies today.

Gary A. Olson
University of South Florida

Acknowledgments

I wish to thank Professor Gary A. Olson for his friendship, encouragement, and helpful review of the earlier draft and insightful suggestions for its improvement. I wish also to extend my thanks to my parents, professors of English in China, who passed on to me a passion for English literature and education in the darkest age in China's history; to my dear friends, Dean Emeritus Maynard M. Miller and Mrs. Joan Miller, who encouraged me to pursue my dream in a new world different from my own; to the president of China University of Geosciences, Professor Pengda Zhao, whose open-mindedness helped overcome the impossible hurdles to my pilgrimage to the West; and to Professor Evelyn Ashton-Jones, who most generously offered her help when I most needed it. To them I am forever grateful.

My deepest gratitude belongs to my husband, Fred, and my son, Qian, whose love and support sustained me through the writing of this book.

Chapter 1

Introduction

I don't feel it is necessary to know exactly what
I am. The main interest in life and work is to
become someone else you were not in the
beginning. If you knew when you began a
book what you would say at the end, do you
think you would have the courage to write it?
                                —Michel Foucault

University open admissions policies in the late 1960s fundamentally
changed American higher education and composition studies. Since
then, the discipline has witnessed a paradigm shift from the
current-traditional way of teaching to the process theories and pedagogies (Hairston 1982). This moving away from a basically teacher-
centered pedagogy toward more student-centered teaching has
brought teacher authority to the limelight of the composition arena.
In the past three decades new schools of thought, such as cognitivism, expressivism, social constructionism, and radical pedagogy,
have offered numerous ways of changing the traditional authoritarian role of the teacher in the classroom.

However, issues concerning teacher authority continue to be
troubling. The cognitivists' process theory helps teachers realize
the distance between the teacher's expectations and the students'
performance traditionally ignored by teachers and therefore
enables teachers to become more involved in students' writing
activities in order to shorten such a distance. Cognitivists, unfortunately, do not address political, social, or cultural issues implicated in the teacher's discourse and teacher's authority in the
classroom. Expressivists, on the other hand, attempt to challenge
the teacher's authority by simply getting rid of the teacher in the
writing classroom, a romantic stance that is articulated by Peter
Elbow in his influential work *Writing without Teachers*. Regarding
teachers and the conventions of their discourse as constraints that

1

block students' thinking and writing, expressivists insist that the teacher's role should be to ensure that students write whatever they think and feel without, at least at first, having to worry about using appropriate grammar, style, or organization. The problem with expressivists' position is that they downplay the significance of the teacher in the writing classroom to the extent that they risk denying the possibility of using the teacher's authority constructively to enhance students' learning.

Social constructionists challenge the traditional teacher's authority by demystifying the teacher's knowledge as social artifact communally created and communally maintained, something that has gained its prestige through the "interpretive community" (Fish 1980). Since knowledge is socially created, social constructionists adopted the collaborative learning method in teaching writing, advocating that teachers should become facilitators and collaborators in the classroom and give up the platform upon which they play the role of transmitters of knowledge. However, social constructionists' emphasis on the academic discourse as the passport to the academic community implies their tendency to privilege the teacher's discourse over the students' discourse without questioning why this should be the case. As a result, the teacher's traditional authority remains essentially intact, even though the collaborative learning approach gives the impression of a student-centered classroom.

Radical educationists' analysis of the relationship between power and literacy and their critique of the traditional classroom as a place of reproducing social injustice and inequality have contributed greatly to a new understanding of the teacher's authority in the classroom. By urging teachers to turn students into subjects (Freire) and agents (Giroux) through dialogic method (Freire, Shor, Holzman, Cooper), radical educationists attempt to change teachers from oppressive figures working for the maintenance of the status quo into critical intellectuals struggling to make society more equal and democratic. However, radical educationists' insistence on substituting for the canon a new canon consisting of "marginal works" (Giroux 1990; Bizzell "Beyond Anti-Foundationalism" 1988; Dasenbrock "What to Teach" 1990; Ewell 1990) and their implicit conviction that radical theories are morally superior to other theories threaten to impose new authority on students in the classroom, an authority that, as Hairston in a recent article argues, can be equally oppressive (Bizzell "Beyond Anti-Foundationalism" 1988, "Foundationalism" 1986, "Classroom Authority" 1991, "Power" 1991; Paine 1989).

The tendency to evade political, social, and cultural issues involved in teacher authority in cognitivists' process theory, the inclination to deny the inevitability and necessity of the teacher's authority in teaching in expressivists' doctrine, and the aspiration to a superficially equal relationship between teacher and students in social constructionists' collaborative learning—all this indicates a failure to see the interrelation between the teacher's authority and the teacher's discourse or the political nature of such a relationship. As a result, these new schools of thought have offered, at best, some seemingly democratic techniques of teaching writing, while leaving the basic assumptions of the traditional teacher's authority intact.

I believe that radical educationists' inquiry into the politics of the dominant discourse has truly touched upon the foundation of the traditional authority of the teacher. As Pierre Bourdieu and Jean-Claude Passeron rightly point out in *Reproduction in Education, Society, and Culture*, the teacher's authority is mainly secured by the teacher's discourse, which "can never be disassociated from the relation of academic authority in which it is manifested" and which is "able to appear as an intrinsic quality of the person when it merely diverts an advantage of office onto the office-holder" (1977, 110). Thus, for radical educationists, the teacher's discourse embodies the ideology of the dominant culture and reflects all the privileges the dominant class enjoys and all the disadvantages the underclasses suffer in a society of inequality (Giroux, Stuckey, and Ohmann).

In the larger social context, the radical educationists' criticism of the dominant discourse is progressive and revolutionary because their contention for power with the dominant discourse is deeply rooted in the Western intellectual tradition, is stimulated by social changes, and is motivated by their vision for a more democratic and equal society. However, I disagree with radical educationists that replacing the teaching of the dominant discourse with the teaching of discourses of the others is a means to change the traditional teacher's authority. Teaching is always "symbolic imposition" (Bourdieu and Passeron 1977), and a change of content does not completely change the basic institutional function of teaching and, therefore, does not change the traditional teacher's authority. As J. Hillis Miller points out, form and style can be as oppressive as content (1993). Since feminism, multiculturalism, deconstruction, and radical theories are all responses to the dominant discourse and are therefore parasitic upon it, avoiding teaching the dominant discourse not only leaves an irretrievable

gap in students' education but also impedes students' development of critical thinking abilities and thus disempowers them.

To this day, composition scholars and teachers are still trying
to deal with the paradoxes inherent in teacher authority: the
conflict between the teacher's desire for democracy and equality in
the classroom and the need for authority in teaching; the incom-
patibility between the teacher's wish to teach discourses of the
others and the goal of the institution to maintain and continue the
dominant discourse and dominant culture; and the contradictions
between the teacher's good intentions and students' diverse and
varied needs. No satisfactory solutions to these dilemmas have
been offered yet.

These dilemmas hereby formed the central concerns of my
research project, an inquiry into the relationships between the
teacher and teaching, the teacher's authority and the authority of
institution, the teacher's authority and the authority of discourse,
and between the teacher's role as social agent for democracy and
as cultural agent for learning in the classroom. Informed by Paulo
Freire's education philosophy, Richard Rorty's edifying philosophy,
Bourdieu and Passeron's theory of cultural reproduction, Bakhtin's
philosophy of language, and poststructural theories in literature
and composition, the inquiry led to the following results:

1. Having examined the inevitability, unavoidability, and
necessity of authority—the authority of the institution and of the
teacher—in teaching, I argue that radical educationists' attempts
to substitute for the canon a new canon or to replace the teaching
of the dominant discourse with the teaching of radical discourses
do not prevent the teacher's authority from being oppressive and
exclusive. We need a new description of the teacher's authority
and the teacher's discourse, a description that will recognize the
double-sidedness of authority and discourse so as to use them
more constructively in the classroom.

2. I argue that the composition discipline's interpretation of
Rorty's notion of normal/abnormal discourse is inadequate and
limited. For example, Kenneth Bruffee retains only the notion of
normal discourse in his pedagogy, neglecting almost entirely the
place of abnormal discourse in teaching and learning ("Collaborative Learning" 1984); John Schilb misunderstands the notion of
normal/abnormal discourse as binary oppositions; and Patricia
Bizzell discounts the significance of Rorty's antifoundational philosophy in teaching, claiming that Rorty can find "no way around
an unequal relation between professor and students" ("Arguing"

1988, 150). After I have reread Rorty's normal/abnormal discourse in light of his edifying philosophy and reexamined the relationships among students' discourse(s), the teacher's discourse, and the dominant discourse, I propose to describe the radical discourses as Responsive Abnormal Discourse and students' discourse(s) as Nonresponsive Abnormal Discourse (1979). I believe that the two forms of abnormal discourse are different from each other in their relations to the dominant discourse, or normal discourse, and that they should be treated differently in the classroom.

3. Based on my analysis of the relationships among normal discourse, Responsive Abnormal Discourse, and Nonresponsive Abnormal Discourse, I suggest that teachers participate in teaching through two-level interactions: the primary interaction between Nonresponsive Abnormal Discourse (students' discourses) and normal discourse, and the secondary interaction between Nonresponsive Abnormal Discourse and Responsive Abnormal Discourse (the teacher's discourse). Since the two-level interaction established a triangular discourse relationship in the classroom, the tendency of normal discourse to become dominant and oppressive in an asymmetrical teacher-student interaction will be effectively resisted by the presence of a third force, the secondary interaction between Nonresponsive Abnormal Discourse and Responsive Abnormal Discourse.

4. Borrowing from Rorty, I describe teachers who participate in the two-level interaction in the classroom as "edifying teachers." Edifying teachers are similar to Rorty's edifying philosophers in that both speak abnormal discourse and both maintain a critical distance from normal discourse and the dominant culture. However, edifying teachers accommodate normal and abnormal discourses in teaching in such a way that the tension between the different, very often conflicting, discourses provides a space, or a context, for students to develop their own discourse. Furthermore, edifying teachers do not try to evade the tension between the authority of the institution and the autonomy of intellectuals but try to find constructive ways to turn the tension into creative power. Nor do edifying teachers try to avoid their conflicting duties of conserving the dominant culture and discourse as cultural agents on the one hand and problematizing and criticizing them as social agents for democracy on the other hand.

Instead, edifying teachers strive to make their seemingly conflicting duties productive in the teaching context. Like Rorty's edifying philosopher, they participate in the hermeneutic and "poetic" activities, trying to make connections between their own culture and other cultures or between their discipline and other disciplines. They strive to "keep space open for the sense of wonder" by insisting on speaking abnormal discourse (1979, 370). They see "*conservation* as the ultimate context within which knowledge is to be understood," instead of seeing conversation as a means of searching for justification of one's discourse as the normal discourse (389). In short, edifying teachers differ from all other types of teachers in their ability to turn the constraints of discourse, authority, and institutional practices into creative and enabling power through communicating with their students across the boundaries of communities, cultures, discourses, and disciplines.

Chapter 2

The New Paradigm and the Questioning of the Traditional Teacher's Authority

> My role—and that is too emphatic a word—is to show people that they are much freer than they feel, that people accept as truth, as evidence, some themes which have been built up at a certain moment during history, and that this so-called evidence can be criticized and destroyed. To change something in the minds of people—that's the role of an intellectual.
>
> —Michel Foucault

American higher education has undergone great changes since the 1960s and 1970s when colleges and universities adopted the open admissions policies. As millions of students—White and Black, Hispanic and Asian, traditional and nontraditional, men and women—flooded into institutions of higher learning, the site of traditional scholarship was confronted with challenges.[1] A teacher of composition at the time at the City University of New York, Mina P. Shaughnessy was among those who were quick to comprehend how the changed student body was to change teaching in college:

> [I]n the spring of 1970, the City University of New York adopted an admissions policy...thereby opening its doors not only to a larger population of students than it had ever before (enrollment was to jump from 174,000 in 1969 to 266,000 in 1975) but to a wider range of students than any college had probably ever admitted or thought of admitting to its campus—academic winners and losers from the best and worst high schools in the country, the children of the lettered and the illiterate, the blue-collared, the white-collared, and the unemployed, some who

7

could barely afford the subway fare to school and a few who came in the new cars their parents had given them as a reward for staying in New York to go to college; in short, the sons and daughters of New Yorkers, reflecting that city's intense, troubled version of America. (1977, 1–2)

Shaughnessy is right: indeed, the college classroom has since then reflected the "troubled version of America," a society that seems to become more and more accustomed to the idea of a "classless society" (Stuckey 1991, 1) and more and more tolerant of cultural multiplicity and diversity. As the well-known anthropologist Clifford Geertz observes in his 1983 collection of essays, *Local Knowledge*, the "hallmark of modern consciousness" is an "enormous multiplicity" of cultural modes and cultural values (161). The modern consciousness, when reflected in the college classroom, becomes the catalyst for change. When the college student population becomes diverse, not only is the class basis for the traditional "unitary 'humanism'" completely absent, as Geertz points out, but the "agreement on the foundations of scholarly authority" has disappeared (161). The traditional teacher is faced with challenges in the classroom, and traditional ways of teaching no longer suffice.

BOURDIEU AND PASSERON'S THEORY OF THE TRADITIONAL TEACHER'S AUTHORITY

In order to understand why the teacher's authority has become a major problem since open admissions, we need first to understand what the teacher's authority is and where it comes from. According to Pierre Bourdieu and Jean-Claude Passeron, the teacher's authority, appearing in the forms of "pedagogic authority" and "personal authority," is actually an "arbitrary power" that "manifests itself in the form of a right to impose legitimately," that exerts "symbolic violence," and that "reinforces the arbitrary power which establishes it and which it conceals" (1977, 13). Since the legitimization of "arbitrary power" is made possible only by domination, the teacher's authority, a legitimized power, is based on dominant cultural legitimacy (22).

Bourdieu and Passeron point out that it is often concealed that the teacher's authority is rooted in power relations because "in preventing apprehension of power relations as power relations, [the dominant culture] tends to prevent the dominated groups or classes from securing all the strength that realization of their strength would give them" (1977, 15). Thus, the teacher's authority always appears as neutral "pedagogical authority" and disinterested "personal authority"—authority clad in the teacher's charisma and idiosyncrasy.

In the classroom, Bourdieu and Passeron observe, the legitimacy of the teacher's authority is indicated by the space the traditional institution arranges for the teacher (the platform, the professorial chair at the focal point on which all gazes converge), a space that represents "material and symbolic conditions which enable him to keep the students at a respectful distance and would oblige him to do so even if he did not wish to." Such a space and distance, accompanied by the teacher's manner, evoke mystery:

> Elevated and enclosed in the space which crowns him orator, separated from his audience, if numbers permit, by a few empty rows which materially mark the distance the laity fearfully keep before the *mana* of the Word and which at all events are only ever occupied by the most seasoned zealots, pious ministers of the magisterial utterance, the professor, remote and intangible, shrouded in vague and terrifying rumor, is condemned to theatrical monologue and virtuoso exhibition by a necessity of position far more coercive than the most imperious regulations. (1977, 109)

And the atmosphere of mystery serves to reinforce the teacher's authority because "[s]uch a context governs teachers' and students' behavior so rigorously that efforts to set up a dialogue immediately turn into fiction or farce" (109). Secured of his superiority,

> The lecturer can call for participation or objection without fear of it really happening: questions to the audience are often purely rhetorical; the answers, serving chiefly to express the part the faithful take in the service, are generally no more than *responses*. (109)

Not only the teacher's space and oratorical manner serve to indicate the teacher's authority, Bourdieu and Passeron point out, the traditional teacher's discourse—"magisterial discourse"—is "the most efficacious and the most subtle" of "all the distancing techniques with which the institution equips its officers" (1977, 110). This magisterial discourse further secures the teacher's authority, for "the distance words create seems to owe nothing to the institution" (110). Protected by the professional use of a professional language, the traditional teacher enjoys privileges that are denied to students:

> There is nothing on which he cannot speak, be it incest or the
> class struggle, because his position, his person, his role imply the
> "neutralization" of his utterances; and also because language can
> ultimately cease to be an instrument of communication and serve
> instead as an instrument of incantation whose principal function
> is to attest and impose the pedagogical authority of the
> communication and the content communicated. (110)

For Bourdieu and Passeron, the teacher's discourse is never as
disinterested and neutral as it seems. In fact, the neutrality is an
illusion, for the teacher's discourse is "able to appear as an
intrinsic quality of the person when it merely diverts an advantage
of office onto the office-holder." It is a "status attribute which owes
most of its effects to the institution, since it can never be dis-
sociated from the relation of academic authority in which it is
manifested" (1977, 110).

In Bourdieu and Passeron's analysis, the teacher's academic
authority is derived from the traditional institution, whose interest
is to conserve the *relation to language and culture* that belongs only
to the dominant classes. In turn, the teacher manifests his "conformity to the dominant model of the relation to language and
culture" in all possible ways, both in and out of the classroom
(1977, 122). In the classroom, through the teacher's monologue,
the teacher teaches the relation to language and culture that
belongs to the dominant classes rather than language and culture
per se, thus rendering service to the dominant classes and groups
from which the traditional institution derives its authority.
According to Bourdieu and Passeron, the teacher's authority has
been unquestionable, despite the minimal efficiency of the pedagogic work of the traditional type:

> The whole logic of an academic institution based on pedagogic
> work of the traditional type and ultimately guaranteeing the
> "infallibility" of the "master," finds expression in the professorial
> ideology of student incapacity, a mixture of tyrannical stringency
> and disillusioned indulgence which inclines the teacher to regard
> all communication failures, however unforeseen, as integral to a
> relationship which inherently implies poor reception of the best
> messages by the worst receivers. (111)

The teacher is "infallible" as long as he or she serves the traditional institution. And the academic institution, as long as it keeps
its allegiance to the dominant classes by transmitting their style, is
able to perpetuate itself and, in turn, designate its authority to the
teacher. It is exactly through the "persistence of its functions,"

Bourdieu and Passeron contend, that the traditional schooling system is able to survive:

> [T]he continuity of pedagogic customs within the continuous history of the education system has been made possible by the continuity of the services rendered by a School which, despite the changes in the social structure, has always managed to occupy homologous positions in the system of relations which link it to the dominant classes. Thus, the constellation of attitudes which was codified in the seventeenth-century ethic of the *honnete homme*—and is not so far removed from the ethic of the "literary gentleman" in the Confucian tradition—owes to the historical permanence of its function the ease with which it has been able to perpetuate itself, at the cost of a few reinterpretations, despite the changing of the content of school curricular and the changing of the classes placed in the dominant position. (1977, 130)

What is perpetuated is the dominant culture's style—a relation to language and culture that is embodied in the following priorities that schools strive to inculcate in their students:

> Consider, for example, the primacy of manner and style; the value attached to naturalness and lightness, conceived as the antithesis of pedantry, didacticism or effort; the cult of the "gift" and the disparagement of apprenticeship, the modern refor-mulation of the ideology of "birth" and contempt for study; the disdain for specialization, trades and techniques, the bourgeois transposition of contempt for business; the pre-eminence con-ferred on the art of pleasing; that is, the art of adapting oneself to the diversity of social encounters and conversation; the attention devoted to nuances and imponderables, perpetuating the aris-tocratic tradition of "refinement" and expressed in the subor-dination of scientific to literary culture, and of literary culture to artistic culture, still more conducive to the indefinite niceties of the games of distinction; in short, all the ways, declared or tacit, of *reducing culture to the relation to culture*, in other words, of setting against the vulgarity of what can be acquired or achieved a manner of possessing an acquirement whose whole value derives from the fact that there is but one way of acquiring it. (1977, 130; emphasis added)

And Bourdieu and Passeron make it clear that the one way of acquiring it is to live as members of the classes that privilege such a relation to language and culture. The teacher, an agent within the institution, teaches nothing else but such a relation, which students either have or do not have upon entering school. In the last analysis, then, the teacher's authority—the platform, the distance between the teacher and the student, the professorial manner, the teacher's monologic way of communication, the master's infallibility and discourse—is but a means to continue and perpetuate the dominant classes' style and power.

Bourdieu and Passeron's analysis of the traditional teacher's authority seems to provide a reasonable explanation why the teacher's authority has been a problem since open admissions. Because open admissions policies drastically changed the composition of the student body in colleges and universities, such changes in student population inevitably altered the traditional goal of higher education. When the teacher began to face a heterogeneous class of "academic winners and losers," "the children of the lettered and the illiterate," "the blue-collared, the white-collared, and the unemployed," instead of a homogeneous group consisting only of White, male, upper-class, Anglo-American students, teaching solely the relation to language and culture that belongs only to the dominant culture and class became problematic. Further, the diverse student population made it tremendously difficult for the teacher to carry out pedagogic acts in the traditional monologic way and to exert academic authority without caring about its consequences. The teacher's authority was questioned as the traditional institution was challenged and forced to change. And the questioning has lasted for thirty years.

THE CHANGING CLASSROOM AND THE QUESTIONING OF THE TRADITIONAL TEACHER'S AUTHORITY

Teachers, once the "infallible masters" whose expectations were the goals for students to reach and whose style and manner were the ideal for students to imitate, find themselves facing in the classroom students of different colors, classes, genders, cultures, and languages. For the first time in their lives, teachers are forced to see that the gap between the transmitter and the receiver is such that it cannot be filled simply by students imitating the master, or, in Bourdieu and Passeron's words, "by teaching without a pedagogy," an elitist approach that derives its power from the institution's function as the preserver of the style of the dominant classes (1977, 126). In the field of composition studies, the current-traditional paradigm—based on the elitist assumption that "no one can really teach anyone else how to write because writing is a mysterious creative activity that cannot be categorized or analyzed" (Hairston 1982, 78)—gradually lost its grip on compositon teaching as a new paradigm began to emerge. Consisting of diverse new theories and pedagogies, the new paradigm showed a general tendency of shifting focus from the composed product to the composing process, from teacher's monologue to student's group work, from the strong concern with usage and style to an interest in understanding how a student essay came into being and why it assumed the form that it did, and from a tradition of teaching writing without a pedagogy to a search for multiple pedagogies that will work in a new age (78). Named by James A. Berlin as "the Renaissance of Rhetoric," the period from 1960 to 1975 witnessed the gathering momentum of the new paradigm that was to change the discipline of composition fundamentally in the years to come (1987).

The new paradigm is formed by several major schools of thought: cognitivism, expressivism, social constructionism, and radicalism, which is a politicized form of social constructionism. Although these schools of thought differ in composition theory, pedagogy, and practice, they share one major assumption: that the traditional way of teaching is inadequate in the new historical period, and that the role the traditional teacher plays in teaching is problematic. As a result, the new schools of thought all contribute, to different extents and in different ways, to changing the traditional teacher's role in the classroom.

The cognitivist school's major contribution to a new conception of the teacher's role in the writing classroom is its inquiry into the process of writing and its emphasis of the teacher's intervention in the recursive stages of the student's writing process. One of the major works of the school is *The Composing Process of Twelfth Graders* by Janet Emig (1971), a "landmark study of student writers" that "called on some of the basic assumptions of the cognitivists" (Berlin 1987, 159–60). In this study, Emig challenges the traditional assumption that teaching writing is a mere mechanical act of requiring students to imitate the master's writing and to produce their own written products. She observes that the stages are the same for all the students investigated and that these stages are recursive rather than linear. Believing that "there are elements, moments, and stages within the composing process which can be distinguished and characterized in some detail" (Emig 1971, 33), Emig calls attention to the possibilities of the teacher's intervention in "the developmental process as well as with the ways in which the process varies among cultures and even personality types" (Berlin 1987, 160). In emphasizing the importance for the teacher to know how students compose and why they compose the way they do,

Emig shows her disapproval of the traditional view that students are solely responsible for their academic performance in the classroom. Implicit in her study is the argument that teachers should step down from their secured space and professorial chair and assist students in the various stages of their composing processes so as to enhance their mental, as well as linguistic, development.

Linda Flower and John R. Hayes further contribute to the cognitivist school's inquiry into the writing process by proposing that writing is a "goal-oriented process" in their important work, "A Cognitive Process Theory of Writing." Basing their conclusions on analysis of protocols recording the choices of both experienced and inexperienced writers over five years, Flower and Hayes describe the mental processes of writing as consisting of three stages: the planning stage, including acts such as generating ideas, organizing ideas, and goal-setting; the translating stage, the process of "putting ideas into visible language"; and the reviewing stage, which includes two subprocesses: evaluating and revising (1981, 372–74). What distinguishes experienced writers from inexperienced writers, Flower and Hayes observe, is whether a writer is capable of setting process goals ("the instructions people give themselves about how to carry out the process of writing") and content goals ("all things the writer wants to say or to do to an audience") in the writing process (377). Because "in the act of composing, writers create a hierarchical network of goals and these in turn guide the writing process" (377), Flower and Hayes call attention to the active role of the writer in producing a text. The significance of their theory, as they announce, is this:

> By placing emphasis on the inventive power of the writer, who is able to explore ideas, to develop, act on, test, and regenerate his or her own goals, we are putting an important part of creativity where it belongs—in the hands of the working, thinking writer. (386)

Like Emig's study of the writing processes of the twelfth graders, Flower and Hayes' study implicitly criticizes the traditional way of teaching writing, especially its emphasis on students' passive imitation of the masters' great pieces. Underlining the importance of the student's initiative in the writing process and the teacher's responsibility to help explore students' creativity in their writing and learning processes, Flower and Hayes seem to reject the "professorial ideology of student incapacity" that Bourdieu and Passeron believe underlies the traditional teacher-student relationship (1981, 111).

If cognitivists' criticism of the traditional teacher's authority is mostly implicit, expressivists' objection to the traditional teacher's authority is unequivocal. For example, in "Making Freshman English a Happening," William D. Lutz argues that teaching writing effectively requires changing both the physical structure of the classroom and the very process by which we attempt to teach writing. "Physically the room insists on order and authoritarianism, the enemies of creativity," he snaps (1971, 35). And the alteration involves not only breaking down the authoritarian classroom atmosphere and creating unique experiences for students but also the "complete restructuring of the university" (35). Berlin summarizes this expressivist position succinctly:

> The happening, of course, provides generously for this, offering "structure in unstructure; a random series of ordered events; order in chaos; the logical illogicality of dreams." This kind of classroom finally "calls for the complete restructuring of the university," including the overthrow of all grading systems and of teacher authority. (1987, 151)

Lutz's position is representative of the "more extreme form" of expressivism, as Berlin thus describes it in "Rhetoric and Ideology in the Writing Class." In the eyes of Lutz and the like-minded, teacher's authority is viewed as synonymous with the corrupt society from which the students should be liberated. "Unsparingly critical of the dominant social, political, and cultural practices of the time," the proponents of expressivism in the 1960s and 1970s demanded that the writing classroom work "explicitly toward liberating students from the shackles of a corrupt society" (Berlin 1988, 485). They insisted on teaching composition as happening, an approach that emphasized resisting the alienating and fragmenting experience of the authoritarian institutional setting by providing students with "concrete experiences that alter political consciousness through challenging official versions of reality." The aim of this approach was to encourage students to resist the "interpretations of experience embodied in the language of others [so as] to order their own experience" (485).

The rejection of the traditional teacher's authority is clearly embedded in these radical expressivists' open rejection of any constraints from society, institution, and language. Although their advocation of overthrowing all grading system and teacher authority is criticized by the moderate wing of the expressionist camp that eventually became dominant, the moderate expressivists have nevertheless carried on "the ideological critique of the dominant culture while avoiding the overt politicizing of the classroom" (Berlin 1988, 485). Like their radical counterparts, the moderate expressivists are also almost exclusively concerned with individual experiences, private thinking, and individualistic language in the writing class. Similarly, their insistence on personal and free writing also indicates their desire to shift power from the teacher to the student.

A good illustration of the moderate expressivists' view on the teacher's authority is Peter Elbow's influential work, *Writing Without Teachers.*[2] In the book, Elbow contends that the teacher is basically an unsympathetic reader of students' writing, someone who vainly adheres to some objective academic standards of good writing and should therefore be dispensed with. For Elbow, a teacher is "*too good* a reader" of student writing in several ways: First, the teacher is usually indifferent to what students have to say in their papers because the teacher usually knows more about the subjects that students are asked to write about. Second, the teacher usually takes no serious interest in what students have expressed in their writing because the teacher usually doesn't expect students' words "to make a dent on him." Third, the teacher doesn't treat students' words like real reading. "He has to read them as an exercise. He can't hold himself ready to be affected unless he has an extremely rare, powerful openness" (1973, 127).

According to Elbow, students are better off in a teacherless writing class, not only because they will get little help from the teacher, but also because a teacherless class gives students the freedom necessary for self-development. By denying the need for a teacher in the writing classroom, Elbow seems to suggest that learning can happen without authority—be it institutional, pedagogical, or personal authority. The students in a teacherless class seem to be perfectly happy: they participate in interchanges between people, between ideas, between "words and ideas, between immersion and perspective," and "between you and the symbols on paper" (1973, xi). In the process of such interactions, spared the negative effects of the teacher's interference and manipulation, the students are able to find their "privately determined truths" and their own identities in the writing process (Berlin 1988, 486). Thus, the teacherless class proves the falsity of the traditional assumption that knowledge can be acquired only through the transmitter, a point that Elbow does not hesitate to make explicitly:

> But in proposing the teacherless writing class I am trying to deny something—something that is often assumed: *the necessary connection between learning and teaching.* The teacherless writing class is a place where there is learning but no teaching. It is possible to be a student and not have a teacher. If the student's function is to learn and the teacher's to teach, then the student can function without a teacher, but the teacher cannot function without a student. (Elbow 1973, ix)

Perhaps no other schools are more determined than expressivists to rid individuals of the economic, political, and social pressures to conform. And perhaps no other schools are more explicit than expressivists in arguing that truth lies deep in each individual rather than anywhere else, not in the master, of course. Thus, in *Writing Without Teachers*, Elbow asserts that his own experience is his main source of writing the book and that it is possible to make "universal generalizations upon a sample of one" (1973, 16). And Donald Murray, another important expressivist, asserts in his *A Writer Teaches Writing* that

> the writer is on a search for himself. If he finds himself he will find an audience, because all of us have the same common core. And when he digs deeply into himself and is able to define himself, he will find others who will read with a shock of recognition what he has written. (1968, 4)

As Berlin rightly points out, "In indirectly but unmistakably decrying the dehumanizing effects of industrial capitalism," the expressivists insist that the "correct response to the imposition of current economic, political, and social arrangements is thus resistance, but a resistance that is always construed in individual terms" (1988, 487). In the classroom, such resistance is directed toward the tyranny of the authoritarian institution embodied in the teacher's authority in the teaching process. Teachers are not necessary; they are useful only when they work as individuals in "an ideal laboratory for learning along with students and being useful to them in that way" (Elbow 1973, x). This stance of the expressivists reveals their determination to break away from any authority that restricts students' freedom of thinking, expression, and search for truth.

Whereas cognitivists indirectly reject the traditional way of teaching and expressivists openly advocate abandoning the teacher's authority in the writing class, social constructionists' criticism of the traditional teacher's authority goes directly to the foundation on which the teacher's authority is based—the conception of how knowledge is generated and maintained. Greatly influenced by neopragmatism, the social constructionist theory posits that "entities we normally call reality, knowledge, thought, facts, texts, selves, and so on are constructs generated by communities of like-minded peers" (Bruffee 1988, 774). "Social construction understands reality, knowledge, thought, facts, texts, selves, and so on as community-generated and community-maintained linguistic entities...that define or 'constitute' the communities that generate them, much as the language of the *United States Constitution*, the *Declaration of Independence*, and the 'Gettysburg Address' in part constitutes the political, the legal, and to some extent the cultural community of Americans" (774). This view of reality, knowledge, and facts as *linguistic entities* and *social constructs* serves as the starting point for social constructionists' inquiry into the role of the teacher in the writing class. For social constructionists, knowledge is never found in the world out there independent of the human existence, as the cognitivist theories imply, nor discovered in the individual's mind or consciousness, as the expressivists claim. Knowledge is created "in the dialectical interaction of the observer, the discourse community (social group) in which the observer is functioning, and the material conditions of existence" (Berlin 1988, 488). Moreover, for social constructionists, not only the dialectical interaction of the observer, the discourse community, and the material conditions of existence depends on language, but the observer, the discourse community, and the material conditions of existence are also "verbal constructs"; they themselves are products of the dialectic interaction. Thus, language for social constructionists becomes "one of the material and social conditions involved in producing a culture" (488–89). The significance of this view lies in a different perception of how knowledge is generated, as Berlin explains:

> This means that in studying rhetoric—the ways discourse is generated—we are studying *the ways in which knowledge comes into existence.* Knowledge, after all, is an historically bound social fabrication rather than an eternal and invariable phenomenon located in some uncomplicated repository—in the material object or in the subject or in the social realm. (489; emphasis added)

The view that knowledge is generated by language through social interactions is the key to understanding social constructionists' criticism of the traditional role of the teacher in the writing class. First, since social constructionism denies that there is a universal foundation behind or beneath knowledge, upon which what we know is built, social constructionism denies that there exists any objective knowledge of certainty or truth. Instead, social constructionists believe that "there is only an agreement, a consensus arrived at for the time being by communitics of knowledgeable peers. Concepts, ideas, theories, the world, reality, and facts are all language constructs generated by knowledge communities and used by them to maintain community coherence" (Bruffee 1988, 777). In other words, for social constructionists, all knowledge is contingent and flexible, depending on communal consensus rather than some reality independent of human consciousness. Following this line of reasoning, the teacher's knowledge, which gives the teacher the supreme authority in the classroom, loses its prestigious status as "truth."

Since for social constructionism the "matrix of thought" is not the individual self but some community of knowledgeable peers and the vernacular language of that community" (Bruffee 1988, 777), social constructionists advocate collaborative learning in the teaching of writing, an approach that is systematically discussed by Kenneth Bruffee in his works.

Ever since the early seventies, Bruffee has been concerned with "the definitions of the roles of teacher and student and the relationship between them that is enforced by classroom procedures" (Berlin 1987, 174). In an early article, "The Way Out," Bruffee proposes collaborative learning for the first time, arguing that this approach is needed to change the classroom conventions that give the teacher all the power in the classroom. What Bruffee opposes is "the dominant pattern of behavior in the English class," an "authoritarian-individualist mode" that includes a number of disturbingly familiar features: "A student talks to the teacher, writes to the teacher, and determines his fate in relation to the teacher individually" (1972, 458–459); a student is not encouraged to relate or collaborate in learning with others. In this class, two teaching conventions are typically followed: either the teacher lectures or the students recite. And, in both cases, the teacher is completely in control of all activities. In the former, the teacher decides on subject matters and shapes the responses permissible. In the latter case, even though students are assigned individual tasks in the form of seminars, laboratory work, writing assignments, team projects, and tutorials, it is the teacher who "continues to be in control of the activities since each student is finally responsible for her own work, and then only to the teacher" (Berlin 1987, 174).

Evidently, what Bruffee sees in the traditional classroom is what Bourdieu and Passeron describe: the absolute authority of the teacher and the absolute obedience of the student. As Bruffee sees it, such a power relationship is secured by the notion that "knowledge is subject matter, a kind of substance which is contained in the mind" and that teachers, having more of this kind of substance in their minds, are responsible to transmit the substance into the students' minds. What's more, "The teacher's responsibility is not only to impart knowledge which was imparted to him, but also to impart knowledge as it was imparted to him" (1972, 460).

Bruffee's collaborative learning aims to change the traditional way knowledge is imparted. Its early version is characterized by "poly-centralization," a scheme consisting of "a number of small groups more or less equal in power contending with one another," aimed at redistributing power in the classroom (1972, 462). As Bruffee states, this approach attempts to turn the teacher from a "philanthropist, munificently bestowing knowledge on his students" to a "*metteur en scene* whose responsibility and privilege is to arrange optimum conditions for other people to learn" (470). The teacher must relinquish control, finding "his purpose as a teacher...in helping people discover, accept, and develop their own intelligence and talent" (470).

If in its initial stage Bruffee's collaborative learning sounds not so different from Elbow's group writing, Bruffee succeeds in differentiating the two in a later article, "Collaborative Learning and the 'Conversation of the Mankind,'" by elaborating on the theoretical basis of his approach. Extending to composition studies Lev Vygotsky's idea that "reflective thought is public or social conversation internalized" (Bruffee 1984, 639), Bruffee proposes that "writing of all kinds" is "internalized conversation reexternalized" (641). This being the case, the task of the writing teacher should be to engage students in "conversation among themselves at as many points in both the writing and the reading process as possible" and to ensure that "students' conversation about what they read and write is similar in as many ways as possible to the way we would like them eventually to read and write" (642). In other words, students learn to read and write by carrying on a conversation among themselves, forming a "community of status equals: peers." This community of peers is supposed to help students to foster "the kind of conversation college teachers value most" and to approximate the discourse "most students must eventually write for in everyday life, in business, government, and the professions" through practicing the "skill and partnership" of reexternalized conversation, writing, among peers (642).

The "community of knowledgeable peers" is an important concept in Bruffee's collaborative learning. It changes the traditional transmittal mode of learning to a dialogic mode: the conversation among knowledgeable peers. This dialogic mode suits Bruffee's goal of teaching writing, the "mastery of a knowledge community's normal discourse," which is the "basic qualification for acceptance into that community." With a "structured conversation" among student peers, the dialogic mode makes accessible the normal discourse of the new community students together hope to enter. Bruffee explains the advantages of this conversational approach:

> Students are especially likely to be able to master that discourse collaboratively if their conversation is structured indirectly by the task or problem that a member of that new community (the teacher) has judiciously designed. To the conversation between peer tutors and their tutees in writing, for example, the tutee brings knowledge of the subject to be written about and knowledge of the assignment. The tutor brings sensitivity to the needs and feelings of peers and knowledge of the conventions of discourse and of standard written English. And the conversation is structured in part by the demands of the teacher's assignment and in part by the formal conventions of the communities the teacher represents, the conventions of academic discourse and standard English. ("Collaborative Learning" 1984, 644)

It seems that in Bruffee's collaborative learning classroom the teacher-student relationship is almost reversed. The tutor (or teacher) becomes an organizer and facilitator, whose major task is to bring to the conversation "sensitivity to the needs and feelings of peers and knowledge of the conventions of discourse and of standard written English." The tutee (or student) becomes his or her own master, having the right to bring "knowledge of the subject to be written about and knowledge of the assignment" ("Collaborative Learning" 1984, 644). As a result, the teacher is no longer the only authority of knowledge in the classroom:

> Because the concept that knowledge is socially justified belief denies that the authority of knowledge lodges in any of these places [i.e. "some touchstone of value and truth above and beyond ourselves," "the great minds," "the objective world"], our authority as teachers according to that concept has quite another

source as well. Insofar as collaborative learning inducts students
into established knowledge communities and teaches them the
normal discourse of those communities, we derive our authority
as teachers from being certified representative of the communities of knowledgeable peers that students aspire to join, and that
we, as members of our chosen disciplines and also members of
the community of the liberally educated public at large, invite and
encourage them to join. Teachers are defined in this instance as
those members of a knowledge community who accept the
responsibility of inducing new members into the community.
Without successful teachers the community will die when its
current members die, and knowledge as assented by that community will cease to exist. (650)

The teacher, no longer the almighty knower, becomes simply a
member of a knowledge community whose mission is to conserve
the community's knowledge by inviting and encouraging new
members to join it. If the teacher has any authority at all, the
authority is derived from the knowledge community that students aspire to join. With this emphasis of writing as a social
process of learning the normal discourse of a specific knowledge
community, collaborative learning demystifies the traditional
way of teaching, challenges the teacher's role as the transmitter
of knowledge, and shifts attention from the teacher's monologue
to the students' conversation as the means to acquiring knowledge and "reacculturation."

Although collaborative learning attempts to change the traditional teacher-student relationship in the classroom through poly-
centralization, social constructionists do not go so far as to inquire
into the political implications of the teacher's discourse. Like
Bruffee, most social constructionists seem to be willing to ignore
the politics underlying the prestigious status of the discourse of
the academic community, which is supposed to be the goal of
college writing courses and students' passport to the discourse
community of the academy. The questioning of the teacher's discourse is pursued by the radicals in the field of composition
studies. Their inquiry into the role of the teacher's authority is not
just confined to teaching but is associated with their political goal
of social justice and equality. For radical scholars and teachers,
the traditional teacher's oppressive authority in the classroom is
rooted in the oppressive power of the dominant culture and class;
the asymmetrical power relationship between the teacher's
discourse and students' discourses reflect the asymmetrical power
relations among different ideologies; and the hierarchical class-

room structure reflects the injustice and inequality in society at large. Inquiring into the relationships among language, ideology, and power, radical theorists and teachers contend that the teacher's authority is the product of the ideology of the dominant class and that the teacher's discourse is an embodiment of the dominant class's ideology and its power. Consequently, they advocate transforming the unequal power relations in the class-room by empowering students, that is, by developing a political consciousness in students through dialogic methods.

Perhaps what distinguishes the radical school from other schools of thought is its insistence on seeing discourse as ideology and seeing ideology as "transmitted through language practices that are always the center of conflict and contest" (Berlin 1988, 478). For radical scholars and teachers,

> Ideology always carries with it strong social endorsement, so that what we take to exist, to have value, and to be possible seems necessary, normal and inevitable—in the nature of things. Ideology also, as we have seen, always includes conceptions of how power should—again, in the nature of things—be distributed in a society. Power here means political force but covers as well social forces in everyday contacts. Power is an intrinsic part of ideology, defined and reinforced by it, determining, once again, who can act and what can be accomplished. These power rela-tionships, furthermore, are inscribed in the discursive practices of daily experience—in the ways we use language and are used (interpellated) by it in ordinary parlance. (479)

This vision of discourse as ideological and political and there-fore powerful has no doubt led to the radical view that teaching is a "political act," which, by privileging the teacher's discourse, forces students into silence and turns them into objects. To counter the oppression of the dominant discourse, radical educationists insist, students must not only be taught to use language to "*formulate* and to *transform*—to give form to feeling, cogency to argument, shape to memory" (Berthoff "From Problem Solving" 647) but also be educated to be "their own agents for social change, their own creators of democratic culture" (Shor 1980, 48).

To achieve the goal of transforming the traditional classroom from the place of reproducing social injustice and inequality into a site of struggling for public democracy and social justice, radical educationists advocate adopting dialogic methods and liberatory learning in composition teaching. Whereas the influence of neo-Marxists such as Louis Althusser, Göran Therborn, and Michel

Foucault is evident in radical pedagogy, radical pedagogy in composition studies owes its greatest debt to Paulo Freire, whose education theory and pedagogic practice have continuously inspired the radical scholars and teachers in the past three decades. In fact, both dialogic method and emancipatory learning advocated by the radical school are expounded by Paulo Freire in his influential works, *Education for Critical Consciousness* and *The Pedagogy of the Oppressed.* For Freire, dialogue is the means to critical consciousness in education because it requires "a horizontal relationship between persons," a "relation of 'empathy' between two 'poles' who are engaged in a joint search." Dialogue is "nourished by love, humility, hope, faith, and trust," and it is "in opposition with the anti-dialogue" that "involves vertical relationships between persons." Antidialogue is "loveless, arrogant, hopeless, mistrustful, acritical"; "it does not communicate, but rather issues communiques" (1973, 45–46). Like Bourdieu and Passeron, Freire sees traditional education as antidialogic, "an act of depositing, in which the students are the depositories and the teacher is the depositor" (1970, 58). This is the banking concept of education, in which "knowledge is a gift bestowed by those who consider themselves knowledgeable upon those whom they consider to know nothing" (58). Such a concept entails oppression, Freire argues, because it projects "an absolute ignorance onto others, a characteristic of the ideology of oppression," it "negates education and knowledge as processes of inquiry," and it assumes the teacher's superiority over the student. The teacher-student relationship fostered by the banking concept of education is hostile:

> The teacher presents himself to his students as their necessary opposite; by considering their ignorance absolute, he justifies his own existence. The students, alienated like the slave in the Hegelian dialectic, accept their ignorance as justifying the teacher's existence—but, unlike the slave, they never discover that they educate the teacher. (58–59)

To change oppressive education to libertarian education, the teacher-student contradiction must first be reconciled, Freire maintains. And dialogue for Freire is the means both to a more equal relationship between the teacher and the student and to a more democratic and emancipatory education. This is so, Freire explains, because only dialogue, which requires critical thinking, is capable of generating critical thinking. For Freire, "without dialogue there is no communication, and without communication there can be no true education." Since dialogue can create a situation in which both the teacher and the student will focus their conversation on the object by which they are mediated, the teacher-student relationship is changed both by the preoccupation with and the participation in the dialogue. Freire explains:

> [T]he dialogical character of education as the practice of freedom does not begin when the teacher-student meets with the students-teachers in a pedagogical situation, but rather when the former first asks himself *what* he will dialogue with the latter *about*. And preoccupation with the content of dialogue is really preoccupation with the program content of education. (1970, 81)

A most important feature of the dialogic relationship between the teacher and the student is that the teacher strives to work *with*, not *for* or *about* the student:

> For the dialogical, problem-posing teacher-student, the program content of education is neither a gift nor an imposition—bits of information to be deposited in the students—but rather the organized, systemized, and developed "re-presentation" to individuals of the things about which they want to know more. (Freire 1970, 82)

What makes the dialogic relationship possible between the teacher and the student, Freire explains, is the "reality to be transformed by them together with other men—not other men themselves" (83). In other words, the teacher's object of action should not be the student. Rather, the teacher and the student should act together upon the conditions that prevent human beings from realizing their "full humanity" (82) or "the thought-language with which men refer to reality, the levels at which they perceive that reality, and their view of the world, in which their generative themes [or realistic themes] are found" (86). Freire is never tired of emphasizing that, only when education is committed to transforming reality through investigation, only when the teacher is committed to working with students through dialogue, will education become authentically liberating and the teacher authentically humanistic and revolutionary.

Freire's view of education as part of the political struggle for humanity and equality in society has certainly won the support and sympathy of radical scholars and teachers in the United States. Criticizing social constructionists' indifferent attitude towards the politics of the status quo in education, C. H. Knoblauch underscores the characteristics Freire has found in the oppressive classroom in Brazil:

The teacher teaches and the students are taught.
The teacher knows everything and the students know nothing.
The teacher thinks and the students are thought about.
The teacher talks and the students listen.
The teacher disciplines and the students are disciplined.
The teacher chooses and enforces his choice, and the students comply.
The teacher acts and the students have the illusion of acting through the action of the teacher.
The teacher chooses the program content, and the students (who were not consulted) adapt to it.
The teacher confuses the authority of knowledge with his own professional authority, which he sets in opposition to the freedom of the students.
The teacher is the subject of the learning process, while the students are mere objects. (1988, 46–47)

The same features also characterize the American classrooms, Knoblauch stresses. Their existence therefore justifies the radical theorists' urge for change in American schools:

Sound familiar? The Department of Education might well envy the succinctness with which its own program for renewed "excellence" in the schools is here replicated, were it not for Freire's insistence that this agenda offers everything we ought to *fear* in a country that claims to venerate freedom. (51)

Knoblauch's desire for change is shared by many other radical educationists, among whom Ira Shor is the one who has contributed greatly to applying Freirean theory in the American context. Apart from applying Freire's dialogic method and liberatory learning to teaching in the American classroom, Shor tries to deal with the traditional teacher's oppressive authority by proposing, in *Critical Teaching and Everyday Life*, the theory of the "withering away of the teacher." The "withering away of the teacher," Shor argues, should be a goal of liberatory learning. As Shor sees it, although "at the start and along the way, the teacher is indispensable as a change agent," "the need to create students into self-regulating subjects requires that the teacher as organizer fade as the students emerge" (1980, 98). Dividing the liberatory process of learning into separation, transformation, and reintegration stages, Shor envisions that the "teacher's profile changes" accordingly, from the "teacher/initiator" role at the start to that of "*peer-discussant*, a member of the dialogue on equal terms with all the others in class" towards the end:

> After catalyzing discussion, at moments of the greatest success, the teacher experiences a dissolution, blending into the group deliberation. At moments of partial or full breakdown, the teacher experiences her or his role reconstituted, separated out for the restoration of the process. (101)

Thus, for Shor, the teacher in a liberating classroom differs from the traditional teacher in that the latter is "always in charge from beginning to end. His or her authority is fixed at an unchanging distance from the students. This authority must be fixed so that the programmed curriculum all the way from Lesson A to Lesson Z can be implemented on schedule, by virtue of the teacher's initiative." Contrary to the traditional practice in which the teacher is "empowered to be active, while students are made reactive" (Shor and Freire, *Pedagogy for Liberation* 1987, 90), the "withering away of the teacher" aims to empower students by gradually strengthening their subject position and weakening the teacher's authority in the teaching process.

In summary, all the schools of thought that belong to the new paradigm have explicitly or implicitly questioned the traditional teacher's authority and directly or indirectly sought to change the traditional way of teaching and the traditional teacher's role in the classroom. Diverse as the theories and pedagogies of cognitivists, expressivists, social constructionists, and radical educationists are, they have brought the issue of teacher authority to the focused attention of the field and offered various alternatives for changing the traditional teacher's authority so that the teacher can better serve the changed student population in the changing American higher education.

A Perplexing Dimension of the Teacher's Authority

After thirty years of searching for new ways to deal with the changes in higher education, composition scholars and teachers, whatever labels they bear, have come to an almost unanimous consensus that the teaching of writing cannot be done by the traditional way of lecturing but that it must make use of talking, small groups, collaboration, dialogue, and other methods of sharing power in the classroom. The communal wisdom achieved in the thirty years of research is that learning to write has to involve a "personal, organic, discovery-centered way of operating" on the part of the student and that teaching writing has to involve a redistribution of the power that was traditionally solely the teacher's in the classroom (Bechtel 1987, 180). However, up until this day no school of thought has yet formed a theory that convincingly describes and delineates the new teacher's authority in the new age. Cognitivists advocate that teachers inquire into the students' writing process and involve themselves in students' writing activities in order to help shorten the distance between teachers' expectations and students' academic performance. Yet cognitivists do not question the political implications of the traditional teacher's authority nor intend to abandon it in the teaching process. On the contrary, with cognitivism's claim of the "transcendent neutrality of science," cognitivism betrays its hidden ideology of the dominant class.[3]

As Berlin identifies the problem, cognitivists' research into child development tends to ignore the influence of children's environmental features on their success in schools, colleges, and the corporate world. Berlin writes,

> That the cognitive skills leading to success may be the product of the experiences of a particular social class rather than the perfecting of inherent mental structures, skills encouraged because they serve the interests of a ruling economic elite, is never considered in the 'scientific' investigation of the mind. (1988, 483)

This avoidance of addressing the social dimension of language indicates cognitivists' assumption that students' problem-solving abilities are related to their mental structures and intelligence rather than to their social, economic, cultural, and linguistic backgrounds. Further, in its insistence on writing as problem-solving and goal-oriented activities, cognitivism implies that teachers, the "university-certified experts, those individuals who have the cognitive skills and the training for problem solving," should be relegated power (483). Thus, in the cognitivist classroom, the teacher may have to give up the comfortable space and step down from the platform to interfere with students' writing process, but the traditional teacher's authority, now further secured by the claim of the scientificity and neutrality of the teacher's knowledge and problem-solving skills, remains the controlling power in the writing class. The teacher's manner and discourse are still the goal for students to reach, for cognitivism makes it clear that only by mastering the teacher's discourse, including the teacher's way of writing, will students be able to write their way to where they want to be and join the community of the competent, the competitive, and the successful (Flower 1985, 4).[4]

Expressivism, on the other hand, errs in its downright denial of the teacher's authority in the classroom. Expressivists over-emphasize students' individual freedom and argue that the teacher should not play any role of a "teacher, critic, assessor, or editor" (Elbow 1987) but that of a kind of private audience in the writing class. Expressivists dismiss the teacher's authority, the real audience, the writing conventions and academic judgment as hostile forces that suppress students' individuality and creativity. Unfortunately, however, they do not offer any strategies to cope with the actual difficulties and problems students experience in college writing. In fact, as Reed Way Dasenbrock recapitulates the critics' view, the expressivists' rather blasé attitude towards errors in students' writing seems to indicate their reluctance to take the teacher's responsibility:

> It should occasion no surprise that subjectivism is generally hostile to a focus on ("superficial") correctness, though this rarely takes the form of a direct claim that errors don't matter. Instead, what is said is something like, "It is more appropriate to worry about that at some later stage." This might seem reasonable in first grade, but in college, there isn't much later left, so what this really means is, "We aren't going to deal with this." (1993, 25)

Further, expressivists' teacherless class implicitly reinforces the elitist assumption that writing cannot be taught because whether a student can write or not depends on whether or not there is something in his or her mind that is worth writing about. For expressivists, the truth lies in individuals' minds awaiting expression, and "writing is a black box: it is making marks on paper and then waiting to see what happens when other people come along and stare at those marks" (Elbow 1973, 133). Further-more, if some students are poorer writers than others, the teacher does not have to feel responsible to help them except for blaming the "distorting effects of a repressive social order" (Berlin 1988, 486). By this logic, the teacher's authority should be abandoned in the writing class, since it helps subject students to the "corrup-tions of the individual authorized by the language of commodified culture" and thus renders them powerless and noncreative (487). The problem with expressivism, however, is that it fails to explain why the teacher should still exist given that writing is unteachable. Its proposal of a "teacherless class" is itself an oxymoron, for the proposal denies and acknowledges simultaneously the inevitability of institutional authority in learning, authority that is embodied in the teacher as well as in a college writing class—a unit of the academic institution. Expressivists are thus caught in a logical fallacy, as they try to abandon the authority of the teacher in the classroom and yet affirm the benefit of the institution (e.g., the assumptions that a writing class provides a context for students to form groups and read each other's writing and that a writing class makes it possible for students to get help from "the strong-lensed person"—perhaps including the teacher [Elbow 1973, 134]).

Social constructionists have contributed greatly to the demystifying of the teacher's knowledge by arguing that it is a social artifact communally created and communally maintained, something that has gained its prestige through the consensus of the "interpretive community" (Fish 1980). In its insistence on the teacher playing the role of a facilitator and collaborator in the classroom, collaborative learning not only challenges the traditional assumption of the teacher as the truth-holder and knowledge-transmitter but also attempts to create a condition in the classroom in which the teacher's authority gives way to the authority of students' collaborative groups—the community of knowledgeable peers. However, the social constructionists' emphasis on academic discourse as the "passport" to the academic community implies their tendency to privilege the teacher's discourse over the students' discourse and the teacher's values and beliefs over the students' values and beliefs without explaining why this should be the case.[5] Observing how literacy plays a fundamental role in distinguishing "insiders" from "outsiders," J. Elspeth Stuckey remarks that literates, including teachers, betray their middle-class complacency, as well as their ignorance of their own biases, through their unquestioned attitude toward the illiterates in society:

> The idea of welcome is widespread; advertising and extending invitations into literacy clubs and communities range across the language/humanities disciplines from developmental specialties (Smith, *Essays*) to the domains of postmodernist literary criticism (Fish). It is as though all one has to do is to invite the illiterate to dinner. (1991, 35)

This criticism may well apply to social constructionists' attitude toward the academic discourse and academic community. Bruffee evidently does not realize his bias when making the following remark:

> Insofar as collaborative learning inducts students into estab-
> lished knowledge communities and teaches them the normal
> discourse of those communities, we derive our authority as
> teachers from being *certified representatives* of the communities
> of knowledgeable peers that students aspire to join, and that we,
> as members of our chosen disciplines and also members of the
> liberally educated public at large, *invite and encourage* them to
> join. ("Collaborative Learning" 1984, 649-50 emphasis added)

For Bruffee and other social constructionists, the teacher is still
superior to students, even though the teacher assumes a role as
facilitator and collaborator in a collaborative learning classroom.
The teacher, belonging to a more prestigious community, will
kindly step down from the platform and invite students to join this
desirable community by learning its normal discourse. However,
why is the academic community more desirable than other communities? Marilyn Cooper ponders:

> We [English teachers] believe in the value of critical thinking,
> cognitive dissonance, and adopting different perspectives—all of
> which are based on the central value of coming to know through
> reading and writing. But that these are the norms of our dis-
> course community, that they are *our* values, is not itself a
> sufficient reason for us to offer them to students too persuasively.
> *Why* are these things valuable to us and to our students? This is
> the question that is not addressed in the discussions of collabor-
> ative learning and discourse communities; it is the question we
> must answer if we are to persuade students to adopt our com-
> munity as their own. ("Unhappy Consciousness" 1989, 55)

But unfortunately social constructionists do not address this
important question in the classroom. As a result, the teacher's
authority in a collaborative learning classroom persists no matter
how the form is changed.[6] The teacher's authority is secured not
only by the teacher's discourse—academic discourse—but by the
academic community to which the teacher belongs.

Radical educationists' insistence on liberatory learning and
dialogic method indicates their desire to change the traditional
teacher's authority into a democratic force that transforms the
oppressive traditional classroom into a site of struggle for social
justice and equality. By urging teachers to turn their students into
"subjects" (Freire) and "agents" (Giroux) through dialogic method,
radical educationists attempt to challenge the traditional way of
seeing the teacher as the "knower," the "transmitter," and the
"depositor" and to change teachers into intellectuals who fulfill

their social responsibilities by pursuing a utopian goal in the classroom rather than helping to maintain the status quo. However, in their critique of dominant culture and dominant discourse, radical educationists reveal their intention to establish a new authority that is morally superior. For example, Henry A. Giroux advocates substituting for the canon a new canon consisting of "marginal works" (1990), Bizzell argues for the need of a new national discourse and a new moral stance that is based on civic virtue and Marxist values ("Beyond Anti-Foundationalism" 1988), and Charles Paine unequivocally announces that radical teachers should be "manipulators" who influence students to accept their progressive beliefs and values through charisma and power (1989, 564). Radical educationists' implicit argument that the teacher's authority based on the new canon or a new discourse is superior to the traditional teacher's authority has generated much criticism. Maxine Hairston speaks for many people when she announces her suspicion that radical educationists' discourse and authority can be equally oppressive in the classroom (1992).[7]

All these theoretical and pedagogical difficulties surrounding issues of the traditional teacher's authority indicate that further inquiry into the teacher's role and authority in the changing society is necessary.

Chapter 3

Reconsidering the Teacher's Authority

> But we know very well that, in [discourse's]
> distribution, in what it permits and what it
> prevents, it follows the lines laid down by
> social differences, conflicts and struggles.
> Every educational system is a political means
> of maintaining or modifying the
> appropriateness of discourses with the
> knowledge and power they bring with them.
> —Michel Foucault

When Hannah Arendt claimed in 1958 that "authority has vanished from the modern world" and that "if we raise the question what authority is, we can no longer fall back upon authentic and undisputable experiences common to all" (81), she seems to have anticipated the dilemma in which composition theorists and teachers have been caught. As I argued in the previous chapter, the endeavor of cognitivists, expressivists, social constructionists, and radical educationists to accommodate varied social and academic experiences of the diverse student population led to various theories and pedagogies that promote a decentered, student-oriented, and dialogic classroom. Implicitly or explicitly, however, all the new schools of thought make claims of authority: the cognitivists' authority, located in the mind and text; the expressivists' authority, focused on the private self, private discourse, and private truth; the social constructionists' authority, found in communal consensus and conventions; and the radical educationists' authority, ensured by utopian goals and personal morals. That compositionists are simultaneously abandoning authority and reclaiming authority is a paradoxical phenomenon that characterizes composition teaching today; it indicates the irresolvable conflict between the progressive teachers' desire to democratize

34 Teachers, Discourses, and Authority

teaching for social justice and equality and the violent dimension of teaching, which, being "symbolic imposition," demands the teacher's authority to ensure students' obedience and participation (Bourdieu and Passeron 1977, 5). I believe that in reclaiming new forms of authority the new schools of thought in composition studies reveal in different ways two major unrealistic assumptions: (1) that the teacher can choose to abandon the institutional authority that oppresses students and reproduces inequality[8]; and (2) that the authority of expertise and personal authority are intrinsically more liberating and democratic than institutional authority and that their use in the classroom will guarantee liberatory and democratic teaching. I argue that these assumptions are dangerous because, on the one hand, they reveal a lack of understanding of the dual character of authority inherent in all forms of authority—that is, authority is always indispensable and dangerous, no matter in what form it appears. On the other hand, this lack of understanding of the ambiguity of authority may lead to progressive teachers' misguided belief that, once they have abandoned institutional authority in their theories and pedagogies (which is impossible, as I shall argue), they are then free from risks of oppressing their students with their authority. To form a pedagogy that truly enables learning and promotes equality and democracy, compositionists need to recognize the complexity of the teacher's authority and the context in which it is used. I believe that such a recognition is a prerequisite for articulating an alternative way of teaching writing that will enable the teacher to fulfill his or her dual task in teaching, to conserve and transform the dominant culture.

THE INSTITUTIONAL AUTHORITY AS NECESSARY EVIL

Composition scholars and teachers have found theoretical support for their resistance against institutional authority mainly in the reproduction theorists' critique of the ideology underlying the discourse and logic of the dominant class's view of schooling.[9] For reproduction theorists, instead of offering possibilities for individual development and social and economic advancement, schools are institutions whose main functions are "the reproduction of the dominant ideology, its forms of knowledge, and the distribution of skills needed to reproduce the social division of labor" (Aronowitz and Giroux 1985, 69). Instead of being politically innocent and academically neutral, schools are reproductive agencies in three senses. Aronowitz and Giroux summarize the major arguments by the reproduction theorists:

First, schools provided different classes and social groups with the knowledge and skills they needed to occupy their respective places in a labor force stratified by class, race, and gender. Second, schools were seen as reproductive in the cultural sense, functioning in part to distribute and legitimate forms of knowledge, values, language, and modes of style that constitute the dominant culture and its interests. Third, schools were viewed as part of a state apparatus that produced and legitimated the economic and ideological imperatives that underlie the state's political power. (70)

The view of the reproduction theorists that schools play a major role in furthering the economic interests of the dominant class and perpetuating the hegemony of the dominant class and culture has no doubt caused progressive compositionists to suspect the authority of the institution.[10] Their suspicion is also sustained by the state's open intervention into schools: for example, through state-established certification requirements, the state is able to create a hierarchy of high-status knowledge—usually the hard sciences—and low-status knowledge—subjects in humanities, a hierarchy based on a "highly technocratic rationality that relies on a logic drawn primarily from the natural sciences" (Aronowitz and Giroux 1985, 92). The state also controls the development of curricula and the formulation of school policies without considering teachers' and parents' opinions in order to "valorize mental labor and disqualify manual labor."[11] Through "the production of 'truth' and 'knowledge' about education,"

> The state appropriates, trains, and legitimates "intellectuals" who serve as experts in the production and conception of school knowledge, and who ultimately function to separate knowledge from both manual work and popular consumption. (93)

Thus, the view is widely accepted that the academic institution serves as the reproduction agent of the state, which represents the dominant class's interests, and whatever power the institution has, it is given by the state to carry out its reproductive missions. It is for this reason that progressive compositionists have questioned, critiqued, or rejected the traditional teacher's authority which, as they believe, derives from the institutional authority that functions to exclude students who come from nondominant class backgrounds and to maintain the hegemony of the dominant culture and ideology in schools.

However, as Aronowitz and Giroux contend, the radical reproduction theories often ignore the other side of the story: that schools are also "relatively autonomous institutions" that do not merely copy the logic of the dominant class or mirror the workings of economic institutions. Schools are "political, cultural, and ideological sites that exist somewhat independently of the capitalist market economy," characterized by diverse forms of school knowledge, ideologies, organizational styles, and classroom social relations. Rather than merely reproducing the hegemony of the dominant class, schools often exist in a "contradictory relation to the dominant society, alternately supporting and challenging its basic assumptions." Rather than having only the delegated power to maintain the status quo, schools also possess power to "influence and shape those limits" set by society within which schools operate (1985, 72). In short, Aronowitz and Giroux view schools as playing a dual role as reproducer and transformer, and their institutional power is a double-edged sword: it can be used to bar students from the higher social classes through institutional measures such as tracking, remedial programs, and standard testing; it can also be used to provide spaces for opposition and resistance by adhering to its liberal democratic ideology and its counterlogic that contain "concerns for human rights that are often at odds with capitalist rationality, its ethos of commodity fetish, and its drive for profits" (94).

Aronowitz and Giroux's conception of the schools' relations to the dominant class and the dual role of the power of the academic institution helps illuminate the relationships between the teacher and the academic institution. The relationship between the teacher and the academic institution shows similarity to that between the dominant class and the academic institution. On the one hand, hired as its agents to fulfill its functions and tasks, teachers are obligated to obey the authority of the institution and carry out its missions of conserving the dominant culture and its forms of knowledge. On the other hand, being also part of the school culture and intellectual tradition in opposition to the dominant culture and ideology, teachers are intellectuals who often challenge and oppose the dominance of the institution and the dominant class over individuals in schools and in society. The relationship between the teacher and the institution is also characterized by the teacher's autonomy as an intellectual, which enables the teacher to alternately support and challenge the institution's basic assumptions. Like the institution they belong to, teachers also have a dual role to play: to conserve the dominant culture and to transform it. And the teacher's power, likewise, can be used either to help exclude students from possibilities of social, economic, and intellectual advancement or to enhance their chances of academic, social, and economic successes. The teacher's power, in this sense, is also a double-edged sword.

Compositionists' struggle to substitute for the traditional teacher's authority new forms of authority can be understood as their efforts to use the teacher's power to transform the dominant culture. But in emphasizing the role of teachers as opponents, compositionists tend to forget their role as cultural agents to conserve the dominant culture. Their denial of the institutional authority in the new forms of authority they claim implies their reluctance to see that the institutional authority can also be used to enhance learning and empower students. They do not want to admit that the institutional authority cannot be thrown away at the will of the progressive teacher, not only because the existence of the academic institution makes its authority inevitable but also because the possibility of education ultimately relies upon it.

Bourdieu and Passeron's examination of the interdependence between academic institution and teaching will help illuminate the point. For Bourdieu and Passeron, teaching requires the existence of institutions for two reasons: first, the arbitrariness of teaching needs an institution to legitimate its practice; and second, pedagogic communication demands juridical authority for its effects.

First, teaching is arbitrary in the sense that, not only are meanings selected to be taught usually chosen in accordance with the material, symbolic, and pedagogic interests of the dominant groups or classes, but the selection of these meanings is based on and legitimized by power relations (Bourdieu and Passeron 1977, 7). In other words, the process of selecting meanings is arbitrarily decided upon, usually by the culture in power, and the meanings selected are also arbitrary—a symbolic system that represents the "structure and functions of that culture" which "cannot be deduced from any universal principle, whether physical, biological or spiritual," nor be "linked by any sort of internal relation to 'the nature of things or any 'human nature'" (8). The "cultural arbitrary" is the product of power; those who are in power decide on the process of selection and the meanings to be selected.

Because pedagogical acts aim to impose this arbitrarily chosen symbolic system upon students, Bourdieu and Passeron explain, they are acts of "symbolic violence" that require a similarly arbitrary power to ensure best results of the inculcation of "the principles of a cultural arbitrary" (1977, 31). According to Bourdieu and

Passeron, the arbitrary power, resting on "the power relations between the groups or classes making up the social formation," has nevertheless to appear as legitimate authority in order to be convincing (10). This is so because only the authority legitimated by the institution—the juridical authority—will make the symbolic imposition easier for the cultural agent.

To demonstrate the importance of power relations that guarantee juridical authority in pedagogical acts, Bourdieu and Passeron compare the father-son relationship in a patrilineal social formation with that in a matrilineal system. In the patrilineal system, they point out, because the son has "explicit, juridically sanctioned rights over his father's goods and privileges," the father also has juridical authority over his son. This juridical authority gives the father sanctions in imposing his pedagogic acts without having to constantly elicit consent from his son for his imposition. In comparison, in the matrilineal society, the son has no rights over his father's goods and privileges, and the father, therefore, has no juridical authority over the son. Hence, the father has only affective or moral sanctions to back up his pedagogical acts when he encounters his son's resistance (Bourdieu and Passeron 1977, 6).

The point that Bourdieu and Passeron try to make with this analogy is that, teachers, having no biological relation with or inherent juridical authority over the student, have to establish their pedagogic relations with their students with the help of the institution. Since teaching "can produce its own specifically symbolic effect only when provided with the social conditions for imposition and inculcation, i.e., the power relations that are not implied in a formal definition of communication,"[12] the existence of the institution provides exactly the "social conditions for imposition and inculcation" (7). Being the delegated authority of the dominant class, the institution provides the teacher with juridical authority; by reproducing within the institution the delegation of authority from which the institution benefits, the educational system "produces and reproduces the conditions necessary both for the exercise of an institutionalized [pedagogic act] and for the fulfillment of its external function of reproduction." By endowing "all its agents with a vicarious authority, i.e., school authority, the institutionalized form of [pedagogic authority]," the institution, with its *institutional legitimacy, "dispenses the agents of the institution from having endlessly to win and confirm"* their pedagogic authority (Bourdieu and Passeron 1977, 63; emphasis added).

Like the patrilineal system that legitimates the father's power over his son, the institution legitimates acts of symbolic imposition of the cultural arbitrary of the dominant class. Owing to the power relations in society that ensure the institution its "institutional legitimacy," the institution is entitled to set up a hierarchical relation of pedagogic communication and delimit what deserves to be inculcated. In the end, the concept that teaching is a process of symbolic violence is obscured by the institution's authority, which "resolves by its very existence the questions raised by its existence" and thus ensures the desired effects of teaching as imposition of an arbitrary symbolic system (Bourdieu and Passeron 1977, 62).

Two examples from history may help further demonstrate Bourdieu and Passeron's contention that teaching demands the existence of the institution as well as its authority: the education crisis in China during the Cultural Revolution and the Literacy Crisis in America during the 1970s and 1980s. What happened in these times reveals, from quite different angles, how the changing of power relations in society can cause crisis in the institution and how the weakening of the authority of the institution can lead to extreme difficulties in teaching.

What characterizes the education crisis during the Cultural Revolution in China between 1966 and 1976 and the Literacy Crisis in America in the 1970s and 1980s is a "Legitimacy Crisis" caused by contradictions between the academic institution and the dominant groups. Given all social, cultural, political, and historical differences between the two crises, they do share one similarity: both happened because the dominant groups had lost their trust in the academic institution and blamed schools and teachers for existing social problems, and both crises led to the weakening of the autonomy and authority of the academic institution and consequent weakening of the teacher's authority in teaching. In both cases, the job of teaching became increasingly difficult, and the difficulties of teaching further led to pressure from the top (the dominant society) and rebellion from the bottom (the victimized students), thus forming a vicious circle in which the weakened autonomy and authority of the institution led to the weakened autonomy and authority of the teacher; the weakened authority of the teacher led to the so-called permissiveness or more oppression in the classroom and to the lowered quality of teaching and learning; the low quality of teaching and learning, in turn, led to students' unsatisfactory academic performance and further to society's dissatisfaction with the academic institution and to the dominant class's criticism and intervention. The vicious circle would continue until the whole educational system became paralyzed and lost its legitimate position in society, as the case during the Cultural Revolution in China. In the end, not only students and teachers fell prey to the disempowerment of the academic institution, but society suffered as a whole.

The education crisis in China between 1966 and 1976 was the climax of Mao Tsetung's series of political movements since 1949 aimed at transforming the superstructure in China to suit the economic basis that was supposed to serve the proletarian classes— workers, peasants, and soldiers.[13] Always critical that the Chinese educational system had been serving the interests of the old, overthrown ruling class and excluding the broad masses from college education, Mao called on the working class, the new ruling class, to destroy the old educational system and build a new one that would serve the interests of the broad masses. Mao accused the Chinese intelligentsia of attempting to restore the lost paradise of feudalists, imperialists, and capitalists through propagating bourgeois ideologies in teaching, and the Cultural Revolution, as he named it, was launched to mobilize workers, peasants, soldiers, and revolutionary students to take over the power of the academics so that the proletariat would become masters of colleges and universities. Cruelly persecuting prominent scholars and professors with various means, persistently denouncing through mass media the "conspiratory crimes" committed by academics to try to overthrow the "dictatorship of the proletariat," abandoning the traditional college entrance procedures and traditional ways of teaching, Mao successfully paralyzed the academic institution with cries of "education crisis." Deng Xiaoping, who had spoken in defense of the autonomy of the academic institution and had been criticized severely by Mao at the beginning of the Revolution but pardoned later, lamented in 1975:

> Out of the 150,000 scientific and technical cadres in the Academy of Sciences, no one dares go into the research laboratories. They are all afraid of being disparaged as "white" specialists. The young are frightened and the old are frightened....Research personnel no longer read books nowadays. (Meisner 1977, 387)

Schools suffered even more severe damages. When the Revolution started in 1966, young Red Guards did what Mao deemed revolutionary:

> Turn the old world upside down, smash it to pieces, pulverize it, create chaos and make a tremendous mess, the bigger the better. (339)

And in the middle phase of the Revolution, in the debris of burned books and destroyed labs, Mao sent workers, peasants, and soldiers into colleges and universities to study, manage, and transform places of old learning into sites of struggling for "liberation, equality, and socialist democracy." The hierarchy in the classroom was turned upside down, with students playing the role as managers and supervisors, telling the teacher to teach what they wanted, forbidding them to teach what they hated. The teacher's authority became nonexistent; teaching depended mainly on the teacher's ability to get along with students and to manage to arouse their interest in the subjects being taught without causing students' resistance or criticism.

My own experience as a teacher of English from 1971 to 1978 is one of the numerous tragic stories of the disempowerment of the academic institution and the teacher. I became a teacher, not because I chose to, but because my parents were well-known college English teachers in the city and also because college-trained English teachers were rare at that time, after Mao had closed all colleges and universities for five years. Despite my lack of credentials as a high school teacher, I was hired to teach English at a high school where most students were children of the workers in a nearby textile factory. Needless to say, teaching English at that time was not an easy job, even though there were signs of China opening its door to America after President Richard Nixon's visit in 1972. The memories of the Red Guards burning books and beating teachers were still fresh, and the reality was that anything that had the least connection with the Western world could still entail suspicion and criticism. Besides, society had little use for English. Having seen how my parents were criticized at the beginning of the Revolution for teaching "the language of imperialists," I had no intention of becoming a teacher of any kind. But my parents convinced me that being a teacher would perhaps be the only chance for me to continue my disrupted education, since, at the time, I would be unlikely to be accepted by any college, coming from a bourgeois family. So I became a teacher, with no credentials and no hope of getting them except by starting at the bottom at the worst time to become a teacher.

And those years taught me how bad it could be to belong to an institution that was the object of contempt and attack in society. The textbooks for English classes consisted mainly of excerpts from newspapers and Mao's works, and I remember how I had a hard time explaining to my students why they had to learn to read Mao's quotations in English when they already had enough of it in Chinese. And I also remember how I was questioned by a worker-teacher for having taught some English songs in class instead of "The East Is Red." Further, not many of my students wanted to be English teachers, and the few who did think of becoming teachers were discouraged either by their parents or by the community to which they belonged.

I still remember with acute pain one of my best students' fate. Tang Li, having been number one in English through her high school years, told her family that she wanted to go to college and become a teacher of English. Her father, a textile worker, shocked me with his unconcealable irritation at her wish. "You're a good teacher and my daughter thinks a world of you," he said to me without a smile. "But I would hate you if she should choose to be an English teacher." Used to his polite smile at parent-teacher meetings in the past, I was dismayed by his bluntness. After a long, awkward silence, he said, "Why should she want to beg for kids to learn the weird stuff that only causes you trouble?!" So, Tang Li succumbed to her father's authority and upon graduation from high school became a worker in the same textile factory. The day before she started working she came to see me, and both of us cried. I wish I had had the power to persuade her father, but the paralyzed educational system and the humiliated teacher had no voice in a society in which education held no value. So, despite all her promise for academic work and her hope of becoming a good teacher, Tang Li had to spend the rest of her life standing in front of a machine, weaving with her hands rather than creating with her brain.[14] She, like thousands and thousands of young people, was victimized by the dominant society's rage at the academic institution, by the institution's loss of its legitimacy in society, and by the nation's loss of faith in education resulting from the institution's loss of its authority and autonomy.

What happened on the American scene during the 1970s and 1980s was very different from what happened in China during the Cultural Revolution, except that the academic institution in America was also attacked by the dominant groups for pursuing different goals in education. A passage from *Back-to-Basics* by Burton Yale Pines explains the cause of the crisis as rooted in the utopian goals in education that marked the 1960s:

> For the half-decade starting with the late 1960s, long-established academic standards were abolished wholesale in a spasm

reminiscent of the Red Guards' destructive rampage through China's classical cultural institutions. (In Shor 1986, 59)

And the dominant class's antagonistic attitude toward the academy can hardly escape notice in the well-known *Newsweek* article, "Why Johnny Can't Write" (1975), which lays the blame on the educational system for students' poor writing skills:

> Nationwide, the statistics on literacy grow more appalling each year....If your children are attending college, the chances are that when they graduate they will be unable to write ordinary, expository English with any real degree of structure and lucidity.... Willy-nilly, the U.S. educational system is spawning a generation of semi-literates. (Sheils 1975, 58)

The criticism was echoed in 1977 in a College Board report:

> More and more high school graduates show up...with barely a speaking acquaintance with the English language and no writing facility at all. (In Shor 1986, 59)

In 1979 by Donna Woolfolk Cross in *Word Abuse*:

> Anyone who teaches English today knows that most students can't write. Their writing skills have been in a steady, downward spiral since the midsixties. (In Shor 1980, 59)

And in 1980 by John Simon in *Paradise Lost* with even greater vehemence. The downhill course the English language is taking is caused by students, minorities, teachers, and television, Simon argues, by what he calls

> the four great body blows: (1) the student rebellion of 1968, which, in essence, meant that students themselves became the arbiters of what subjects were to be taught, and grammar by jingo (or Ringo), was not one of them; (2) the notion that in a democratic society language must accommodate itself to the whims, idiosyncrasies, dialects, and sheer ignorance of underprivileged minorities, especially if these happen to be black, Hispanic, and later on, female or homosexual; (3) the introduction by more and more *incompetent English teachers, products of the new system of even fancier techniques of not teaching English*; and (4) television. (1980, xiv; emphasis added)

Whatever might have been the causes for the literacy crisis in America, the dominant groups obviously believed that the academic institution, as well as teachers, should be responsible for students' unsatisfactory literacy levels. Ronald Reagan's first secretary of education, T. H. Bell, summed up the tone for the 1980s with his charge that schools had devoted too much attention to "bringing up the bottom" (Faigley 1992, 68). And Senator Edward Zorinsky testified (in a hearing before the Senate Subcommittee on Elementary, Secondary, and Vocational Education) that "schools are creating illiterates" and that reforms could not be left up to the educators (Hourigan 1992, 21). Education was under siege, as Carl Klaus describes in "Public Opinion and Professional Belief":

> No matter where I turn, whether to television or newspapers or weekly magazines or institutional newsletters or professional journals or academic colleagues, I hear the same feverish cry: "Johnny Can't Write" (and apparently Jenny can't write either). Walter Cronkite says so, and so does the *Iowa City Press Citizen*, and the *Des Moines Register*, and *The New York Times*, and *Time Magazine*, and *Newsweek*, and the *Reader's Digest*....Suddenly it seems as if the whole country is about to take arms against a sea of stylistic troubles and by opposing end them [sic]. (1976, 335)

And the whole country did take arms against the sea of troubles supposedly created by intellectuals: the career education in the early 1970s, the back-to-basics movement in the mid-1970s, and the education reform in the 1980s were all measures taken by the dominant class to restore the traditional authority in the academy disrupted by the intellectuals' utopianism and political activism in the 1960s. Demanding that schools teach basic skills and standard English as well as reinforce standard testing and remedial programs, the dominant class turned teachers into "test-givers, test-scorers, bad-news messengers, and remedial instructors" and created a situation that indicated the teacher's powerlessness. As Ira Shor describes the situation,

> Teachers found less room to test alternate pedagogy because the official pressure to teach to the tests was formidable....Teachers no less than students suddenly found themselves on the defensive in the face of so much punitive surveillance from the authorities. Their competency was being intensely probed in a society where business and government had to hide their own dismal incompetence. (1986, 90)

As the academic institution's authority was weakened and the teacher's autonomy restricted, teaching became difficult. When "order is demanded by the top and freedom by the bottom," when school is accused of producing "stupefaction," "mediocrity," and "semi-literates" and is forced to change its curricula to satisfy the dominant class, teachers are caught in a dilemma: "If teachers build opposition, they risk their jobs. If they impose schoolish regimens, students make their jobs impossible to live with" (Shor 1986, 83). Thus, what seems to be the teachers' fault—the much criticized tendency of teachers' "permissiveness"—indicates the consequences of the disempowerment of the academy and the teacher: simultaneously attacked for his or her incompetence in maintaining the literacy standards and expected to impose more effectively the cultural arbitrary (in this case the basic skills and standard English), the teacher was required to accomplish more with less pedagogical authority. Facing the pressure from the top and the resistance from the bottom, teachers had to play the role of pacifists so that teaching could still continue. The result is a sad scene in the academic world, as Earnest Boyer observes in his important study of high schools during the 1983 Reagan reform:

> "Beaten down" by some of the students and unsupported by the parents, many teachers have entered into a...corrupting contract that promises a light work load in exchange for cooperation in the classroom. (In Shor 1986, 81)

And the credibility of Boyer's observation is confirmed by Theordore Sizer's tour of schools in the period of literacy crisis, during which he saw students "run schools" and noted that

> The agreement between teacher and students to exhibit a facade of orderly purposefulness is a Conspiracy for the Least, the least hassle for anyone. (In Shor 1986, 81)

For Christopher Jencks, the phenomenon indicates a Legitimacy Crisis: "Teachers stopped bugging students who did not want to work. In return, these students were expected not to organize open revolt against the school's nominal authority" (In Shor 1986, 80). In the end, both teachers and students became victims of the teacher's weakened authority. Christopher Lasch thus laments:

> Hoping to avoid confrontations and quarrels, [teachers] leave students without guidance, meanwhile treating them as if they were incapable of serious exertion. (In Shor 1986, 81)

The weakened authority of the institution finally has exacted its toll on the teacher and the student, whose relationship in the classroom changes from hierarchical to superficially equal, not because the equal relationship will more effectively help students to learn, but because the teacher does not want to lose his or her job and therefore has to resort to pacifist strategies. Like the Sophists, "teachers who proclaimed their educative practice as such (e.g., Protagoras saying 'I acknowledge that I am a professional teacher—*sophistes*—an educator of men') without being able to invoke the authority of an institution," teachers in the shadow of the Literary Crisis could not entirely convince their students that they have juridical authority over them in pedagogical acts (Bourdieu and Passeron 1977, 62). Further, as the institution lost its authority and autonomy, teachers also lost their authority and autonomy and hence their power to oppose the reproduction of inequality and injustice in society. The difficulties of teaching in America during the Literacy Crisis in the 1970s and 1980s and the impossibility of teaching in China during the Cultural Revolution from 1966 to 1976 serve to show that compositionists' wish to completely abandon institutional authority in teaching is wishful thinking. Employed by the institution to carry out its missions, teachers rely on the institution for authority to perform pedagogic acts. As long as teachers have to play the role of cultural agents for the institution, they will never be able to sever their ties to the institution completely. As long as teachers want to have power to oppose the dominant society, they have to belong to the academic institution and become part of its oppositional tradition. It is a dual role that the teacher has to recognize and learn to cope with.

THE AMBIGUITY OF THE AUTHORITY OF EXPERTISE AND PERSONAL AUTHORITY

Since teaching demands institutional authority, and since the teacher's authority is inevitably related to the authority of the institution, I will further examine the implications of compositionists' assumption that authority based only on the teacher's expertise or charisma is intrinsically more liberatory and empowering. I argue that, despite compositionists' attempt to change the traditional, hierarchical relationship between the teacher and the student through challenging institutional authority, the new forms of authority implicitly favored or openly endorsed by the new theories and pedagogies can also threaten to oppress students in the classroom, if the dual character of these forms of authority and the context in which they are used are ignored. By examining the complexity of the teacher's authority, I attempt to demonstrate that the authority of expertise favored by cognitivists, expressivists, and social constructionists and the personal authority promoted by radical pedagogues, can be as potentially oppressive as the traditional teacher's authority, if the institutional authority that constitutes part of the teacher's authority is not recognized.

As I have argued in the previous chapter, the emphasis of cognitivists on the research into the workings of the mind in the composing process and on the teacher as an expert of scientific, neutral discourse reveals their belief that what makes the new teacher differ from the traditional teacher is that the new teacher relies on the authority guaranteed by his or her expertise in teaching. Similarly, for expressivists, what gives the teacher authority in the class is the absence of institutional constraints and the teacher's ability to discover private truth and to express it in his or her writing.[15] For social constructionists, the teacher's authority is secured by the privileges of academic discourse and discourse community. Since students' well-being supposedly will be ensured by their mastering the teacher's academic discourse and joining the teacher's discourse community, teachers, rather than having to rely on institutional authority in teaching, need just to keep their arms open to those underprivileged and show their welcome and good will by helping students master academic discourse. In short, in these theories and pedagogies, the teacher's expertise is the guarantee of the teacher's authority. The authority of expertise is preferred because it is assumed that, since the teacher's expertise is what students need in life, authority based on this expertise must also be good for students.

The danger about the assumption that the authority of expertise is better than other forms of authority lies in its tendency to write off the complexity involved in all forms of authority. Not only does this assumption ignore the teacher's relation to the academic institution and to the job of teaching, but it also suppresses the power relations implicated in the authority of expertise. For example, one may well ask: What justifies cognitivists' inquiry and intervention into students' writing processes as legitimate pedagogical acts? What gives expressivist teachers the right to require their students to write about their personal experiences and private feelings and then discuss their writing with others despite some students' unwillingness to do so? What determines that students should approximate the teacher's academic discourse, instead of vice versa? And what entitles the radical teacher to claim that he or she has more charisma, better moral values, greater passion, or worthier goals in life than his or her students that he or she should change not only their ways with words but also their ways of life? The answer to these questions is "the institution." For, no matter how radical a theory and a pedagogy a teacher espouses, he or she cannot alter the fact that it is the institution's acknowledgement of the teacher's knowledge as legitimate that gives the teacher the authority of expertise.

In their article, "On Authority in the Study of Writing," Peter Mortensen and Gesa E. Kirsch make a useful definition of two kinds of authority: the "power to enforce obedience," and the "power to influence action, opinion, belief." This theoretical distinction of two kinds of power can be mapped into two functional categories: the "authority of office" and the "authority of expertise" (1993, 559). For Mortensen and Kirsch, the power to enforce and the power to influence action, opinion, and belief are "interrelated in practice," since "the power to enforce obedience is often presumed to derive from expertise," whereas "the power to influence action, opinion, or belief may sometimes conceal the power to enforce obedience—the latter power only becoming apparent should influence fail" (570). According to the authors, authority in hierarchical institutions such as the academy is "the *legitimate* force that attenuates raw power: authority conditions the power to persuade, the power to coerce, the power to initiate or mandate action" (560). This authority is a mixture of the authority of office and the authority of expertise, quite similar to Max Weber's "legal authority," which is an "impersonal, rational authority inherent in *specific social positions* and secured by *the possession of expertise*, defined as technical knowledge" (1993, 560; emphasis added). In other words, the authority in the academy, including the teacher's authority, possesses both the impersonal authority that pertains to positions and the rational authority secured by knowledge.

Bourdieu and Passeron's view of the teacher's authority is similar; they see it as a mixture of the "school authority"—"the authority of the agent of the educational system"—and "pedagogic authority"—"the authority for carrying on an education in a diffuse and unspecified way" (1977, 63). Being "a legitimacy by position" guaranteed by the institution and "socially objectified and symbolized in the institutional procedures and rules defining [the teacher's] training, by the diplomas that sanction it, and by the legitimate conduct of the profession," the teacher's authority is defined by Bourdieu and Passeron as containing both "school authority" and "pedagogic authority," which resemble the authority of office and the authority of expertise (63).

That the teacher's expertise is clearly an institutionalized entity is also argued by Aronowitz and Giroux:

> Behind this facade of credentialized expertise and professionalism lies a major feature of dominant ideology—the separation of knowledge from power. Poulantzas states, "The knowledge-power relationship finds expression in particular techniques of the exercise of power-exact devices inscribed in the texture of the state whereby the popular masses are permanently kept at a distance from the centers of decision making. These compromise a series of rituals and styles of speech, as well as structural modes of formulating and tackling problems that monopolize knowledge in such a way that the popular masses are effectively excluded. (1985, 93–94)

It is not hard to see that the cognitivists' problem-solving discourse with its particular scientific structures; the expressivists' private discourse with its typical structurelessness and idiosyncrasy; and social constructionists' academic discourse with its special concerns, conventions and modes can all monopolize knowledge in such a way that a large number of students can be effectively excluded.

Foucault's analysis of disciplines further illuminates the institutional dimension of the teacher's expertise. For Foucault, disciplines, the matrix from which the teacher's expertise derives, are the results of "the complex patterns of structuralization and distributions of power that influence the way in which a society selects, classifies, transmits, and evaluates the knowledge it considers to be public" (Goodson and Dowbiggin 1990, 105). Disciplines are "socially approved structures of knowledge [that] legitimize the relations of power between professional and client," and they fulfill the institutional task similar to that shared by nineteenth-century asylums and public schools—namely, "the task of creating, transforming, and disciplining forms of behavior and character in order to produce mechanisms for what Foucault has called 'constant policing.'" Because disciplines emerged out of the power relations between the state and profession, the disciplines become "general forms of domination" which create subjected and practiced bodies, "docile bodies" (105–06). In this analysis, the teacher's expertise, being part of disciplines, functions similarly as the institutional authority in producing docile bodies.

In the same analysis, cognitivists' expertise based on neutral, scientific discourse; expressionists' expertise on private discourse; social constructionists' expertise on academic discourse—all can function to produce docile bodies in the classroom because of the inherent power relations embodied in disciplines and knowledge. The teacher's expertise can be used to exclude or punish, to domesticate or transform students because the teacher-student relationship is inscribed in the institution, which guarantees that the student is the one who does not know and has, therefore, to be worked on and changed. To reach their democratic and utopian goals in teaching, radical educationists opt for personal authority that is characterized by "obedience [that] is owed to the *person*" and that often appears in "traditional" and "charismatic" forms, as in the case of an ancient monarch or modern dictator (Mortensen and Kirsch 1993, 560). However, like cognitivists, expressivists, and social constructionists, radical educationists erred in assuming that institutional authority oppresses, while personal authority does not.[16] For example, in "Relativism, Radical Pedagogy, and the Ideology of Paralysis," Charles Paine argues from a radical position that endorses personal authority. He maintains that if a teacher (a "relativist teacher") wants to "develop and maintain an emancipatory vision" when surrounded by students who are comfortable with their world and do not want to change things as they are, the teacher *must* "accept the role as manipulator" and "influence (*perhaps manipulate is the more accurate word*) students through charisma or power" (1989, 563; emphasis added). As to what gives the teacher the power to manipulate students, Paine believes it is the teacher's commitment to "his or her own beliefs, values, and loyalties about what is right and wrong in the world," as well as his or her desire to "bring about change through individual action or socially, by influencing the beliefs and values of other persons" (563). In other words, what makes the teacher powerful and charismatic is the teacher's "personal beliefs—but held with strong convictions nevertheless" (564). The students, whose values and beliefs are perhaps held with less strong convictions, as Paine implies, should then be subjected to the teacher's personal authority and become, ideally, converts. For Paine, the success of the teacher is indicated by "the degree to which [he or she is] able to influence students" with "charisma and power," and "the real value of emancipatory education can only be measured by the degree to which students are *converted*" and become "committed to emancipatory causes and activities" like the teacher (564; emphasis added).

Paine cites Giroux and Freire to support his arguments, but he seems to have missed Giroux's belief that the teacher's authority can never be mere personal power or charm; it is always political, implied in the existence of the institution and secured by power relations in society, a view that is similar to that held by Bourdieu and Passeron (Aronowitz & Giroux, *Education Under Siege*, 1985). For Giroux, the radical teacher needs to use his or her authority to transform the oppressive system rather than students, a view that bears Freire's influence (Giroux, *Border Crossings*, 1992). This same point is also missed by Paine in his interpretation of Freire's view of the dialogic teacher-student relationship. As Freire emphasizes in all his works, the emancipatory teacher will never seek to *convert* his or her students. For example, in *Education for Critical Consciousness*, Freire sees "extension," a form of education that opposes "*conscientizacaō*," as "cultural invasion" because it is characterized by the educator's seeking to "impose his system of values on its members" through "the manipulation—never the organization—of the individuals" (1973, 113). The truly liberatory educator, Freire argues, will aim to change one's environments rather than change human beings in the process of education. The students' change in consciousness results not from the educator's propaganda but from their interaction as subjects with the educator and the real world. In fact, Paine's converting students with charisma and power does not differ much from what Freire calls the "invading agent," who turns the students into objects through "manipulating, steering and domesticating" activities (115).

Left unexamined in Paine's argument for personal charm and power is the power relationship between the teacher and students confirmed by the institution, a power relationship that Paine is reluctant to face in his argument for emancipatory education. Patricia Bizzell is more outspoken than Paine on this issue. When persuasion seems inadequate to the task of moving students in the direction of her own "left-oriented political goals," Bizzell argues in "Power, Authority, and Critical Pedagogy," the teacher should resort to authority to ensure students' obedience. However, Bizzell would not admit that the authority she relies on is secured by the institution. On the contrary, her authority, she says, is granted by the students at the beginning of the course through her successful use of a democratic process of persuasion. According to Bizzell, what makes her authority differ from coercion is her promise to her students that their "best interests ultimately will be served" by the authority they have granted her. This authority then allows her to change the teacher-student relationship to "a less dialogic one," a relationship that enables the teacher to force students to comply with the teacher in practices that are found "uncongenial" or "even painful" by students. What ensures students' endurance of pain is their faith in the teacher, who is devoted to serving the common good by achieving her own "left-oriented political goals" in teaching.[17]

It is not hard to see that the authority Bizzell advocates is another version of the personal authority Paine favors. Locating authority in the intrinsic goodness of the teacher, Bizzell manages to dress up the institutional authority in the claims of the teacher's civic virtues, left-oriented political goals, and good will. However, Bizzell's claims imply that the teacher is morally superior to the students and therefore should have the power to think and act on their behalf. The danger of such an assumption lies in this: that the teacher can be an oppressor without realizing it, believing that whatever he or she does will ultimately serves students' best interests.[18] Further, as Min-Zhan Lu correctly senses it, it is "self-serving" for the teacher to believe that his or her own "representations of the 'needs' and abilities of the students" are "self-evident 'facts' devoid of political interests" (1993, 900). Lu argues convincingly that:

> [A] classroom treating the teacher's knowledge of the student as self-evidently "factual," supposedly inherent in the "object's own integrity" and "its own nature dictating how it is best known," risks leading students to passively accept the teacher's knowledge. Thus, students are more likely to be "silenced by the teacher's political agenda" if they are not asked or allowed to reflect on the role both students and teachers have played in espousing it. (900–01).

When students are "silenced by the teacher's political agenda," the power that silences them stops being the authority Bizzell endorses. Only coercive power will silence the students, an institutional power that grants authority to the teacher's political agenda. Seen in this light, Bizzell's authority does not differ much from the traditional teacher's authority: for the authority of both depends on the teacher's prestigious discourse, and both justify their superiority to their students by the position they hold in the institution. Like the traditional teacher's authority, personal authority can also oppress in the classroom context.

Paine's and Bizzell's arguments are derived from the radical school's view of the teacher's authority, which has been formed in the course of the radical educationists' struggle against the hegemony of the dominant groups in society and in schools in the past two decades. In order to counter the negative effects generated by the series of education reforms that have weakened the teacher's authority and made teaching difficult, radical educationists like Paine and Bizzell attempt to use personal authority in lieu of institutional authority to achieve their democratic and emancipatory goals in schools. However, in their struggle to break away from oppressive institutional authority, radical educationists risk the danger of suppressing the institutional authority implicated in the teacher's personal authority and consequently of suppressing students with personal authority in the classroom.

Bourdieu and Passeron do not deny the existence of charismatic forms of personal authority in teaching, yet they see it as part of the authority of office, as encouraged and secured by the institutional authority for better effects of symbolic imposition:

> The most typically charismatic feats, such as verbal acrobatics, hermetic allusion, disconcerting references of peremptory obscurity, as well as the technical tricks which serve as their support or substitute, such as the concealment of sources, the insertion of studied jokes or the avoidance of compromising formulations, owe their symbolic efficacy to the context of authority the institution sets up for them. And if the institution tolerates and so strongly encourages disrespect for the accessories and even the institutional rules, this is because pedagogic action must always transmit not only a content but also the affirmation of the value of that content, and there is no better way of doing so than by diverting onto the thing communicated the glamour which the irreplaceable manner of communicating it secures for the interchangeable author of the communication. (1977, 125)

And Bourdieu and Passeron are not alone with this view. Max Weber makes a similar connection between the teacher's charisma and the institution: "The priest dispenses salvation by virtue of his office. Even in cases in which personal charisma may be involved, it is the hierarchical office that confers legitimate authority upon the priest as a member of a corporate enterprise of salvation" (In Bourdieu and Passeron 1977, 63). Emile Durkheim's remark confirms Weber's observation: "The teacher, like the priest, has a recognized authority, because he is the agent of a moral body greater than himself" (In Bourdieu and Passeron 1977, 63–64).

So, the teacher's authority, no matter whether it appears in the form of the authority of expertise or personal authority, contains some potential danger of oppression, as does institutional authority. William E. Connolly rightly remarks, "We must expect that every operative set of authoritative norms contains arbitrary elements within it," arbitrary in the sense that any authority brings with it constraints and exclusions. "While indispensable to this way of life there are other forms of living, admirable in their own way, in which this specific set would not be necessary." As Connolly sees it, all forms of authority are potentially oppressive, because "every good way of life imposes arbitrary limits, exclusions, losses, burdens, and sacrifices on its members to sustain itself," and because "these burdens are likely to be distributed asymmetrically across lines of gender, class, generation or region." That authority is ambiguous is exactly because of its dual character: that it is both indispensable and dangerous, that it regulates and suppresses, as the following examples illustrate:

> To honor equality (an admirable thing) is also to demean excellence in certain ways; to institutionalize individualism is to sacrifice the solace and benefits of community; to exercise freedom is to experience the closure that accompanies choice among incompatible and often irreversible projects; to secure stable identities through gender demarcation is to exclude the hermaphrodite from such an identity and to suppress that in others which does not fit neatly into its frame; to prize the rule of law is to invite the extension of litigiousness into new corners of social life; to institutionalize respect for the responsible agent is to show institutional disrespect for those unqualified or unwilling to exercise responsibility; to give primacy to mathematization in the social construction of knowledge is to denigrate individuals whose thought escapes that mold and to depreciate ways of knowing which do not fit into its frame. And lest the point be misread, to reverse these priorities would be to install another set of losses and impositions. (1987, 21)

Unless radical educationists realize how the personal authority they endorse may impose arbitrary limits, exclusions, losses, burdens, and sacrifices on their students in the classroom, their strong desire to democratize education and their good will to serve their students' best interests would not alone guarantee a classroom free from ideological and psychological oppression. For the same reason, the authority of expertise can also limit, oppress, exclude. Only when the teacher fully realizes how all kinds of authority, in the classroom context, will inevitably serve to ensure the teacher's pedagogic authority over the student, will the teacher be able to see the complex implications of various new theories and pedagogies and explore better ways of teaching.

A brief discussion of the relationship between the teacher and the student in the classroom context will further illustrate why it is dangerous for the teacher to ignore the institutional authority inherent in all forms of authority. In the hierarchy of the dominant society, the academic institution, the teacher, and the student, the student is at the very bottom. Unlike the relationships between the dominant society, the academic institution, and the teacher, the relationships between the student and the academic institution and the teacher is marked by an absence of all the salient features of the other relations: the institutional responsibilities and obliga tions each reproduction agent bears for the higher institution, the delegated power each agent possesses to perform various task and duties, the autonomy each agent enjoys that allows divers forms of knowledge and oppositional views and ideas, and th freedom, though limited, to challenge and resist the authority of the institution higher on the hierarchy. Students, especially thos who were not born into the dominant class, do not belong to th academic institution; nor do they share with the teacher th intellectual tradition that stands legitimately in opposition to th dominant society and dominant ideology.[19] Although students ca also resist the institution's or the teacher's authority, the resistance usually results either in breaking the school rules, po academic performance, or dropping out of school.[20] Because of t powerless position of the student in the academic institutio expressivists, social constructionists, radical compositionists, a even cognitivists all attempt to downplay or even eradicate instit tional authority in their theories and pedagogies, believing th once institutional authority is absent from the classroom, t teacher and the student will then enjoy an equal relationship th makes teaching democratic and learning pleasant. Neverthele contrary to what they wish, the denial of institutional author also hides the danger of ignoring the dual character of other for of authority that may likewise lead to oppression and inequalit the classroom.

Thus, we have circled back to the place where we first start asking the same question: If teaching requires the teach authority, if the teacher's authority, no matter in what forn appears, has the potential danger of oppression and exclusior the teacher has the obligation to impose the cultural arbitrary the responsibility to oppose the hegemony of the dominant cl culture, and ideology in education, what can the teacher d fulfill both tasks in teaching? Connolly's question is also pertin

since "any authoritative set of norms and standards is, at its best, an ambiguous achievement, it excludes and denigrates that which does not fit into its confines," "which achievements are worthy of our endorsement once the ambiguity within them is recognized" (1987, 21)? Now that the ambiguity within the teacher's authority, as well as within the authority of expertise and personal authority is recognized, the next step will be to form an alternative description of the teacher's authority in the writing class, a task that forms the focus of the next chapter.

Chapter 4

Rethinking the Relationship of Discourses in the Classroom

> We must make allowance for the complex and
> unstable powers whereby discourse can be
> both an instrument and an effect of power,
> but also a hindrance, a stumbling block, a
> point of resistance and a starting point for an
> opposing strategy.
>
> —Michel Foucault

I have argued that the teacher's authority, no matter in what forms it appears, is always a composite of institutional authority, the authority of expertise, and personal authority. I have also argued that, because the teacher-student relationship in pedagogic communication is based on power relations existing in society, teachers cannot abandon the institutional authority immanent in the role they are expected to play as cultural agents. The recognition of the inevitability of the teacher's judicial authority over the student enables teachers to realize the indispensability of institutional authority in teaching and the ever-existing potential danger of its use in the classroom. This realization, in turn, will help teachers avoid the pitfall of assigning all the evils to institutional authority, while using other forms of authority with blind convictions that would likewise threaten to oppress despite their progressive goals in teaching and good intentions for students. With the foregoing arguments as premises, I want to explore further how teachers can use their authority in teaching for the purpose of enhancing learning and empowering students.

Given the power relations between the teacher and the student in pedagogic communication, certain discourses privileged by various theorists and educationists can all be used to secure the teacher's authority and to limit, exclude, and oppress students. To arrive at a better understanding of how teachers can use the

authority of discourse as a means to fulfill their emancipatory and
democratic goals in the writing class, therefore, requires that we
explore the relationships among the teacher's radical discourse, the
dominant discourse, and the students' discourse(s). Using Richard
Rorty's distinction between normal discourse and abnormal
discourse as the theoretical framework, I will show how the three
kinds of discourse form a continuum, with the dominant discourse
occupying the middle ground, from which the teacher's radical
discourse and the students' discourse(s) extend toward the opposite
ends. Because the students' discourse(s) and the teachers' discourse are differently related to normal discourse, I refer to the
former as Nonresponsive Abnormal Discourse and the latter as
Responsive Abnormal Discourse.

Discourse as the Site of Struggle

In a few lines in *Yearning*, the feminist writer bell hooks accurately
reflects the postmodern academics' obsession with discourse[21]:

> Language is also a place of struggle. We are wedded in language,
> have our being in words. Language is also a place of struggle.
> Dare I speak to oppressed and oppressor in the same voice? Dare
> I speak to you in a language that will move beyond the boun-
> daries of domination—a language that will not bind you, fence
> you in, or hold you? Language is also a place of struggle. The
> oppressed struggle in language to recover ourselves, to reconcile,
> to reunite, to renew. Our words are not without meaning, they
> are an action, a resistance. Language is also a place of struggle.
> (1990, 146)

Indeed, the rhetorical turn in the twentieth century, with its
rejection of the traditional view of philosophy as epistemology and
foundation, has made discourse "an absolute sphere." The questioning of the Kantian notion of the essence of the mind, the
suspicion of an independent world out there that can be objectively observed and described, and the suggestion that truth is not
the representation of reality but a holistic coherence of beliefs
settled by an ongoing social debate—all this leads to a new view of
philosophy as hermeneutics, as just another narrative and conversation among numerous other narratives and conversations of
humanity. Discourse is an absolute sphere in the sense that, as
John D. Caputo puts it,

> If the philosophy as epistemology wanted to create a master,
> canonical discourse, the new hermeneutics seeks only to

recognize the plurality of discourses and is content to keep a civil conversation going. There is strict method in neither the natural sciences (Kuhn) nor the human sciences (Gadamer), but simply diverse spheres of discourse, some of which assert themselves for a while as normal. There is no hard and fast distinction between the human sciences and the natural sciences, nor between man and nature. Sartre was only half right: not only does man have no essence, nature has none either. The natural and the human sciences do not differ as explanation from understanding; rather a hermeneutically governed conversation is going on in all the disciplines, none of which can be canonized as representing truth Being. The real mistake is to think that there is a "deep nature"— whether it be matter or spirit or Being—and hence an absolute sphere of discourse. (1985, 251)

Within this sphere of discourse, social, cultural, political, and intellectual battles have been fought with words rather than with guns and swords. Discourse becomes power and social control in the modern time, replacing centralized power of monarchy in preenlightenment days. As Carolyn Ericksen Hill tersely summarizes Foucault's view, "power resides now more in dispersed forces of knowledge and discourse called disciplines—bureaucratic, institutional, or academic ones—than in centralized legal authority" (1990, 95). In other words, Hill cites Foucault, today power is more subtle than in the days of monarchy, "woven invisibly into our psyches and locally diffused in relations between people." It is exercised "through internalizing the laws and regulations" provided by those experts, who, "by representing the authority of disciplines, know and can teach the truth for the sake, supposedly, of those they teach" (95). In a sense, power has become the power of discourse, as Hill explains:

> More than power *in* people, then, authority may better be thought of as moving *between* them, regulating the way they talk with and relate to each other. The margins between center and edges are no longer easily stabilized, even though power may *feel* outside of us in some other center. It is the discourses we use that attempt the stabilizing, claims Foucault, and discourses can destabilize too. (95)

In schools, the struggle has been focused on the dominant discourse founded on the "great books," the canon. In the past three decades, the canon's predominantly white, middle-class, masculine bias has been exposed and critiqued from different angles by feminists, deconstructionists, Marxist theorists, and cultural critics. In the field of composition studies, the battles over the canon have generated debate over what to teach in first-year English courses. There are those who, like Erika Lindemann, believe that first-year English should "provide opportunities to master the genres, styles, audiences, and purposes of college writing." So they argue that first-year English should "offer guided practice in reading and writing the discourses of the academy and the professions" instead of preoccupying it with "grammar, or the essay, or great ideas" (1993, 312). There are also those who believe that the emphasis of first-year English on academic discourse restricts college education to mere job training and thus denies students "most important conversations" that "take place *outside the academy*—that is, how to vote and love and survive, how to respond to change and diversity and death and oppression and freedom" (Tate 1993, 320). For this reason, as Gary Tate argues, literature—fiction, poetry, drama—should be included in the first-year writing courses.[22] There are still others who view first-year English as sites for resistance and opposition; therefore, they argue that marginal discourses in the writing classes should be the major content of teaching and that such marginal discourses should be used as weapons against discourses of oppression. For these people, any nonmainstream, noncanonical, nonacademic discourse is potentially liberatory and should be encouraged in the writing class.[23] Further, the nonfoundationalists' objection to any inclination to rely on a certain conceptual scheme or theory in teaching writing and their warning against new forms of essentialism in the writing class makes it difficult for composition teachers to decide what kind of discourse can be taught without entailing oppression or exclusion.[24] Thus, as the canon is examined, evaluated, questioned, and changed, new questions keep surfacing with the concern that the new canon and new essentialism can be just as hegemonic, exclusive, and biased as the old canon (Morgan 1990, 6).[25]

Besides the debate over the canon, the special relationship between reading and writing in the writing class has also complicated the issue of the canon. For example, for literary professors, one of the major obligations of the teacher is to "display a way to do something," as J. Hillis Miller emphasizes in his interview with Gary A. Olson (1994, 124). However, while it is possible for a literature professor to display how to read a canonical text in a literature class whose major goal is interpretation and comprehension, it is almost impossible for a writing teacher to display how to write a good paper before students produce any written drafts. Thus, Jasper Neel's annoyance at Miller's remark is understandable:

> What Miller does not seem to understand is that the only mean-
> ingful texts in the composition class already belong to the
> students. One cannot teach composition by "displaying" one's
> "interaction with the text at hand" because no text at hand exists
> as an object of study whose power and beauty allow for a
> professional explication. (1994, 157)

Neel may be wrong to assume that the teacher's displaying his or her interaction with a representative student paper will not be taken seriously as pedagogy (157–58), but his point is worth heeding that teaching writing requires more than just displaying how to read a canonical text. It is also worth noting that a teacher's interaction with a student paper is different from his or her interaction with canonical texts, a point that assumes different relations of the teacher's discourse to the dominant discourse and to student discourse.

Radical scholars' criticism and rejection of canonical knowl-edge and the "great works," compositionists' disagreement over the major goals and content of first-year composition, and antifounda-tionalists' distrust of any tendency to establish new canons or new schemes have created a difficult situation for composition scholars and teachers. Patricia Bizzell would not conceal her anxiety over such a situation. She criticizes antifoundational critics for creating "a sort of pedagogical bad faith" in their deconstructive approach to canonical texts and foundational knowledge, and she sees their insistence on enlarging the canon with works by previously mar-ginalized and politically disenfranchised groups as a hidden tendency to escape from the struggle of ideologies to philosophical abstraction ("Beyond Anti-Foundationalism" 1988, 670). Bizzell recommends that we find "the collective will to collaborate on a pluralistic national discourse that would displace [E. D.] Hirsch's schemes while addressing the same lack he delineates," because "our task is to aid everyone in our academic community, and in our national community, to share a discourse." She urges that we must not only critique and deconstruct but also go on to "develop a positive or utopian moment in our critique, an alternative to Procrustean schemes for national unity" (665). Bizzell is unam-bivalent about her convictions:

To take the next step in our rhetorical turn, we will have to be more forthright about the ideologies we support as well as those we attack, and we will have to articulate a positive program legitimated by an authority that is nevertheless non-foundational. We must help our students, and our fellow citizens, to engage in a rhetorical process that can collectively generate trustworthy knowledge and beliefs conducive to the common good— knowledge and beliefs to displace the repressive ideologies an unjust social order would inscribe in the skeptical void. (671)

Bizzell's desire for a "positive program" may well touch a responsive chord in many composition teachers who share her anxiety over the field's lack of an agreed-upon content to teach in the first-year writing class. Bizzell's acknowledgment of the need of authority to legitimate such a program is also insightful. However, Bizzell's suggestion of establishing a "positive program" and a "national discourse" based on "civic virtue" and Marxist values has also encountered criticism and rejection ("Beyond Anti-Foundationalism" 1988, 671). For example, Nancy McKoski criticizes Bizzell for representing a "strong modernist reaction to postmodern critique" with her "call for intellectuals to represent and teach a unified academic discourse and culture in order to provide for a shared political discourse at the national level." McKoski perceives Bizzell's desire for a national discourse as revealing her belief that "only a totalizing, universalizing, rationalistic (masculinist, Western) politics is 'genuine.'" She also considers Bizzell's proposal a refusal to "regard the historical significance of postmodern politics, which she writes off as the quietistic liberal or anti-foundational belief in pluralism and difference" (McKoski 1993, 339).

Andrew and James Sledd also reject Bizzell's interpretation of an antifoundationalist position, which, they argue, is based on her misinterpretation of antifoundationalism as assigning all the power to rhetoric:

Anti-foundationalists argue, Bizzell reports, that "whatever we believe, we believe only because we have been persuaded." Accordingly, "foundational knowledge is really the product of cultural activity, shaped by ideology and constituted, not merely conveyed, by rhetoric." Rhetoricians, in such a view, are of immense importance, for "persuasive language creates truth by inducing belief; 'truth' results when rhetoric is successful." (1991, 717–18)

Andrew and James Sledd's objection is well justified, for they are right to argue that Bizzell's interpretation of antifoundationalism as assigning all the power to rhetoric is a misunderstanding. In fact, what Bizzell reports as an antifoundationalist position is exactly what antifoundationalists are suspicious of. For example, in his interview with Olson, Jacques Derrida warns against "rhetoricism"—"a way of giving rhetoric all the power, thinking that everything depends on rhetoric as simply a technique of speech" (Olson 1994, 135). Derrida points out that, on the one hand, "we should not neglect the importance of rhetoric, as if it were simply a formal superstructure or technique exterior to the essential activity." On the other hand, he says, "This doesn't mean that everything depends on verbal statements or formal technique of speech acts," because the "possibility of speech acts, or performative speech acts, depends on conditions and conventions which are not simply verbal." Derrida especially warns against the "inherent danger of rhetoricism in the teaching of rhetoric":

> When you teach rhetoric you are inclined to imply that so much depends on rhetoric. But I think that a self-conscious and trained teacher, attentive to the complexity, should at the same time underline the importance of rhetoric and the limits of rhetoric— the limits of verbality, formality, figures of speech. Rhetoric doesn't consist only in the technique of tropes, for instance. First, rhetoric is not confined to what is traditionally called figures and tropes. Secondly, rhetoric, as such, depends on conditions that are not rhetorical. In rhetoric and speaking, the same sentence may have enormous effects or have no effects at all, depending on conditions that are not verbal or rhetorical. I think a self-conscious, trained teacher of rhetoric should teach precisely what are called "pragmatics": that is, the effects of rhetoric don't depend only on the way you utter words, the way you use tropes, the way you compose. They depend on certain situations: political situations, economical situations—the libidinal situation, also. (135–36)

Derrida's clarification may well serve as a diagnosis of the problem I see in Bizzell's and many other compositionists' defense of their own position: in rejecting the dominance of the canon, they are often carried away by their belief in the righteousness of their own "positive program," "national discourse," or something else that is supposedly to be more progressive and less oppressive than the canon.[26] But in arguing for their own alternatives, they tend to forget that "the effects of rhetoric don't depend only on the way you utter words, the way you use tropes, the way you compose. They depend on *certain situations: political situations, economical situations—the libidinal situations, also*" (Derrida 1991, 136; emphasis added).[27] By this logic, the effects of a certain discourse, whether it is the dominant discourse founded on the canon or the radical discourse based on Marxist values, depend not only on how they are articulated and defended but also on the situations in which they are articulated. In the writing class, whether a certain discourse has a positive or negative effect on students depends on how the teacher and students are related to this discourse—politically, economically, socially, culturally, and linguistically—and how they interact with this discourse. Thus, to argue convincingly whether one discourse is preferable than the others requires an examination of the relationships of various discourses in the classroom and an analysis of the way in which they interact with one another. For my own purpose, I want to invoke Rorty's vision of the relationship between normal and abnormal discourse to illuminate the complex relationships among the teachers' discourse(s), the students' discourse(s), and the dominant discourse in the writing classroom.

RORTY'S NOTION OF NORMAL AND ABNORMAL DISCOURSE

Richard Rorty's neopragmatism has greatly influenced social constructionists' thinking, and his notion of normal and abnormal discourse has provided a rationale for Bruffee's influential argument for collaborative learning in the writing class. In "Collaborative Learning and the 'Conversation of Mankind,'" Bruffee identifies Rorty's normal discourse with "the sort of writing most people do most in their everyday working lives," and argues that "teaching normal discourse in its written form is central to a college curriculum" (1984, 642, 643). From this premise Bruffee proposes that the best way to teach normal discourse is through collaborative learning, for collaborative learning "provides the kind of social context, the kind of community, in which normal discourse occurs: a community of knowledgeable peers." For Bruffee, Rorty's notion of normal discourse justifies his claim that teaching writing consists of two major goals: to help students master the normal discourse, or "academic discourse" in social constructionist terms; and to provide a context, a community of knowledgeable peers, for students to practice and master the normal discourse exercised in established knowledge communities in the academic world and in business, government, and the professions (644).

Bruffee understands (or misunderstands) Rorty's abnormal discourse as a "knowledge-generating discourse." For Bruffee, abnormal discourse is a more desirable discourse compared with normal discourse, which only "maintains knowledge" but is "inadequate for generating new knowledge" (1984, 647). However, although abnormal discourse is necessary to learning, Bruffee dismisses it from his agenda, claiming that it cannot be directly taught. The solution for Bruffee is that we must teach "the tools of normal discourse" in such a way that "students *can* set them aside, if only momentarily, for the purpose of generating new knowledge, for the purpose, that is, of reconstituting knowledge communities in more satisfactory ways" (648).

Bruffee's endeavor to apply Rorty's notion of normal and abnormal discourse to the teaching of writing is pioneering in the field. However, his interpretation of Rorty is unfortunately inadequate and inaccurate. Although Bruffee is right, as confirmed by Rorty's interview with Olson, that normal discourse should be taught in the writing class and that abnormal discourse cannot be taught, Bruffee nevertheless simplifies the relationship between normal and abnormal discourse and dismisses the latter altogether in teaching.[28] If, as Bruffee claims, abnormal discourse is "knowledge-generating discourse," whereas normal discourse is just to "maintain knowledge" but is "inadequate in generating new knowledge," Bruffee's ignoring the place of abnormal discourse in his pedagogy indicates a weakness, especially when he announces that the goal of his collaborative learning approach is to generate new knowledge. Bruffee states that normal discourse can be taught simply as tools to generate abnormal discourse, but he never explains how a discourse, supposedly to be constitutive of our thinking and being, can be taught merely as tools to generate another discourse of quite different nature.

Further, Bruffee's conversational model, devoid of the tension between normal and abnormal discourse in Rorty's notion of conversation, overemphasizes the importance of communal consensus as the goal of conversation and entails much criticism of Rorty in composition studies. That Bruffee's conversational model should be considered equivalent to Rorty's philosophical concept of conversation is, indeed, a grave misunderstanding of Rorty. For example, Giroux criticizes Rorty for ignoring power, struggle, and individual will in his notion of conversation (Green 1990, 155). However, Giroux does not seem to understand that Rorty's abnormal discourse exists exactly to resist the hegemonic power of normal discourse and to struggle for individual voices. Joseph Petraglia criticizes Bruffee's conversational model for failing to show how competing communities arrive at consensus and to acknowledge possible coercion involved in conversation (1991, 50). And Bruffee's failure results mainly from his inadequate interpretation of Rorty, for Bruffee fails to realize that for Rorty the conversation is both means and end in itself, a human pursuit of knowledge, a humanizing process in which space for new wonders is kept open, a hermeneutic endeavor to confront and embrace the incompatible values, ideas, and language games, a way of human existence and growth. Consensus is not the goal of Rorty's conversation: there may be hope for consensus, but dissensus is the dynamic, the enjoyment, the moment that should be seized and valued in conversation.

The absence of tension in Bruffee's conversational model has also attracted feminists' criticism. For example, Evelyn Ashton-Jones argues that the conversational model as described by Bruffee and John Trimbur "assumes that society disregards gender in matters of meaning-making, that women have unobstructed access to democratic discourse in society at large and in writing groups" (1995, 20). Justified as her criticism is, the criticism cannot be extended to Rorty's notion of conversation. Since Rorty's abnormal discourse may well include the feminist discourse, the gender subtext is then part of Rorty's conversation. Ashton-Jones's and the others' criticism of the conversational model indicates that a rereading of Rorty's notion of conversation is highly necessary.

Taking Bruffee as the point of departure, I want to inquire further into the relationship between normal and abnormal discourse so as to define the role of abnormal discourse in the writing class. Since the concepts of normal and abnormal discourse are embedded in Rorty's antifoundationalist philosophy, I will take Rorty's discussion of the relationship between systematic and edifying philosophy as the place to start.

In *Philosophy and the Mirror of Nature*, Rorty presents two philosophical worlds different from each other: systematic philosophy, which "centers in epistemology," and edifying philosophy, which "takes its point of departure from suspicion about the pretensions of epistemology" (1979, 366). Systematic philosophy, as Rorty explains, is the mainstream of the Western philosophical tradition, the paradigm of "*knowing*—possessing justified true beliefs, or, better yet, beliefs so intrinsically persuasive as to make justification unnecessary." This tradition is characterized by philosophical revolutions produced by philosophers excited by new cognitive feats and attempting to refashion the rest of culture on the model of the latest cognitive achievements (366–67).[29] Its goal is always to search for a proper line of inquiry so that all inquiry will be reshaped on this successful model, "thereby permitting objectivity and rationality to prevail in areas previously obscured by convention, superstition, and the lack of a proper epistemological understanding of man's ability accurately to represent nature" (367).

In contrast, Rorty's edifying philosophy is on the "periphery of the history of modern philosophy," characterized by figures who, without forming a tradition, "resemble each other in their distrust of the notion that man's essence is to be a knower of essences." Rorty lists Goethe, Kierkegaard, Santayana, William James, John Dewey, the later Wittgenstein and the later Heidegger as among the edifying philosophers, who

> have kept alive the suggestion that, even when we have justified true belief about everything we want to know, we may have no more than conformity to the norms of the day. They have kept alive the historicist sense that this century's "superstition" was the last century's triumph of reason, as well as the relativist sense that the latest vocabulary, borrowed from the latest scientific achievement, may not express privileged representations of essences, but be just another of the potential infinity of vocabularies in which the world can be described. (367)

These edifying philosophers—"peripheral, pragmatic," as Rorty thus describes them—are skeptical primarily about systematic philosophy, about the whole project of universal commensuration" (Rorty 1979, 368). In discourse, method, and perception of knowledge, edifying philosophers form a sharp contrast to systematic philosophers. Rorty thus outlines their differences:

> Great systematic philosophers are constructive and offer arguments. Great edifying philosophers are reactive and offer satires, parodies, and aphorism. They know their work loses its point when the period they were reacting against is over. They are *intentionally* peripheral. Great systematic philosophers, like great scientists, build for eternity. Great edifying philosophers destroy for the sake of their own generation. Systematic philosophers want to put their subject on the secure path of a science. Edifying philosophers want to keep space open for the sense of wonder which poets can sometimes cause—wonder that there is something new under the sun, something which is *not* an accurate

representation of what was already there, something which (at least for the moment) cannot be explained and can barely be described. (369–70)

Not only do edifying philosophers violate the rules of normal philosophy (the philosophy of the schools of their day) by being reactive and destructive, but they also violate "a sort of meta-rule" by simply offering "another set of terms, *without* saying that these terms are the new-found accurate representations of essences" (370).[30] Unlike systematic philosophy, whose goal is to build and eternalize what it has found, edifying philosophy questions the found truth with an attempt to find new, better, more interesting, more fruitful ways of speaking so as to "take us out of our old selves by the power of strangeness, to aid us in becoming new beings" (360). The discourse of edifying philosophers is therefore abnormal discourse, in the sense that it intentionally puts aside the conventions of the discourse of systematic philosophy and that it exists as reactive, deconstructive, and peripheral to normal discourse.

Rorty thus defines normal and abnormal discourse:

Normal discourse (a generalization of Kuhn's notion of "normal science") is any discourse (scientific, political, theological, or whatever) which embodies agreed-upon criteria for reaching agreement; abnormal discourse is any which lacks such criteria. (1979, 11)

Rorty sees no substantial difference between his notion of normal discourse and Thomas Kuhn's normal science. Normal science is the "practice of solving problems against the background of a consensus about what counts as a good explanation of the phenomena and about what it would take for a problem to be solved," Rorty writes. Normal discourse, likewise, is "that which is conducted within an agreed-upon set of conventions about what counts as a relevant contribution, what counts as answering a question, what counts as having a good argument for that answer or a good criticism of it." Normal discourse, as well as normal science, is concerned with the product—the sort of statement—which "can be agreed to be true by all participants whom the other participants count as 'rational'" (320).

Nonetheless, Rorty's abnormal discourse is more complex than his definition makes it appear to be. According to Rorty, abnormal discourse differs from Kuhn's notion of "revolutionary" science in that revolutionary science is the "introduction of a new 'paradigm' of explanation"; it is what Kuhn desires as "a viable alternate to the traditional epistemological paradigm," a competing paradigm with the paradigm of normal science (1979, 324–25). Rorty's abnormal discourse, on the other hand, does not seek to be a new epistemological paradigm. Its product can be "anything from nonsense to intellectual revolution, and there is no discipline which describes it, any more than there is a discipline devoted to the study of the unpredictable, or of 'creativity'" (320).

In other words, Rorty's abnormal discourse, like edifying philosophy—sometimes the two terms are interchangeable in Rorty's discussion—does not seek to generate knowledge in the sense that normal discourse, or systematic philosophy, does. For Rorty, abnormal discourse exists for the purpose of keeping the conversation from closing down and keeping discourses from perpetuating themselves as normal discourse. Abnormal discourse does not seek knowledge or truth but renders new descriptions through wisdom; it does not intend to engender new normal discourse or competing paradigms. It exists for the sense of wonder, as Rorty puts it, for the sake of our full humanity in an age when it is threatened by obvious danger:

> The fear of science, of "scientism," of "naturalism," of self-objectivation, of being turned by too much knowledge into a thing rather than a person, is the fear that all discourse will become normal discourse. That is, it is the fear that there will be objectively true or false answers to every question we ask, so that human worth will consist in knowing truths, and human virtue will be merely justified true belief. This is frightening because it cuts off the possibility of something new under the sun, of human life as poetic rather than merely contemplative. (1979, 388–89)

So the hope abnormal discourse offers lies in that it exists as a "protest against attempts to close off conversation by proposals for universal commensuration through the hypostatization of some privileged set of descriptions" (377). It exists as a humanizing force, trying to avert the danger that "some given vocabulary, some way in which people might come to think of themselves, will deceive them into thinking that from now on all discourse could be, or should be, normal discourse." According to Rorty, this perpetuation of discourse will result in freezing-over of culture, which would be the "dehumanization of human beings." To prevent such a condition from becoming real, abnormal discourse, as well as edifying philosophy, opts for "the infinite *striving* for truth over 'all of Truth'" (377). Its main goal is to keep a conversation going, to see human beings as generators of new descriptions rather than beings one hopes to be able to describe accurately, and to see human beings as both *en-soi* and *pour-soi*, as both described objects and describing subjects (378).

Although abnormal discourse is reactive to and deconstructive of normal discourse, Rorty makes it clear that their relationship is one of interdependence instead of confrontational. This point is not only essential for a correct understanding of Rorty's notion of normal and abnormal discourse but is also important for my later discussion of the relationships between the dominant discourse and the teachers' and students' discourses. According to Rorty, abnormal discourse is "always parasitic upon normal discourse, the possibility of hermeneutics is always parasitic upon the possibility (and perhaps upon the actuality) of epistemology, and edification always employs materials provided by the culture of the day" (1979, 366). Abnormal discourse depends on the existence of normal discourse for being reactive; it is aware that "it falls into self-deception whenever it tries to do more than send the conversation off in new directions." Rorty emphasizes that even if "such new directions may, perhaps, engender new normal discourses, new sciences, new philosophical research programs, and thus new objective truths," they are "not the point of edifying philosophy, only accidental byproducts."[31] Abnormal discourse does not contend with normal discourse for power, Rorty stresses:

> The point is always the same—to perform the social function which Dewey called "breaking the crust of convention," preventing man from deluding himself with the notion that he knows himself, or anything else, except under optional descriptions. (1979, 378–79)

Abnormal discourse is parasitic upon normal discourse, not only in the sense that the creation of abnormal discourse always depends upon normal discourse, but also in that abnormal discourse tends to use normal discourse as a means to an end. In generating abnormal discourse, the edifying philosopher has to start from the "point of view of some normal discourse," as Rorty so admits and so practices. In writing *Philosophy and the Mirror of Nature*, for example, Rorty acknowledges that his book, an exemplary text of abnormal discourse in the tradition of Wittgenstein, Heidegger, and Dewey, is "largely written in the vocabulary of contemporary analytic philosophers, and with reference to problems discussed in the analytic literature."[32] Further, Rorty is extremely explicit about the importance of recognizing abnormal discourse's parasitic relations to normal discourse in education. As he explains, before we can generate abnormal discourse we have to pass through "stages of implicit, and then explicit and self-conscious, conformity to the norms of the discourses going on around us" (1979, 365). For Rorty, abnormal discourse can be produced only with a sound understanding of normal discourse, because

> To attempt abnormal discourse *de novo*, without being able to recognize our own abnormality, is madness in the most literal and terrible sense. To insist on being hermeneutic where epistemology would do—to make ourselves unable to view normal discourse in terms of its own motives, and able to view it only from within our own abnormal discourse—is not mad, but it does show a lack of education. (366)

In other words, to generate abnormal discourse requires a realization that abnormal discourse makes sense only in opposition to the tradition of normal discourse and that we are taking a "conscious departure from a well-understood norm" when we adopt the attitude of edifying philosophers (366). And such realization can come only from an education in normal discourse, as Rorty emphasizes:

> Education has to start from acculturation. So the search for objectivity and the self-conscious awareness of the social practices in which objectivity consists are necessary first steps in becoming *gebildet*. We must first see ourselves as *en-soi*—as described by those statements which are objectively true in the judgment of our peers—before there is any point in seeing ourselves as *pour-soi*. (365)

For Rorty, the creative process of abnormal discourse is incorporated in normal discourse, or in our interaction with normal discourse, to be more precise. To produce abnormal discourse as *pour-soi* (the describing subject), we have to experience being *en-soi* (the described object) first and to understand how we are described by others in their discourse. Abnormal discourse, in this sense, is a response to others' descriptions of ourselves; the response could be criticism, revision, or alternative descriptions of others' descriptions.

Abnormal discourse is thus parasitic upon normal discourse in almost every way: goals, content, form, creative process. However, such a parasitic relationship does not prevent abnormal discourse from being critical of normal discourse. What is most important about abnormal discourse lies in its consciousness of the discourse's tendency to normalize itself and in its self-conscious struggle to resist such a tendency by insisting on the peripheral position in relation to normal discourse. With his emphasis that abnormal discourse does not aim to produce a competing paradigm with that of normal discourse but to keep normal discourse from perpetuating itself and the conversation of humankind from closing off, Rorty's notion of normal/abnormal discourse offers a useful theoretical framework with which the authority of the teacher's discourse can be reconceived and described.

RESPONSIVE ABNORMAL DISCOURSE AND NONRESPONSIVE ABNORMAL DISCOURSE

The traditional teacher's discourse was synonymous with the dominant discourse until the intrusion of deconstructionist, feminist, cultural, and Marxist theories into the academy, which has broken the homogeneous world of the dominant discourse into a world of conflicts and heterogeneity. Consequently, the teacher's discourse no longer exists as a unified symbolic system that embodies only the ideology of the dominant culture but becomes a "jumbling of varieties of discourse," as Clifford Geertz aptly describes it (1983, 19). The academic discourse, the term social constructionists use to represent the teacher's discourse, has undergone change not only in ideology but also in its deep structure and intellectual practices. Deconstructionists, for example, have changed our view of language forever with such notions as "logocentrism," "differance," "deferral," and "supplement": The traditional faith in Western philosophy as the master metadiscourse and in the power of language as means to represent truth has been shaken by the powerful notion of logocentrism, which, as Derrida claims in *Of Grammatology*, characterizes the discourse of Western philosophy (1976). The revelation of logocentrism as resting upon "a self-sealing argument regarding the representative relationships that exist between the minds, the world, and language" undermines the belief that there is absolute truth out there that can be re-presented in words and in the mind (Crowly "A Teacher's Introduction," 1989, 3).

Language creates meaning by simultaneously establishing and undermining the presence of the sign, a phenomenon that is explained by the notion of differance, which can mean to differ and to defer. The meaning of language is thus created through a "violent hierarchy," in Derrida's words, because, instead of representing the one-on-one relationship between the signifier and the signified, the signifier obtains its meaning by privileging one meaning and suppressing the other, as in binaries such as love/hate, good/evil, presence/absence. At the same time, the signifier defers, puts off, postpones the presence of the signified, complicating the notion of sign, of representation (Carino 1992, 285; Tompkins 1988, 743–44).

Feminists not only reject the male hegemonic ideology and male values and beliefs but also the masculine conventions of following linear, hierarchical, or discursive models of structure. Cultural critics have challenged the traditional view of teaching English as a systematic inquiry into classical and Anglo-American literature in order to find the truth of human affairs. They view the discourse of English as "a cultural phenomenon, situated within an ideological matrix, that has been evolving since the early nineteenth century." They are concerned mainly with "ideological transformations at work at the English department as we know it comes into being," the connections between power and knowledge, and between "English" as a cultural force and as a body of knowledge (Davis 1990, 258–59). Marxist critics and educationists have also contributed to the change of academic discourse with their theories of "discourse awareness," human agency in learning, emancipatory education, power relations in school and society, and critical literacy. In short, the teacher who speaks a radical academic discourse in the postmodern age does not speak the same language as did the traditional teacher. The teacher's discourse in the postmodern age resembles the age itself, diverse, complex, and heterogeneous, a protest against the hegemonic power of the dominant discourse and culture. For this reason, then, it is no longer accurate to identify the teacher's radical discourse with the dominant discourse. For the same reason, I label the teacher's radical discourse Responsive Abnormal Discourse to differentiate it from the students' discourse, Nonresponsive Abnormal Discourse. And I will also discuss the differences between these two kinds of abnormal discourse later in this chapter.

By Rorty's definition, abnormal discourse is "what happens when someone joins in the discourse who is ignorant of these conventions or who sets them aside." And the "product of abnormal discourse can be anything from nonsense to intellectual revolution" (1979, 320). If we describe the teacher's discourse as abnormal discourse, it should be because the teacher intentionally sets aside the norms and conventions of the dominant discourse, as a deconstructionist teacher would reject the New Critics' strictly linguistic and structural analysis of the canonical texts, a feminist teacher would refuse to write in a linear and discursive manner, a cultural critic would abandon the educational concern of the dominant class for universality and opt for the local and the immediate, and a Marxist teacher would dismiss the dominant ideology of educational neutrality and disinterestedness as mere lies. On the other hand, the students' discourse (although it may appear in numerous forms), especially the discourse of those from underprivileged groups, can be often described as products of students' ignorance of the conventions and norms of the dominant discourse.[33] While the conspicuous differences between the teacher's discourse and the students' discourse have never passed unnoticed, little attention has been paid to how they are related to each other and to the dominant discourse respectively.

Some compositionists believe that the teacher's discourse is so different from the students' discourse that requiring students to learn the teacher's discourse is not only unnecessary but even harmful. For example, in "Reflections on Academic Discourse: How It Relates to Freshmen and Colleagues," Elbow objects to the idea of teaching academic discourse in first-year composition classes mainly because it is so different from the language students speak. Elbow claims that he does not like academic discourse characterized by the convention of explicitness and straight-forward organization, by its deployment of hypotaxis rather than parataxis, by its note of insecurity or anxiety hidden behind stylistic and textual conventions, and by its mannerism for the sake of display, even though he admits that he loves "what's *in* academic discourse: learning, intelligence, sophistication" (1991, 146–47). For Elbow, all these conventions of academic discourse— voice, register, tone, diction, syntax, and mannerisms—are "various aids to authority," used either to "impress those who have authority over us" or to "distinguish ourselves from our peers" (148). Since first-year students need only to learn what's *in* academic discourse instead of academic discourse, Elbow argues that they should be allowed to learn a new intellectual stance or take on difficult intellectual goals without having to learn a new language and style and voice at the same time (149). Consequently, Elbow argues that the first-year composition should encourage nonacademic writing and move students toward "a kind of polyphony—an awareness of and pleasure in the various competing discourses that make up their own" (153).

While Elbow is right in assuming that students should not be forced to give up their own discourse in order to learn the teacher's academic discourse, he is wrong in believing that learning a new intellectual stance can be separated from learning the language in which this stance is articulated. His notion of "academic" and "nonacademic" writing is also problematic, for it does not distinguish between "the discourse that renders rather than explains" (1991, 153) produced by teachers, which may well be part of academic discourse, and nonacademic writing generated by students, which may differ considerably in quality and sophistication. Moreover, Elbow is unable to describe how the teacher, who supposedly should abandon teaching the conventions and norms of academic discourse in the classroom, can help students achieve the kind of polyphony that is supposedly associated with various competing discourses. It is not hard to see that the difficulty of Elbow's position lies in his assumptions that thoughts and language can be separated and that teaching academic discourse, the discourse he himself speaks, contributes little to students' development and articulation of a new intellectual stance.

The tendency to view the teachers' discourse as the ally of the students' discourse is often found in radical educationists influenced by Marxist theories. Because of their egalitarian goals in education, radical educationists argue that their oppositional discourse should become the major content of teaching so that the hegemony of the dominant discourse and ideology in schools will be resisted and changed. For example, in *Teachers as Intellectuals*, Giroux advances a critical pedagogy to counter the hegemony of the dominant discourse. The central questions this critical pedagogy asks will be the "questions of how we help students, particularly from the oppressed classes, recognize that the dominant school culture is not neutral and does not generally serve their needs." This critical pedagogy requires that teachers ask "how it is that the dominant culture functions to make them, as students, feel powerless." It asks teachers to be responsible to reveal "the myths, lies, and injustices at the heart of the dominant school culture and build a critical mode of teaching that engages rather than suppresses history and critical practice" (1988, 7). And it urges teachers to examine "their own perspectives about society, schools, and emancipation" (9).

Giroux believes that teachers should share with students the same oppositional discourse which "would instruct students and teachers alike about their status as a group situated within a

society with specific relations of domination and subordination."
He emphasizes that teachers "should help students, particularly
from the oppressed classes, recognize that the dominant school
culture is not neutral and does not generally serve their needs"
(*Teachers* 1988, 8, 7).

In *Schooling and the Struggle for Public Life*, Giroux further
contends that, in order to use teacher voice to empower students,
teachers need to treat the histories, experiences, subjective interests,
and languages of different cultural groups as "particularized forms
of production" (1988, 142). He emphasizes that only when teachers
realize how power, dependence, and social inequality enable and
limit students around issues of class, race, and gender, will teachers
be able to understand students' diverse responses to analysis of a
particular classroom text. Giroux insists that, for schooling to be
empowering, teachers need to "affirm and critically engage the
polyphonic languages their students bring to schools" (143).

What unites the teacher and students, as Giroux sees it, is
their shared goal to resist the oppression of the dominant discourse. But several important questions are left unanswered: for
example, how can the teacher, speaking academic discourse, even
though it is radical, engage the polyphonic languages of the
students? How can teachers, hired as institutional agents to
impose the dominant culture and discourse, play the same roles
as intellectuals and as educators in and out of the classroom?[34]
Giroux's failure to answer these questions accounts for the loss of
much of its impact on classroom teaching. As Robert Con Davis
rightly points out, the dilemma of teachers-as-political-deviants is
rooted in their dependence on the social function of bourgeois
institutions and their commitment to far-reaching change within
and beyond them. In other words, oppositional pedagogues "play a
fundamental role in producing the dominant culture but are committed nonetheless to offer "students forms of oppositional discourse...at odds with the hegemonic role of the university." Thus,
Davis asserts, the dilemma of oppositional pedagogy is "precisely
that of trying to destroy and reconstitute an activity even while
performing it" (1990, 249).

Bourdieu and Passeron's analysis of utopianism in education
further illustrates my point. For Bourdieu and Passeron, requiring
teachers to reveal to students the violent nature of education and
to admit to them that education does not serve their needs is
almost like asking teachers to shoot themselves in the foot.
Bourdieu and Passeron maintain that teaching, which "aimed to

unveil, in its very exercise, its objective reality of violence and thereby to destroy the basis of the agent's pedagogic authority, would be *self-destructive*" (1977, 12; emphasis added). This is so because any attempt by the teacher to unveil the violent nature of pedagogic acts and of pedagogical authority to students will put the teacher in a dilemma that makes teaching impossible:

> The paradox of Epimenides the liar would appear in a new form: either you believe I'm not lying when I tell you education is violent and my teaching isn't legitimate, so you can't believe me; or you believe I'm lying and my teaching is legitimate, so you still can't believe what I say when I tell you it is violent. (12)

Because Giroux's utopian pedagogy idealizes the pedagogic relationship between the teacher and the student and between the teacher's discourse and students' discourse, Davis observes that

> Giroux et al. avoid the resistance of textual and institutional practice too well, are too eager in their uptopianism, and disappear into the future (fictive) institutes they have projected as pedagogical ideals. (1990, 256)

I argue that both Giroux's insistence that teachers teach radical discourse and engage students' polyphonic languages in the classroom and Elbow's rejection of academic discourse in favor of students' nonacademic discourse in the writing class reveal a rather wistful belief that teachers can freely choose whatever discourse they want to speak in the process of teaching. They seem to be unaware of the useful point Bourdieu and Passeron have made: that the teacher speaks academic discourse instead of the students' discourse is decided less by the teacher than by the teacher's relationship to the dominant class, culture, and discourse. "It is impossible to imagine a teacher able to maintain his own discourse and his students'," Bourdieu and Passeron argue, because the teacher's discourse, as well as the students' discourse, is the "ensemble of the relations between this system (the school system and the academic tradition) and the structure of class relations." Thus, Bourdieu and Passeron remind us, to change one's discourse means to change one's relation to language. And to change one's relation to language, "one only has to imagine all the prerequisites which would be objectively implied in setting up a different relation to language in all school practices" (1977, 126). In other words, expecting teachers to engage students' polyphonic languages in teaching implies expecting teachers to adopt students' relation to the dominant discourse and the dominant culture, a relation that is quite different from the teacher's. Such a task, therefore, is far beyond the teachers' ability to accomplish, no matter how radical and progressive they are.[35]

We need to understand that the teacher's discourse, whether it appears in the form of Giroux's critical pedagogy or Elbow's non-academic writing, is dependent upon the dominant discourse and therefore unable to sever its tie with the dominant discourse completely. We also need to understand that the students' discourse, despite its ignorance of the conventions and norms of the dominant discourse, is not entirely antagonistic or unrelated to the dominant discourse and ideology, as radical educators seem to think.[36] It is in their respective relations to the dominant discourse that the teacher's discourse and the students' discourse differ, a point that is worth exploring if we want to reconceive the relationships between the teacher and the student and between their discourses.

DIFFERENCES BETWEEN RESPONSIVE ABNORMAL DISCOURSE AND NONRESPONSIVE ABNORMAL DISCOURSE

One of the most important differences between Responsive Abnormal Discourse (the teachers' discourse) and Nonresponsive Abnormal Discourse (the students' discourse) in relation to normal discourse is that the former is developed through the teacher's experience in and interaction with normal discourse, whereas the latter, the students' discourse, shows a lack of such experiences and interactions with normal discourse. A comparison of a passage from a feminist text and a paragraph from a Hispanic student paper will suffice to illustrate the point. In "The Laugh of the Medusa," Hélène Cixous writes,

> Listen to a woman speak at a public gathering (if she hasn't painfully lost her wind). She doesn't "speak," she throws her trembling body forward; she lets go of herself, she flies; all of her passes into her voice, and it's with her body that she vitally supports the "logic" of her speech. Her flesh speaks true. She lays herself bare. In fact, she physically materializes what she's thinking; she signifies it with her body. In a certain way she *inscribes* what she's saying, because she doesn't deny her drives the intractable and impassioned part they have in speaking. Her speech, even when "theoretical" or political, is never simple or linear or "objectified," generalized: she draws her story into history. (1980, 251)

In this passage, Cixous's use of paratactic structures instead of hypotactic structures indicates her intentional endeavor to avert from the male, linear, logical textual development. The contrast of such words as "woman," "body," "flesh," and "voice" with "logic," "theoretical," "political," "objectified," and "generalized" reflects the tension between the female discourse seeking to express herself and the male discourse attempting to silence her voice. The idea expressed in the passage may be strange, that a woman should support the "logic" of her speech with her body and speak truth with her flesh. But the strange idea is exactly Cixous's articulation of her rebellion against the dominant discourse that traditionally excludes women's writing with the pretext that women cannot think or write in linear, logical, objective, theoretical or abstract manners. The piece, therefore, is connected, though oppositionally, to the dominant discourse in many ways: semantically, syntactically, rhetorically, ideologically, and stylistically.

Cixous's writing forms a sharp contrast with a paper written by Jose, a young Hispanic student, in my first-year composition class:

> It is true that a dog is the best friend a man could ever have. Belcha has been more than a dog to me, more than a pet. She was like a friend; you can count on. Every time I felt sad and want to be alone there she was sitting right next to me, as if she understood what I was going thru. Her light brown eyes were penetrating and humane like two ardent balls of fire. She realized in a way giving all her attention to every single word I said. I am very proud of having Belcha, because something inside her makes me had particular feelings for her. I could not describe in a piece of paper, since feelings are shown not written. Belcha significated a friend and individual to me.

Jose's description of his dog is somewhat touching, and he himself comes across in the paper as a sensitive and sincere young man capable of understanding and appreciating the friendship Belcha shows him. However, apart from the obvious grammar, spelling, punctuation errors and misused words, Jose's writing shows a simplicity that indicates his inexperience with complex sentence structures rather than his choice to avoid them. A potential complex sentence in the passage is structurally erroneous: "She realized in a way [that] giving all her attention to every single word I said [would make me feel better?]." And another cause-effect sentence hardly makes any sense: "I could not describe in a piece of paper, since feelings are shown not written." On the whole,

Jose's paper shows a circular development rather than the linear, coherent development that composition teachers want to find in college students' narrative papers. However, this passage also reveals Jose's attempt to conform to the rules of good writing prescribed in the textbook: the topic sentence appears at the beginning of the paragraph, followed by examples and descriptions to illustrate the writer's point. It is a piece of writing that speaks loudly of the student's unfamiliarity with the great works in the English language.

This comparison of the passages by Cixous and Jose serves to show that Responsive Abnormal Discourse is characterized by the writer's familiarity with the norms, conventions, ideologies, and major concerns of normal discourse as well as by the writer's intention to ignore or abandon them. Nonetheless, the writer's ability to ignore or abandon them to produce Responsive Abnormal Discourse does not come merely from the writer's willfulness but develops in the process of the writer's intimate interaction with normal discourse. In this sense, Responsive Abnormal Discourse depends on normal discourse for its creation and existence, for without the writer's experience with normal discourse it would be impossible for Responsive Abnormal Discourse to find its subject matters or means of articulation. Its relationship to normal discourse is therefore parasitic and derivative.

Nonresponsive Abnormal Discourse, on the other hand, gives all kinds of indication of the writer's lack of intentional rebellion against the rules or major concerns of normal discourse. Nonresponsive Abnormal Discourse is related to normal discourse *innocently*, aware of the latter's awesome presence and power, but unaware of its content and secrets, a relationship resulting from the writer's lack of interaction with normal discourse.

Responsive Abnormal Discourse can be also reactive and oppositional to normal discourse, as in the case of Marxian and cultural critical theories. However, even in its most oppositional and rebellious moment, Responsive Abnormal Discourse cannot escape from its dependence upon normal discourse for its creation and existence. J. Hillis Miller provides a good example to illuminate this point. In "Nietzsche in Basel: Writing Reading," Miller analyzes the style of Friedrich Nietzsche's early writings on rhetoric and makes this observation: Nietzsche, a master of German style, nevertheless employs a style that "hardly conforms to normal standards of correctness in these early writings" marked by a nonconventional use of tropes, an "erasure of the traditional relation between literal and figurative language," for the sake of articulating a new theory of language (1993, 316, 320). Nietzsche's desire to criticize in his lectures the long tradition of Western metaphysics beginning with Aristotle and Quintillian nevertheless conflicts with his duty as a professor "to repeat what the authors he is telling his students about said and believed." As a result, Miller points out, Nietzsche has to resort to a "counter-mode of composition" through the anti-Aristotelian use of figure, through the use of fable, and through the radical irony implicit in the inconsistencies of the course on rhetoric (325). And one of the costs of Nietzsche's using this "counter-mode of composition" in his lectures is his loss of the following of students in classical philology.

The point Miller tries to make with his analysis of Nietzsche's early writing is that the Aristotelian tradition "cannot be success-fully challenged in conceptual polemics" and that "a change in concepts about rhetoric and the intellectual tradition to which it belongs demands a change in style" (1993, 325). Using Nietzsche's early writing as an example, Miller argues that the ideology of the dominant culture is not only hidden in ideas but also in the standards of correctness and clarity of composition, in style, in every aspect of discourse. Miller warns, therefore, that

> The danger is that teachers of composition may assume that the reading chosen for the course can be liberating while the formal instruction in the rules of correct composition remains the same. This does not work. It does not work because the formal aspect of composition is even more powerful in imposing an ideology than is the thematic content of what is read. This is parallel to the way those in women's studies, minority discourse, or multiculturalism are in danger of falling into the hands of those they challenge if their language repeats in symmetrical mirror image the modes of language of the hegemonic discourse they would contest. Real change will come only through changes that go all the way down to the ground, so to speak, changes in language that challenge all that system of assumptions about language I have described. (315)

Implicit in Miller's warning is the same point that Bourdieu and Passeron have made: that the dominant discourse, with its ideology, knowledge, style, values, standards, and conventions, has so pervasively influenced all aspects of our lives that changing one of the components of the dominant discourse does not ensure a clean cut with its influences. Because of the omnipresence of the dominant discourse, Miller considers it "difficult to conceive just what an alternative way of writing might be like, a way based on difference and radical heterogeneity rather than on models of sameness and unity" (315).

Miller's view is enlightening. Challenging the dominant tradition and discourse is not easy because academics are constituted by the dominant discourse in numerous ways: the content, the form, the standards of correctness and clarity of the dominant discourse all embody dominant ideologies from which the people writing in that language have no escape. His view also offers a different angle for us to examine the relationship between Nonresponsive Abnormal Discourse and Responsive Abnormal Discourse as well as their different relations to normal discourse. The complexity of the relationships may well be conceived at an abstract level through Miller's eyes: Responsive Abnormal Discourse may be like Nietzsche's early writing on rhetoric: critical in content, nonconventional in form, and rebellious in assumptions about the standards of correctness and clarity, written in what Miller calls a countermode of composition as a conscious endeavor to challenge the dominant discourse. Or it can be like Giroux's critical pedagogy: revolutionary in content, yet quite traditional in form, conforming perfectly to the standards of correctness and clarity of the dominant discourse, written in a typical academic style that Elbow disapproves.[37] In fact, the Giroux type of Responsive Abnormal Discourse is the most often seen in composition studies.

Despite its dependence on normal discourse, the critical stance the Responsive Abnormal Discourse takes against normal discourse nevertheless creates a space for wonder and new possibilities. Again, Giroux's critical discourse serves as a good example here. A consistent concern in Giroux's works is the relationship between traditional educational discourse and its relations to the dominant ideology and culture. For Giroux, as for Foucault, Bourdieu and Passeron, and Freire, traditional educational discourse shows its affinity to the dominant discourse in all the following aspects: rationality, problematic, ideology, and cultural capital. In terms of rationality, traditional educational discourse is "rooted in the narrow concerns for effectiveness, behavioral objectives, and principles of learning that treat knowledge as something to be consumed in schools as merely instructional sites designed to pass onto students a common culture and set of skills that will enable them to operate effectively in the wider society" (*Teachers*

1988, 6). Dominated by the logic of technical rationality, the problematic of the traditional discourse of schooling centers on questions about the "most thorough or most efficient ways to learn specific kinds of knowledge, to create moral consensus, and to provide modes of schooling that reproduce the existing society." Such a problematic, Giroux notes, keeps traditional teachers from asking *why* questions: why might a certain predefined goal be beneficial to some socioeconomic groups and not to others, or why do schools tend to block the possibility that specific classes will attain a measure of economic and political autonomy (6)?

Giroux criticizes the ideology of traditional educational discourse for being "relatively conservative," for it ignores questions concerning relationships between knowledge and power or between culture and politics. In deciding which forms of knowledge, language practices, values, and modes of style should be labeled as cultural capital and should be privileged in schools and society, traditional educational discourse helps perpetuate the dominant discourse and the dominant culture through schooling. As Giroux sees it, the rationality underlying the traditional educational discourse is "limited" and "crippling":

> It ignores the dreams, histories, and visions that people bring to schools. Its central concerns are rooted in a false notion of objectivity and in a discourse that finds its quintessential expression in the attempt to posit universal principles of education that are lodged in the ethos of instrumentalism and a self-serving individualism. (*Teachers* 1988, 6)

Giroux contends:

> Rather than attempt to escape from their own ideologies and values, educators should confront them critically so as to understand how society has shaped them as individuals, what it is they believe, and how to structure more positively the effects they have upon students and others. Put another way, teachers and administrators, in particular, must attempt to understand how issues of class, gender, and race have left an imprint upon how they think and act. Such a critical interrogation provides the foundation for a democratic school. (9)

In *Schooling and the Struggle for Public Life*, Giroux further develops his critical pedagogy into a "pedagogy of cultural politics," still centering it on the struggle of language. He cites as opponents of dominant educational discourse the discourse of production, the discourse of textual analysis, and the discourse of lived cultures. Through these deviating discourses, he claims, the means by which cultural processes are produced and transformed can be examined.[38] According to Giroux, the discourse of production is important in that its analyses of the state, the workplace, foundations, publishing companies, and other embodiments of political interests that directly or indirectly influence school policy provide us with a larger network of connections within which schools are understood and analyzed as historical and social constructions and as embodiments of social forms that always bear a relationship to the wider society. The discourse of production helps to "alert teachers to the primacy of identifying practices and interests that legitimate specific public representations and ways of life" (*Schooling* 1988, 137). In other words, it enables teachers to understand how the process of schooling is formed in relation to how the wider forms of production are constructed, manifested, and contested both in and out of schools, an understanding that is indispensable for teachers and students to transform processes of schooling that disempower them.

What Giroux describes as the discourse of textual analysis refers to "a form of critique capable of analyzing cultural forms as they are produced and used in specific classrooms." For Giroux, "not only does the discourse of textual analysis draw attention to the ideologies out of which texts are produced, but it also allows educators to distance themselves from the text in order to uncover the layers of meanings, contradictions, and differences inscribed into the form and content of classroom materials." Giroux identifies the special significance of the discourse of textual analysis as lying in several respects: First, it provides teachers and students with the "critical tools necessary to analyze those socially constructed representations and interests that organize and emphasize particular readings of curriculum materials." Second, it "opens the text to deconstruction" and interrogation, as part of a wider process of cultural production. Third, by making the text an object of intellectual inquiry, the discourse of textual analysis posits an active role of the reader as a producer of meanings. It also changes the traditional view of the text as "endowed with an authorial essence waiting to be translated or discovered" to the view of the text as "an ensemble of discourses constituted by a play of contradictory meanings," some of which are visibly privileged and some of which are suppressed (*Schooling* 1988, 138–39). Most importantly, the discourse of textual analysis, with its emphasis on dialogue and social action and its assumptions drawn from the works of Bakhtin and Freire as well as from the wider tradition of deconstructive criticism, provides a mode of analysis that "does not assume that lived experiences can be inferred automatically from structural determinations." The assumptions underlying the discourse of textual analysis form part of Giroux's critical pedagogy, as Giroux succinctly summarizes them:

> These assumptions include treating the text as a social construct that is produced out of a number of available discourses; locating the contradictions and gaps within an educational text and situating them historically in terms of the interests they sustain and legitimate; recognizing in the text its internal politics of style and how this both opens up and constrains particular representations of the social world; understanding how the text actively works to silence certain voices; and, finally, discovering how it is possible to release possibilities from the text that provide new insights and critical readings regarding human understanding and social practices. (141)

These assumptions are indispensable to the development of the discourse of lived cultures, another part that constitutes Giroux's critical pedagogy. As Giroux explains it, the discourse of lived cultures should "interrogate the ways in which people create stories, memories, and narratives that posit a sense of determination and agency." Giroux calls what the discourse of lived cultures studies "the cultural 'stuff' of meditation, the conscious and unconscious material through which members of dominant and subordinate groups offer accounts of who they are in the ways in which they present their different readings of the world. It is also part of those ideologies and practices that allow us to understand the particular social locations, histories, subjective interests, and private worlds that come into play in any classroom pedagogy" (*Schooling* 1988, 142).

According to Giroux, the discourse of lived cultures enables teachers to "view schools as cultural and political spheres actively engaged in the production and struggle for voice" and to develop a critical understanding that will turn them into agents who consciously demystify and resist the domination of the privileged voices of the white middle and upper classes. The teacher's critical understanding, Giroux argues, will allow students from subordinate groups to "authenticate their problems and lived experiences through their own individual and collective voices" (*Schooling* 1988, 143). Fully aware of the double-sidedness of "teacher voice," Giroux points out that teacher voice can either be used to sustain or challenge the dominant schooling processes, to marginalize or empower students.

Giroux's critical pedagogy has no doubt shed light on our understanding of the struggles centered on language in society, schools, and classrooms. By revealing the power relations underlying the dominant discourse through the discourse of production, the discourse of textual analysis, and the discourse of the lived cultures, Giroux's critical pedagogy aims to demystify the neutrality and disinterestedness that the traditional educational discourse claims to possess. In the classroom, Giroux's critical pedagogy aims to help overcome one of the most harmful shortcomings of teachers as found by Dan C. Lortie in his study of teachers, namely, their subjective, idiosyncratic approach to teaching and their lack of self-consciousness of their own subjectivity and bias in teaching (1975). In emphasizing the importance for teachers to understand students' dreams, histories, cultures, and languages and to affirm and engage in the polyphonic languages their students bring to schools, Giroux's critical discourse attempts to open new possibilities and offer hope for those from subordinate groups to succeed in schools dominated by the traditional educational discourse. Although it depends on normal discourse for its existence, Giroux's oppositional, or abnormal, discourse nevertheless maintains a critical distance from normal discourse.

Compared with Responsive Abnormal Discourse, the students' discourse, Nonresponsive Abnormal Discourse, lacks such a critical distance from normal discourse even though students want to resist the oppression of the dominant culture and discourse. In *Education Under Siege*, Aronowitz and Giroux cite incidences of students' resistance against school or teacher authority to show how students' resistance is seldom well articulated in their discourse but is often realized through breaking rules. Moreover, the students' oppositional behavior often reveals the influence of the dominant ideology underlying the structure of social domination and results in students' loss of opportunities to obtain freedom through learning (1985, 100–01). In *Reclaiming Pedagogy*, Patricia Donahue and Ellen Quandahl mention how students, when assigned to analyze television advertising, tend to echo the teacher's thinking in their writing assignments. Donahue and Quandahl argue that this tendency reveals students' inability to interact critically with texts by professional writers. The result of students' echoing the teacher, Donahue and Quandahl point out, is the "reproduction of preexisting 'truth,'" a characteristic that I believe marks Nonre-sponsive Abnormal Discourse (1989, 9).[39] Unlike Giroux's critical discourse, which is the product of his interaction with the domi-nant discourse and his criticism of it, the students' discourse is seldom able to pose a critical stance against the dominant ideology or discourse.

RECONCEIVING THE DISCOURSE RELATIONSHIPS IN THE CLASSROOM

In "Arguing about Literacy," Bizzell dwells on the composition discipline's changing view of literacy—the shift from "literal literacy" as characterized by the Great Cognitive Divide theory articulated by Walter Ong to "cultural literacy" proposed by E. D. Hirsch and to "academic literacy" favored by social construc-tionists. She expresses her perplexity over problems created by the challenges of academic literacy that come from "lower classes, foreign born, non-White, and/or female": If one wishes to support these "oppositional forces" and to teach academic literacy through a collaborative effort, she says, how can the professor initiate the students into the currently acceptable academic practices without risking forcing them into conformity and submission, given the "persuasive power" that the professor "automatically" has because of the prestigious status of academic literacy (1988, 150)? Bizzell evidently is not satisfied with the existing collaborative model, which, she points out, does not truly guarantee that professor and students are equal partners in the process of teaching and learning academic literacy. Bizzell certainly sounds anything but optimistic when she says:

> I do not know that anyone has yet articulated a truly collabor-ative pedagogy of academic literacy, one that successfully inte-grates the professor's traditional canonical knowledge and the students' non-canonical cultural resources. Certainly I cannot do so. It is extremely difficult to abrogate in the classroom, by a collective act of will, the social arrangements that separate pro-fessors and students outside the classroom. Integration has not been achieved if students are simply allowed to express affective responses to canonical knowledge as conveyed by the professor or if the professor simply abdicates the role of guide to tradition and encourages the students to define a course agenda from their own interests. For example, we might expect Richard Rorty to favor a pedagogy that raises questions about canonical knowl-edge and opens the academy to new cultural resources. This has been his project in his own scholarly work. Yet in discussing

pedagogy, even Rorty can find no way around an unequal relation between professor and students. (150)

However, in Bizzell's rather pessimistic recounting of the conundrum, I see a solution emerging: if we stop viewing the teacher's canonical knowledge or normal discourse as the absolute opposite of students' noncanonical cultural resources or their Nonresponsive Abnormal Discourse but, instead, see normal discourse (or academic literacy) as a connecting point between students' Nonresponsive Abnormal Discourse and the teacher's Responsive Abnormal Discourse—a means to an end but not the end itself—we perhaps will be able to articulate a more satisfactory relationship between the teacher and students based on a new concept of the discourse relationships in the classroom.

Having examined the relationships between normal discourse and Nonresponsive Abnormal Discourse and between normal discourse and Responsive Abnormal Discourse, I believe that the usual binary oppositions that have dominated our view of the teacher's discourse and students' discourse—academic/nonacademic, canonical/noncanonical, literate/illiterate—can be modified by a continuum of discourses: On the continuum, Nonresponsive Abnormal Discourse appears on the left pole, signifying the entering college students' innocence and ignorance of the conventions of normal discourse. However, since most of these students have lived in America and received their education in American schools before coming to college, they must have had a considerable amount of contact with the dominant culture and discourse, even though they may not have paid attention to such contact. In this case, their discourse, Nonresponsive Abnormal Discourse, must bear the influence of the dominant culture and discourse to some extent and in some ways. For this reason, I imagine that normal discourse should appear in the middle of the continuum, thinly connected to Nonresponsive Abnormal Discourse. Since the radical teacher's Responsive Abnormal Discourse is derived from normal discourse and aspires to break away from the constraints of normal discourse, I put it on the right pole of the continuum, its relation to normal discourse indicated by a thicker line. The continuum looks like the diagram on the next page.

The arrows indicate how I imagine the discourses should be related to one another in the classroom. I propose a two-level interaction among Nonresponsive Abnormal Discourse, Responsive Abnormal Discourse, and normal discourse: Since Nonresponsive Abnormal Discourse can develop into Responsive

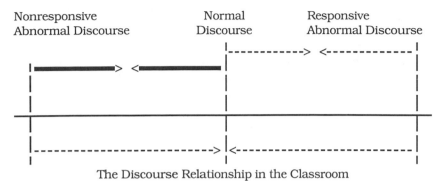

The Discourse Relationship in the Classroom

Abnormal Discourse only through its interaction with normal discourse, I will describe the interaction between Nonresponsive Abnormal Discourse and normal discourse as *primary* interaction. Since Responsive Abnormal Discourse cannot exist without a preexisting interaction with normal discourse (hence its parasitic relationship to normal discourse), since it cannot be described systematically, and since it can never interact with Nonresponsive Abnormal Discourse without the intervention of normal discourse, the interaction between Responsive Abnormal Discourse and Nonresponsive Abnormal Discourse can only be *secondary*, subordinating to the primary interaction between Nonresponsive Abnormal Discourse and normal discourse. The two-level interaction forms a triangular discourse relationship that differs substantially from the oppositional and hierarchical relationship between the teacher's discourse and the student's discourse in the traditional classroom:

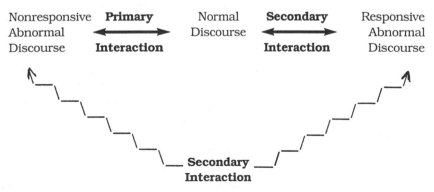

Triangular Discourse Relationships

While the discourse the teacher speaks and is obligated to teach—normal discourse, academic literacy, canonical texts, standard English, or whatever else—may assume a more authoritative position in the classroom and exert constraints upon the student's Nonresponsive Abnormal Discourse, the teacher's other discourse, Responsive Abnormal Discourse, with its critical distance from normal discourse, will check normal discourse's tendency to dominate and oppress Nonresponsive Abnormal Discourse. The teacher's Responsive Abnormal Discourse will also interact with Nonresponsive Abnormal Discourse in reading, writing, and collaborative activities, but this interaction can never be performed without the presence of normal discourse. Thus, with the secondary interaction between Responsive Abnormal Discourse and Nonresponsive Abnormal Discourse, normal discourse will not be able to assume absolute authority in the classroom, for its claim of possessing the ultimate Truth for students to discover will be problematized and challenged by Responsive Abnormal Discourse, its claim of holding the objective standards to evaluate students' academic performance will be examined and questioned by Responsive Abnormal Discourse, and its prestigious position of being the only desirable goal for students to aspire to will be scrutinized and modified by Responsive Abnormal Discourse. In short, the hegemonic authority of normal discourse will be effectively resisted with the secondary interaction between Responsive Abnormal Discourse and Nonresponsive Abnormal Discourse in the classroom. With its conscious critical distance from normal discourse and its aim to keep the conversation going, Responsive Abnormal Discourse serves as a humanizing force to ensure that the primary interaction moves in the direction of empowering and strengthening the powerless Nonresponsive Abnormal Discourse rather than silencing or excluding it.

It is important to stress that the secondary interaction between Responsive Abnormal Discourse and Nonresponsive Abnormal Discourse cannot become the primary interaction in the classroom. For, to turn the secondary interaction into the primary interaction threatens to deprive students of opportunities to experience and interact with normal discourse, opportunities that are of vital importance for the production of Responsive Abnormal Discourse. Further, the direct interaction between the two abnormal discourses without a preceding interaction between Nonresponsive Abnormal Discourse and normal discourse would leave a gap in students' education, a gap that makes the production of Responsive Abnormal Discourse impossible. Besides, to replace normal discourse with Responsive Abnormal Discourse in the primary interaction is to assign Responsive Abnormal Discourse the status of normal discourse without acknowledging the danger of doing so. If Responsive Abnormal Discourse forgets its own nonepistemological claim and edifying goal, it will inevitably lose its significance as a liberating and humanizing force in keeping the conversation going and in "preventing man from deluding himself with the notion that he knows himself, or anything else, except under optional descriptions" (Rorty 1979, 379).

With this understanding of the relationships among Responsive Abnormal Discourse, Nonresponsive Abnormal Discourse, and normal discourse, it is then not so difficult to see why students' interaction with the canonical texts should constitute major reading, writing, and collaborative activities in the writing class. This interaction, however, does not aim at reproducing imitative texts and repeating the found truth but at keeping the conversation going in schools so that students who speak Nonresponsive Abnormal Discourse will not be silenced and denied opportunities to create Responsive Abnormal Discourse. The teachers' Responsive Abnormal Discourse, be it feminism, deconstruction, critical pedagogy, or cultural studies, interacts at a secondary level with students' Nonresponsive Abnormal Discourse, not only to ensure that the conversation is not stopped and students' sense of wonder is not suppressed, but to reveal how the knowledge of normal discourse can be used for democratic goals in teaching and how the dominant ideology and culture can be effectively resisted with words. With this conception of the relationships of discourses, we are now able to move forward to discuss how the two-level interaction can resist the dominance of normal discourse and the oppressive power of institutional authority embodied in the teacher's authority and to help enhance students' ability to develop their own critical stance in their discourse.

Chapter 5

Discourse as Enabling Constraints

> Whether it is issues in the elaborate linguistic
> machines of seventeenth-century "projectors"
> like Bishop Wilkins, or in the building (a la
> Chomsky) of a "competence" model of
> language abstracted from any particular
> performance, or in the project of Esperanto or
> some other artificial language claiming univer-
> sality, or in the fashioning of a Habermasian
> "ideal speech situation" in which all assertions
> express "a 'rational will' in relation to a com-
> mon interest ascertained without deception,"
> the impulse behind the effort is always the
> same: to establish a form of communication
> that escapes partiality and aids us in first
> determining and then affirming what is
> absolutely and objectively true, a form of
> communication that in its structure and
> operations is the very antithesis of rhetoric.
> —Stanley Fish

I have examined the interrelationship among normal discourse, Responsive Abnormal Discourse, and Nonresponsive Abnormal Discourse, and I have attempted to show that these discourses, though different and even in conflict with one another, never-theless are connected in such a way that they depend on one another for existence and meaning. My examination has led me to argue that the teaching of writing needs to involve two levels of interactions: the primary interaction between Nonresponsive Abnormal Discourse and normal discourse, and the secondary interaction between Responsive Abnormal Discourse and Nonre-sponsive Abnormal Discourse, if we want to prevent the teacher's authority and the authority of whatever discourse favored by the teacher from becoming exclusive and oppressive in the classroom. With this understanding, I will further discuss why the primary interaction between students' Nonresponsive Abnormal Discourse and normal discourse is of special importance in first-year composition classes and how the two-level interaction works to resist the possible oppression and exclusion of the teacher's discourse in the process of moving students out of their Nonresponsive Abnormal Discourse so that they can generate their own Responsive Abnormal Discourse.

Lena's Story as an Indication of the Need for Primary Interaction in the Writing Class

Lena was an extremely quiet student in one of my Composition I classes. She almost never spoke in class and group discussions, and she did not write as well as the majority of the students I taught. Troubled by her often grammatically correct but logically disconnected writing and her conspicuous silence and obvious anxiety in class, I arranged a meeting with her. She was frank and told me that the way we read texts in class intimidated her, for she could never figure out how other classmates could say so much about a short story or a poem that to her had been nothing but just another reading assignment to get over with. She said that she had disliked reading and had never read anything for pleasure and that for the first time in her life she realized that she was at a disadvantage in college because her "below average reading skills" (in her own words) had caused her difficulties not only in my class but in other classes as well.

Lena's aversion to reading is not uncommon among first-year students, nor is her anxiety over her reading and writing skills, which most entering students will undergo for a period of time. However, I was truly shocked when she told me that she had "always" been in the top math and reading groups and was "exempt from reading classes during junior high and high school." Later, when I read her paper titled "My Dislike for Reading," my initial surprise turned into smoldering anger, anger at the wrong that was done to Lena sometime in her life when she was too young to know its consequences. Lena's paper in its entirety reads:

> Throughout the first to twelfth grades, I was an honor-roll student. I was always in the top math and reading groups. I was exempt from reading classes during junior high and high school.

However, after I began my studies in college, I realized that I was a poor reader.

As a child my parents never stressed reading as being an important element that I would need later on in life. They never read bedtime or any other type of stories to me. I was never encouraged to read, so I didn't.

I didn't attend headstart. So, when I began kindergarten, I didn't know my alphabets, how to count, or how to spell, let alone read. I didn't begin learning to read until I was in the first grade. First, I began learning little, three little words, such as cat, dog, run, etc. Throughout elementary, I remained in the top reading groups. There wasn't much reading to be done in elementary. During the middle of the sixth grade, I took the MAT6 test. This test determined what type of classes I would take in the seventh grade. After the sixth grade, I didn't have to take another reading class because I scored high on the MAT6 test.

Throughout junior high and high school I never really read, but somehow I managed to maintain a B-average. I only did enough to get by. Take my history class for example, I would define the vocabulary words and skim through the text to answer questions. The only assignments that I remember reading and thoroughly, I might add, were Antigone and Beowulf.

Now that I'm in college, not being a good reader makes it harder to keep up with the assignments. Sometimes I read and reread the same word or phrase endlessly in order to get some type of understanding. After awhile, I'll get frustrated, and then I'll stop reading whatever it is that I'm reading. Many poor reading habits have also contributed to my poor reading skills. I skim through the text that I'm reading. I very seldom read for pleasure.

I hope to improve my reading skills by reading for pleasure. I will also begin looking up words in the dictionary to find the meanings. I hope that I will become a better reader by practicing, and maybe even like it.

Lena's tone is apologetic, as if it were her deliberate wrongdoing that she was not reading and writing satisfactorily. I would have thought so myself in the past, but facing her paper I was forced to ask: Shouldn't we, teachers of English and of writing, feel apologetic that we have been so resigned from our duty as teachers that we have let a student go unnoticed for ten years with B's, having seldom bothered to show her how reading could be enjoyable and how books could make a difference in her life?

Lena's paper also raised a series of questions that I had rarely thought of before: If students like her come to my writing class, should I be responsible just for improving her writing or should I also be responsible for teaching her how to read? Further, where can I draw the line between reading and writing in a writing class even if I wanted only to focus on helping improve students' writing ability and skills? If the conventional wisdom is still accepted as true that one's writing always reflects one's reading, then I certainly should not shrug off the obligation of teaching reading. Yet how can I teach reading and writing within a limited amount of time so that reading does not take over writing, so that reading and writing will enhance each other?

Lena and her story called my attention for the first time to a subject that compositionists have been reluctant to dwell on: reading in the writing class. How is reading associated with writing in a writing class? What are the purposes, methods, and types of reading tasks that writing students encounter, and how do they differ from those in a literature class? What are effective ways of teaching reading in a writing class to aid students to write better? These questions have seldom been asked or looked into in recent scholarship.

As I thought about the reading I assigned my students, I was astonished at its complicatedness. Just consider the varied types of reading students have to do in a writing class: literary texts or texts by professionals on specific social, political, cultural or academic issues; chapters in textbooks on the subjects of composition and rhetoric, ranging from writing processes, modes of discourse, rules and strategies, grammar and style, to audiences and logic; instructions for writing assignments; literature for research projects; articles for journal responses; the teacher's comments on papers; the classmates' drafts and revisions; and written responses to one another's writing products among peers in a group. In addition, in the course of reading, as Sharon Crowley observes, students are also busy reading the teacher to determine what he or she "wants": they read the assigned textbooks or articles to find out what the teacher wants them to know; they read the teacher's assignments to determine what the teacher wants them to do (1989, 36). Compared with reading in English classes in high schools where students are often spoon fed the meanings of literary texts, reading in first-year college composition courses undoubtedly constitutes a much more demanding task for students.

Not only do the varied kinds of texts make reading hard for the student, the constantly shifting goals of reading also complicate the task. For example, as students' writing assignments change from narrative to persuasive, the reading of texts accordingly has to shift its emphasis from techniques concerning narratives to elements of persuasive writing. Likewise, reading for research projects requires quite different strategies from reading chapters on Stephen Toulmin's model of argument or on the writing process. Also, reading and evaluating one another's drafts involves thinking and skills that students seldom consciously apply to reading literary texts or textbooks. It is almost too obvious to be worth mentioning that reading in the writing class can be maddening to any entering college student because it requires a flexibility and an ability to switch methods, strategies, and emphases of reading over which most new college students do not have mastery.

So the task of teaching reading in the writing class is by no means easy. And so it seems that writing can by no means be taught without being accompanied by the teaching of reading. Can we ask students to write an analytical paper without showing them what an analytical paper looks like or how people actually use those rules in their writing in different ways? Can we require students to write a convincing persuasion paper by simply telling them to use ethical, emotional, or logical appeals instead of showing them how these appeals can be used successfully or unsuccessfully? Can we assign students to do a research project without helping them to find out what other people have already said on the subject they choose to study? Can we judge their writing as good or poor without telling them what our methods of reading and criteria of evaluation are? Can we require them to revise and improve their writing without making them see the differences between good and poor texts through comparison and analysis? If the answers to these questions are positive, then we cannot but see the complexity, as well as the necessity, of teaching reading in the writing class. In other words, we have to recognize the need for the primary interaction in reading, including reading canonical texts and learning about the conventions, methods, values, and criteria that are incorporated in the written text.

CHANGING THE "STABILIZED SOCIAL AUDIENCE" THROUGH PRIMARY INTERACTION

Examining student papers, Hill lists several types of writing that typically reflect first-year students' workings of mind: (1) the Jimmy type; (2) the corporate type; (3) the "fifth-grade teacher" type; and (4) the Maury type. In all these types, Hill sees a similar pattern of fixity and avoidance, a reluctance to get out of one's old world and to face the new audience that he or she is addressing. Hill describes the Jimmy type of writing as being able to talk about only one thing in one way. In the specific case of Jimmy, his father was the center of his world, as well as the obsession of his papers. Hill thus describes Jimmy's writing:

> When Jimmy needed to write about a topic other than his father, he would often wander down side paths, tell side stories (as in the paper about the supermarket's deli), and forget his point or his purpose....It was as if he had no ability to follow an independent line of thought when his mind moved away from its source of power, whether the power was Catherine [the teacher] in the classroom or his father at home. It was a mind accustomed to walking in someone else's footsteps, seeking always the comfort of staying safely within that other's conceptual borders. (1990, 4)

Hill describes the corporate type of writing as characterized by the mind-set common in organizational settings or corporate cultures: entire groups in the work world seem more dedicated to learning better ways to save face and avoid conflict about what they write than to learning new ways to understand the conflict and negotiate it (1990, 33). "This cultural interest in not making waves," Hill observes, "sometimes motivates writers more strongly than interest in grappling with and finding patterns in the discovered content, or the data they collect from research." Hill sees the problem with this type of writing as lying in the writer's helplessness and resignation:

> As rhetorical triangles go, this one is lopsided, with the power and purpose a writer senses seemingly resting in the hands of the audience rather than being shared among writer, material, *and* audience. (33)

In the "fifth-grade teacher" type of writing, Hill notices a mere concern for facts and categories of facts but never for their connections or significance. The fifth-grade teacher in question believes that having students categorize their questions about animals at a zoo is a way of teaching thinking skills. Hill wonders "how students could think 'critically' without questioning the questions, without engaging the value-making parts of their minds" (36). But unfortunately the fifth-grade teacher and most first-year college students are seldom bothered by the question that troubles Hill.

In the case of her student, Maury, Hill finds a tendency to "stereotype others and refuse to revise life texts." Hearing Maury "swallow Muslims and Hindus as antagonists in his system of values" and "falsify their beliefs in order to center his own," Hill "only winced" (Hill 1990, 37). It is not hard to imagine how students like Maury would write: they are usually full of convictions, and they never have a moment of doubt about the righteousness of their beliefs and values. They shut out others' voices and hear only their own. They are confident.

In all these types of writing, Hill sees people "who seemed to be thickening their own mental boundaries, closing down some life-giving activity, and questioning at the edges of their belief systems" (1990, 38). Hill writes,

> The corporate writers appeared to want a voice with their bosses, but they did not have an expectant frame of mind about negotiating boundaries in that world of discourse nor did they imagine the possibility of change. The fifth-grade teacher did not expand critical thinking into a questioning of contexts for the project. Those fifth-graders were being asked to narrow their focus and learn conventional, conflict-free schemes of classifying information. They were not being asked to widen their thinking at the same time, not being encouraged to notice and question some inherent oppositions in the context, not to notice, for instance, restricted movements of the animals as opposed to their own nonconfined ones....
>
> And Maury my student did not question his relationship to Hindus, being content to make a conceptual life apart from them, where strengthening a faith seems to happen through excluding foreign others rather than engaging with their ideas....(38)

Hill's perceptions are valuable, not only because they have accurately identified the major problems in most first-year students' writing but also because they point to the need for change at a much deeper level than just the formal and technical elements of writing. What is at stake is the change of students' frame of mind, a task that is interrelated with changing students' writing. But how can teachers implant a desire for change in students instead of forcing students to change by simply resorting to their authority? Further, how can teachers help students change without prescribing to them what these changes should be and without imposing their own values and beliefs upon students? I believe that a truly democratic way is to expose students to others: other descriptions, other perspectives, other conventions, other beliefs and values, other texts and utterances. For those students coming from underprivileged social backgrounds, the most important *other* cannot but be the mainstream culture and discourse. This means that, in the writing class, exposing students to others requires, first and foremost, exposing them to normal discourse individualized in various texts written by professional, academic writers.

Mikhail Bakhtin's theory of utterance enables us to see why primary interaction is important. According to Bakhtin, our inner world, as well as our consciousness, is shaped by the social milieu surrounding us, and our experiences are created and formed by the social circumstances in which our experiences are received, apprehended, and evaluated.[40] For Bakhtin, a person's inner world has a social dimension, because "each person's inner world and thought has its *stabilized social audience* that comprises the environment in which reasons, motives, values, and so on are fashioned" (1973, 86; emphasis added). Similarly, a person's consciousness is also social in the sense that "*outside objectification, outside embodiment in some particular material* (the material of gesture, inner word, outcry), *consciousness is a fiction*" (90). Bakhtin sees the forming of consciousness as forming the "inner speech," and he believes that a person's inner speech is structured only when all its terms and intonations "have gone through the stage of expression and have, so to speak, passed the test of expression." Bakhtin explains,

> Thus what is involved here are words, intonations, and inner-word gestures that have undergone the experience of outward expression on a more or less ample social scale and have acquired, as it were, a high social polish and lustre by the effect of reactions and responses, resistance or support, on the part of the social audience. (93)

This view of a person's forming of consciousness as a process of testing out his or her use of words on the social audience leads Bakhtin to posit that "*the organizing center of any utterance, of any experience, is not within but outside—in the social milieu surrounding the individual being*" (93). From these premises Bakhtin develops his important thesis about utterance:

> The actual reality of language-speech is not the abstract system of linguistic forms, not the isolated monologic utterance, and not the psychophysiological act of its implementation, but *the social event of verbal interaction* implemented in an utterance or utterances. (94; emphasis added)

Bakhtin conceives utterances as implementation of the "social event of verbal interaction." For him, individuals' consciousness and inner worlds are shaped exactly by their verbal interaction with the "stabilized social audience" that comprises their environment of living and communication. Since compositionists have generally agreed that teaching writing should focus on developing students' critical thinking and critical consciousness, an agreement that implies the assumption of students' preexisting noncritical consciousness, a change from that non-critical consciousness to critical consciousness will then involve a different kind of verbal interaction with a different kind of "social audience" in a different environment of communication. In other words, if students' utterances reveal their noncritical consciousness, we should be able to infer from their utterances that the social events of verbal interaction implemented in them, the stabilized social audience they were addressing, and the social milieu in which their utterances are shaped do not encourage the kind of critical consciousness and critical thinking valued in the academy. This means that if we want to change students' consciousness as well as their utterances, we will also have to change social events of verbal interaction, social audience, and social circumstances so that they will nourish critical consciousness and critical thinking as well as different kind of utterances.

Seen from Bakhtin's perspective, Jimmy's obsession with one topic and one way of talking about it indicates his unawareness of the limitation of his topic and utterances, his inability to reflect intelligently upon the significance of his or his father's life and experiences, and his insensitivity to different purposes of writing and different audiences for whom he was writing. Reflected in his writing is the dominant influence of the "stabilized social audience" existing in his consciousness, and one can easily envision a world in which Jimmy moved around with his tales about his father, winning approval from family members, friends, peers, and perhaps his father's employees. Jimmy did not know why he wanted to talk about his father so much, nor did he consider whether his teacher would be interested in knowing all the details about his father's deli. He lived one life in the shadow of his father, so that was all he could talk about. Similarly, Maury's antagonism against Muslims and Hindus may well have been the influence of his environment, in which judgments passed on religions different from his own might have often been negative and biased. Like Jimmy, Maury did not know why he hated Muslims and Hindus.

He was not aware that his bias made him less willing to treat people with different religious beliefs as fellow human beings. He did not care to know how the religions of Muslims and Hindus differ from his own religion. And his inner world was formed on an uncritical acceptance of the views of his stabilized social audience. For students like Jimmy and Maury, whose inner world seems to be a carbon copy of their daily life and immediate experiences, interacting with literary texts and texts written by professionals on social, cultural, and political issues constitutes an important way of helping them "rise above the language of the day to become fully human" (Bruffee 1988, 788).

On the other hand, the corporate mind-set and the fifth-grade teacher's thinking reflected in student writing indicates students' uncritical acceptance of the dominant ideology and positivist thinking. Gerald Graff attributes Americans' distaste for conflict and confrontation to the old American tradition, and to the country's affluence and geography that make escape and avoidance possible.[41] However, Graff argues, as conflicts over race, gender, and ethnicity are becoming more frequent and conspicuous in society, as the academy has become deeply diversified and openly political with "a mind-boggling juxtaposition of clashing ideologies," Americans as well as college students have to learn to cope with conflicts and confrontations (1992, 7). In the humanities, political and cultural conflicts and confrontations are embodied in the text, and the best way for the teacher of writing to help students cope with conflict and confrontation in the academy has to begin with teaching them how to read conflicting ideas and competing interpretations. Critical thinking, after all, can grow only from dealing with conflict and confrontation of different perspectives. And it is in the process of interacting with texts in which conflicting ideas and values are interwoven and verbalized that students will learn to break away from the confinement of their old, simplistic way of looking at the world and of writing. Bruffee paraphrases Rorty to emphasize the importance of knowing alternative perspectives:

> In Rorty's view, however, we rise above the language of the day not by learning to think and write abstractly or by appealing to "something higher—Reason rather than Prejudice, Truth rather than Convention." Instead, we rise above the language of the day by using it "as one option among others." We should therefore not regard the "liberality of mind and critical thought" that we try to develop in our students as capacities to deal in abstractions but as capacity to seek out and understand "alternative perspec-

tives." "Critical thinking," Rorty argues, "is playing off alternatives
against one another, rather than playing them off against criteria
of rationality, much less against eternal verities." (1988, 788)

For Rorty, as for Bruffee, critical thinking means the capability of
playing off alternatives against one another, a capacity that
students with the corporate mind-set and the fifth-grade teacher's
thinking do not possess. If in the academic institution alternatives
and disputes invariably appear in words and distributed in texts,
teaching writing inevitably involves teaching students how to read
and interpret conflicts, confrontations, alternatives, and negotiations in the text. Further, if academic discourse, or normal discourse, is addressed to the academic audience rather than
students, teaching writing also demands that the teacher describe
to students the characteristics of the audience that is new to them.
Most important, if teachers want to fulfill the dual role of cultural
agents and progressive intellectuals in the writing class, they will
have to be aware of the potential danger of their own discourse
and perspective becoming coercive and exclusive in the writing
class. The best way to prevent such danger will be by allowing
students to interact with different discourses, different perspectives, and different belief systems so that they come to their own
choices and conclusions. In short, to change students' consciousness and their ways of writing requires interactions between
students and the teacher, and the focus of the interactions should
always be the written text, texts in normal discourses and in
abnormal discourses, texts that are microcosms of different
worlds.

Stories about "Outsiders": Critical Consciousness Versus Critical Literacy

A story about outsiders is quoted in Aronowitz and Giroux's
Education Under Siege, a story told by Michelle Fine about drop-
outs from alternative high schools in New York City's South Bronx.
The story goes like this:

> Fine had assumed that the students who dropped out of these
> schools were victims of "learned helplessness," but she dis-
> covered instead that they were *the most critical and politically
> astute students* in the alternative schools: "Much to our collective
> surprise (and dismay) the drop outs were those students who
> were most likely to identify injustice in their social lives and at
> school, and most ready to correct injustice by criticizing or

challenging a teacher. The drop outs were least depressed, and had attained academic levels equivalent to students who remained in school. (1985, 98; emphasis added)

Aronowitz and Giroux see in Fine's story the irony of students' unsuccessful struggle for freedom and its disastrous consequence of their being denied "political and social avenues conducive to the task of radical reconstruction" (1985, 98). As I see it, Fine's discovery also undercuts the role of critical and political consciousness in learning, a role that radical educationists believe to be of essential importance. Fine's story can be read as a warning against a premature critical and political consciousness, a consciousness that, divorced from its means of expression, will only lead the outsiders to their final exclusion from the academic world and a more fulfilling life. Fine's story can also be interpreted as underscoring the importance of critical literacy, which consists of not only an awareness of the domination and oppression of mainstream culture and normal discourse but also an ability to carry out "discursive resistance" against such domination and oppression. The difference between critical consciousness and critical literacy is almost transparent: the former leads to the victimization of the "outsiders"; the latter, to their empowerment and greater freedom.

In *Political Literacy: Rhetoric, Ideology, and the Possibility of Justice*, Fredric G. Gale posits that the possibility of justice in society is closely associated with critical literacy, which differs from mere critical and political consciousness in that

> Critical literacy is the process of acquiring a more critical self-consciousness, the ability to discern in any cultural structure the ideology its founding and maintaining rhetoric accepts unconsciously. Critical literacy grants people power to think critically about language, to recognize its opacity, and to use language for their own liberation. Critical literacy grants both the power to recognize structural contradictions and the power to represent oneself effectively in a political transformation. (1994, 144)

The critical literacy that Gale sees as the basis for justice in society owes its power to two things: the ability to discern and recognize the ideology underlying a cultural structure and its contradictions, and the ability to use language to represent oneself effectively in a political transformation. In fact, Gale cites Edward White's claim that the major task of American education is to empower the American people with critical literacy:

> The foundations of American education are based on a distinctly
> political agenda, emerging as they do from such thinkers as
> Thomas Jefferson, who saw public education as essential for a
> functioning democracy. Since democratic theory derives all power
> from the people, and [in theory] only grants power to government
> with the consent of the governed, an educated populace is
> required; an uniformed consent is no consent at all. This political
> theory puts a premium on education defined as thinking and
> judging for oneself. (144)

The question is, how can teachers of writing help develop
critical literacy in students, students whose political consciousness impedes rather than enhances their ability to represent
themselves effectively in written words? The complicatedness of
the question seems to have been indicated by John U. Ogbu's
studies of different minorities and their school success. In
"Cultural Diversity and School Experience," an article based on his
and others' anthropological research, Ogbu observes that minorities' school success is not so much determined by cultural and
language differences as by the relationships between the minority
groups and the majority group. According to Ogbu, academic
performance problems of minority students are due to complex
forces not only in schools but also in broader historical, economic,
and sociocultural domains.

Ogbu classifies minority groups into three types by their
historical and sociocultural characteristics: 1. *Autonomous minorities*, people who are minorities primarily in a numerical sense.
They may possess a distinctive ethnic, religious, linguistic, or
cultural identity, but they are not socially, economically, and politically subordinated. Autonomous minorities do not experience
disproportionate and persistent problems in learning to read and
to compute partly because they usually have a cultural frame of
reference that demonstrates and encourages school success. This
group includes Jews and Mormons (1991, 30). 2. *Immigrant
minorities*, people who have moved more or less voluntarily to the
United States because of a desire for more economic well-being,
better overall opportunities, and/or greater political freedom.
These expectations continue to influence the way the immigrants
perceive and respond to schooling in the host society. For this
reason they do not experience lingering, disproportionate school
failure, even though they often encounter initial difficulties due to
cultural and language differences. Another reason is that the
immigrants are often characterized by a cultural difference that

does not discourage crossing cultural boundaries (to be discussed later). The Chinese and Punjabi Indians are representative examples (30). 3. *Castelike or involuntary minorities*, people who were originally brought into the U.S. through slavery, conquest, or colonization. Thereafter, these minorities were relegated to menial positions and denied true assimilation into the mainstream of American society. American Indians, African Americans, Mexican Americans, Native Hawaiians, and Puerto Ricans are examples. It is involuntary minorities or nonimmigrants who usually experience more difficulties with social adjustment and academic achievement in school (31).

Ogbu remarks that, when he compares immigrant and involuntary minorities, he finds that "they not only differ in features that distinguish their cultures from the culture of the 'mainstream' America, but also that their cultures embody contrasting cultural or collective identities, folk theories of how to succeed in the U.S., and degrees of trusting relationships with the public schools and the white Americans who control them" (1991, 31). Ogbu observes that "these differences accompany minority children to school and contribute to their patterns of social adjustment and academic performance" (31). The involuntary minority groups tend to perform less successfully in schools because they are conscious of their status as outsiders, Ogbu points out, and

> The relationship between minority bearers of secondary cultural differences and white Americans and the institutions the latter control is characterized by conflict and distrust. The minorities are more or less skeptical over whether they can trust the schools to educate their children in the same way they educate white children. They interpret school rules and standard practices as an imposition of white culture that does not necessarily meet their "real educational needs." For them the schools appear to approach the education of these minorities defensively—through control, paternalism, or even contest—strategies which divert attention from efforts to educate the children. (40)

As Ogbu sees it, the real issue of education lies not so much in which language or dialect schools teach as in whether students who have experienced inequality in their lives will be given equal opportunities in education and in society. Ogbu's observation is valuable:

> One real issue in the school adjustment and academic performance of minority children is not whether the children possess a different language or dialect, a different cognitive style, a different style of socialization and upbringing, although all these

are important. But the real issue is twofold: First, whether or not the children come from a segment of society where people have traditionally experienced unequal opportunity to use their education or school credentials in a socially and economically meaningful and rewarding manner; and second, whether or not the relationship between the minorities and the dominant group members who control the public schools has encouraged the minorities to perceive and define school learning as an instrument of replacing their cultural and language identity with the cultural and language identity of the dominant group but with no equality of reward or true assimilation. (40)

If, according to Ogbu, students' school failure is directly related to their living among people who have historically suffered oppression and discrimination and to their awareness of an unequal opportunity of social and economic reward between minorities and the dominant race, how can teachers cope with the anger and distrust that minority students bring with them to the writing classroom?

Radical educationists argue that teaching texts written by minorities or minority dialects will change minority students' hostility and distrust, but, with the preoccupation that they will not be taught the same things that White students are learning, a radical teacher's eagerness to teach minority literature or criticize dominant ideology will perhaps reinforce students' suspicion and resistance. A story told by Kathleen Weiler about a feminist teacher's experience with a Black student is a good example to illustrate my point. Reading a selection from *The Autobiography of Malcolm X*, the teacher intended to use young Malcolm's encountering racial discrimination in a public school to illustrate a theory of socialization. The Black student, however, misunderstood the teacher's discussion as "naming a racist experience and condemning it outright" and became offended. The teacher, thinking that the Black student was being disruptive, ignored his angry questions in class. The next day, the black student dropped out of her class (Giroux *Schooling* 1988, 145).

For Giroux, this incident indicates the dangerous tendency of the teacher's voice and authority to silence rather than give expression to the student's anger, concern, and interests. "Regardless of how politically or ideologically correct a teacher may be," Giroux cautions us, "his or her 'voice' may be destructive for students if it is imposed on them or if it is used to silence them" (Giroux *Schooling* 1988, 144–45). Nevertheless, the story may also be interpreted as the failure of the interaction between the teacher's radical discourse and the student's Nonresponsive Abnormal Discourse. Blind to the Black student's needs and desires, the teacher's choice of a Black text and her way of teaching it impinged upon his fragilely maintained "marginality" and forced him to drop out of the class rather than enabled him to reflect upon his own experiences critically.

This incident, like Fine's story, further underlines the importance of critical literacy. Critically and politically conscious though students may be, they nonetheless lack effective means to resist the domination and oppression of the institution. Their awareness of injustice, consequently, turns them into ultimate outcasts of the academic world rather than empowers them to constructive actions that would change the injustice. The incident, together with Fine's and Ogbu's studies, also suggests the need of a way of teaching that will not only effectively disarm students' hostility and distrust but also positively engage students' desires, dreams, and needs in learning. Further, all these stories seem to support my argument that both normal discourse and Responsive Abnormal Discourse should be taught in such a manner that students' interaction with normal discourse will not only take them out of their old, familiar world and discourse, but also enable them to create their own Responsive Abnormal Discourse and new possibilities in life.

THE TWO-LEVEL INTERACTION AS MEANS TO CRITICAL LITERACY

Since students who are outsiders speaking Nonresponsive Abnormal Discourse are confined to their old discourse and mental boundaries and restricted by the stabilized social audience existing in their consciousness, it is important for them to interact with normal discourse—that is, texts that embody the disciplinary matrix of rhetoric and composition or, rather, texts written in academic discourse.[42] In first-year composition classes, this primary interaction has two goals: First, it strives to bring students into direct contact with a discourse different from their own, a discourse of the "other" whose perspectives, ideologies, values and beliefs, and ways of thinking and writing differ significantly from those of Nonresponsive Abnormal Discourse. The contact and interaction will serve as a means and a force to help students break away from the restrictions of their home discourse and the existing stabilized social audience, as they become acquainted with the new discourse and the new social audience it addresses.

Second, the primary interaction will provide opportunities for students to develop their critical literacy through reading and writing activities. Rather than making the teacher the only voice in the classroom, students are made aware of multiple voices and views through interacting with written texts. The primary interaction aims, in a Bakhtinian sense, to aid students in seeking a higher form of experience and a better way of communication.

That students' interaction with normal discourse is of vital importance can be illuminated by Bakhtin's differentiation between the "I-experience" and the "we-experience." As Bakhtin sees it, the social nature of discourse determines that the comprehension of a specific experience depends on the comprehension of the social context in which the experience is communicated. Rejecting the traditional view of seeing experience as the foundation of expression, Bakhtin argues that it is expression that organizes experience (1973, 85).[43] In this way, Bakhtin makes experience part of discourse, which provides an "evaluative context" for experiences to be apprehended. From this premise, Bakhtin proceeds to differentiate between two kinds of experiences in terms of their relationship to discourse, the I-experience and the we-experience. The I-experience is isolated from the ideological structure of discourse, Bakhtin explains, and

> The "I-experience" actually tends toward extermination: the nearer it approaches its extreme limit, the more it loses its ideological structuredness and hence, its apprehensible quality, reverting to the physiological reaction of the animal. In its course toward this extreme, the experience relinquishes all its potentialities, all outcroppings of social orientation, and, therefore, also loses its verbal delineation. Single experiences or whole groups of experiences can approach this extreme, relinquishing, in doing so, their ideological clarity and structuredness and testifying to the inability of the consciousness to strike social roots. (1973, 88)

What Bakhtin classifies as I-experience bears characteristics of lacking ideological structuredness, social significance, and verbal delineation. The consciousness formulated from the I-experience, therefore, is unable to make association between what the individual has experienced and its social causes and social significance. In the case of hunger, for example, the I-experience refers to instances that "hunger is apprehended by one of a disparate set of hungry persons whose hunger is a matter of chance (the man down on his luck, the beggar, or the like)." Consequently, such chance happenings can hardly have any social impact upon the addressee to whom these experiences are communicated. Thus, the meaning of the I-experience is often random and isolated:

> The experience of such a declassé loner will be colored in some specific way and will gravitate toward certain particular ideological forms with a range potentially quite broad: humility, shame, enviousness, and other evaluative tones will color his experience. The ideological forms along the lines of which the experience would develop would be either the individualistic protest of a vagabond or repentant, mystical resignation. (1973, 88)

On the opposite pole of the I-experience is the "we-experience," which is "differentiated," and "not by any means a nebulous herd experience" (1973, 88). For example, hunger expressed as the we-experience will not be any "haphazard" experience but experienced at large, by a member of an objectively and materially aligned and united collective (for example, a regiment of soldiers, workers in their association within the walls of a factory, hired hands on a large-scale, capitalist farm, or a whole class). In cases like this, the social significance of the experience and expression of hunger cannot be missed by the addressee, and

> The experience of hunger this time will be marked predominantly by overtones of active and self-confident protest with no basis for humble and submissive intonation. These are the most favorable grounds for an experience to achieve ideological clarity and structuredness. (1973, 89)

Bakhtin evidently values the we-experience for its "ideological differentiation, the growth of consciousness," which, he claims, is "in direct proportion to the firmness and reliability of the social orientation." The we-experience is desirable, because "[t]he stronger, the more organized, the more differentiated the collective in which an individual orients himself, the more vivid and complex his inner world will be" (1973, 88).[44]

From Bakhtin's perspective, Lena's writing would have been more powerful if she had been able to associate her lost opportunities in learning how to read and write with issues of class and race and with problems of the testing and tracking system in schools. If she had read Mike Rose's *Lives on the Boundary* and Shirley Brice Heath's *Ways with Words*, she would probably have been able to see that her poor reading and writing ability was more a result of a social environment in which access to books was hard to obtain and of a school system that emphasizes mechanical skills and standard tests more than critical literacy for supplying society with a functional labor force. Unfortunately, Lena was not guided to interact with texts written by professional writers early enough in her life, and her writing, suffering from the lack of a firm orientation in a differentiated collective and the absence of an effective way of organizing her personal experiences, stayed at the level of the I-experience.

Similarly, Hill's students' inability to grow out of their old belief systems and their fixed ways of thinking and writing and the New York dropouts' failure to articulate their desire for justice and equality and to stage constructive discursive resistance also indicate the need for students to interact with normal discourse so that they can move from the I-experience to the we-experience in writing. If we agree with Bakhtin that the we-experience carries more power than the I-experience, if we also agree with Gale that an educated populace is the requirement for a democratic society and that critical literacy is the basis for justice, it is hard to imagine that teachers who are truly progressive can deny the importance of the interaction between students' Nonresponsive Abnormal Discourse and normal discourse.

I want to emphasize that primary interaction as a way of teaching and learning needs to be taught in the writing class. Gerald Graff's criticism of the conservative argument that great works should be chosen because good books teach themselves helps explain my point. Observing that students' problems in schools are "not with some particular set of books and ideas but with books and ideas as such" (1992, 94),[45] Graff warns that "It is easy to forget that for most American students the problem has usually been how to deal with books in general, regardless of which faction is drawing up the reading list" (11). For Graff, the students' problem lies not only in that many students from underprivileged groups are estranged from "life of the mind stuff"—that is, life of intellectuals and their "intellectualspeak"— but also in the "peculiarly analytical ways in which the academy expects students to read and talk about all texts, regardless of their cultural standing" (95). To a student who has had little contact with the intellectualspeak and who is not interested in the life of the mind stuff, Graff points out, "however deep their [academics] ideological antagonism, they will still be just a couple of professors speaking a language light-years from his own about problems he has a hard time regarding as problems" (93).

To solve students' problems with books and ideas, Graff contends, the most important thing for the teacher to do is not to argue endlessly over what texts students should read but to find ways of making texts easier and more interesting to read. When "even the sternest traditionalist will usually concede that it is foolish to refuse to teach *any* book, however noncanonical, if it figures to interest a student who otherwise would not read at all," (Graff 1992, 94) what excuses can a truly progressive teacher find to justify his or her reluctance to put serious efforts into making their students interested in books and ideas?

Graff's argument for teachers to focus on how to make books accessible rather than merely arguing about what books to teach seems to sound amazingly similar to the conservative view expressed by David P. Bryden in an article pungently titled "It Ain't What They Teach, It's the Way That They Teach It." However, the similarity stops right here, at the title. For, whatever good reasons Bryden may have for arguing that how to teach is more important than what to teach, his premises differ from Graff's in significant ways. For example, Graff's argument for emphasizing how to teach reading is based on his acknowledgment of the legitimacy of the canon debate and conflicts on campuses. What Graff tries to change is the separatism of the established curriculum—"with each subject and course being an island with little regular connection to other subjects and courses"—that denies students "a view of the interactions and interrelations that give each subject meaning" (1992, 13, 12). In contrast, Bryden bases his argument on his denunciation of multiculturalism as well as deconstructionists, feminists, neo-Marxists, multiculturalists, and liberal professors in universities in general (1991, 50). Adopting a posture of being neutral and nonpolitical, Bryden defends the canon with the argument that the canon does not require the teacher to "adopt any particular political slant" and that "traditional courses in Western civilization have been taught by scholars of every ideological hue" (42). However, Bryden's accusation of multiculturalism and radical and liberal scholars for having caused political conflicts on campuses and having turned the politically neutral university into a political battleground undercuts his argument for political neutrality and his posture of political disinterestedness. With their drastically different positions on the issues of conflicts and confrontations in the academic world, Graff's and Bryden's answers to the same question, how to teach students to read, cannot but differ significantly.

For Bryden, the answer to the "how to" question is already embedded in the answer to the "what to" question. As Bryden answers the question "what to teach," he has already presumed that the canon should be chosen because the canon has all the intrinsic good qualities: the universal truth it reveals, the neutral aesthetic standards it maintains, the appropriately difficult language it employs, and the easy hold it has upon the human heart. For Bryden, therefore, a professor wise enough to choose the great works is pre-empted by success. "All else being equal," Bryden asserts, "some courses and some books are indeed far better than others. Let us continue to defend them" (1991, 52–53). We defend them, not just because they are better books, but because they define better ways of teaching—that is the major message that Bryden tries to convey in his article. In other words, Bryden is not concerned with how to teach reading because he assumes that once a teacher has found a good book for students, the good book will teach itself.

And this view brings Bryden awfully close to Allan Bloom's view of reading and teaching as expressed in *The Closing of the American Mind.* Bloom holds that "a liberal education means reading certain generally recognized classic texts, just reading them, *letting them dictate what the questions are and the method of approaching them*—not forcing them into categories we make up, not treating them as historical products, but trying to read them *as their authors wish them to be read*" (1987, 344; emphasis added). In other words, Bloom, like Bryden, believes in the standard story that a good book essentially teaches itself. For Bloom, as for Bryden, the Great Works are the key to both questions of what to teach and how to teach.

Like many progressive teachers, Graff maintains a completely different stance on the issue. He faults Bloom's argument for two reasons. First, Graff points out, books, no matter how great they are, cannot completely dictate what the questions are or the method of approaching them. This is so because reading usually involves interactions between the questions posed by the text and the questions we bring to the text from our own differing interests and cultural backgrounds (Graff 1992, 74). Concurring with Rorty that reading is inevitably *selective,* Graff further argues that Bloom's "just read the books" theory is "disastrous when it guides the teaching of literature, where texts are not simply read but made the objects of sophisticated conversations in which students are expected to participate." Moreover,

> What the theory obscures is that no matter how humble and self-effacing teachers may try to be, they inevitably teach *themselves* in the process of teaching Plato, Dante, or any other text or subject. (74)

And it is not hard to imagine that Bryden will never be able to reflect upon his own biases in teaching the Great Works, as he is unable to detect his own political interests in arguing against any changes in curricula and on campuses. As for Bloom, Graff points out that Bloom's own reading of Plato and Dante indicates that he "is not reading these writers as they wished to be read but is *applying* them to a set of contexts they did not and could not have anticipated" (73). In other words, Bloom cannot help bringing his own questions to the texts when he reads Plato and Dante, despite his belief that readers should only concern themselves with the questions dictated by the books.

Graff also objects to Bloom's claim that Great Works teach themselves for another reason—that is, that it implicitly dismisses the question of how reading should be taught as irrelevant. For Graff, not only does reading need to be taught but it has to be taught in such a way that students are able to interact with not only the text but also the ongoing critical conversation about the text and the critical vocabulary of talking about the text. Recalling his reading experience as a literature student, Graff describes his own reading as a "curiously triangular business":

> Getting into immediate contact with the text was for me a curiously triangular business; I could not do it directly but needed a conversation of other readers to give me the issues and terms that made it possible to respond. (1992, 70)

Here Graff is talking about the primary interaction between the reader and the text, or Nonresponsive Abnormal Discourse with normal discourse. What distinguishes Graff's view of reading and Bloom's view of reading is that the latter assumes a mechanical relationship between the reader and the text while the former acknowledges that reading involves interactions among the reader, the text, and the conversations of other readers. For Graff, the interaction between the reader and the text has to be accompanied by the interaction between the reader and the conversations of other readers, for without this interaction between the reader and the conversations of other readers the student will hardly be able to find relevance in reading a book, no matter how great the book is. Be it Homer's *Iliad*, Conrad's *Heart of Darkness*, or Eliot's *The*

Waste Land, the student needs to know what questions are raised in the book and what questions are raised by other readers in order to bring any questions of his or her own to the reading of the text.

For the same reason that Graff critiques Bloom's view of reading, Hill objects to E. D. Hirsch's sixty-three-page list of nouns and noun phrases in *Cultural Literacy*. She writes:

> My own agenda is to oppose this book's message not because it supports people's learning more about mainstream culture (I support that too), not because it claims learning takes place through clusters of values (I believe that also), or even because Hirsch believes reading is a social and socializing process (I do not question that it is). Rather I oppose his deceptive claim that he is giving the nation a way to read and write better—become more literate—through social and cultural means, when what he seems to me to be doing is giving the nation a way to *numb potentially active mind by making sure they stay in little boxes of nouns devoid of verbs and mutual encounters.* (1990, 16; emphasis added)

For Hill, as for Graff, the more important question is how learning (or teaching) should be pursued rather than whether mainstream culture should be learned at all (the latter is no question to Hill). What Hill opposes are the assumptions underlying Hirsch's list: that these nouns are cues for some mental entities, that a knowledge of the cues might start students down the road toward literacy in the mainstream culture, that the schemata are facts, information, and "clusters of associations" that can be taught through dictionary-like explanations (Hill 1990, 16). What is wrong with Hirsch's list and these assumptions, Hill explains, is that they represent a "simple, reductive solution to the undeniable problems our students have with writing and reading" rather than "introducing students to the complexities, conflicts, and irregular rhythms of life in a democratic society" (17). For Hill, learning involves active interactions between the learner and the things to be learned, for

> No list of cultural concepts can possibly sink into a nation's young heads and make them "literate" until they, and especially we, begin to notice what those concepts are *doing* in all our lives with each other and with us. (18–19)

For Graff and Hill, reading and learning should be active inter- actions among the reader (learner), the text, and the conversations of others. This interaction is what I call Primary Interaction, which is characterized by its epistemological goal and by its view of the writing class as a *universitas*—"a group united by mutual interest in achieving a common end" (Rorty 1979, 318)—and by the hope of finding the common ground on which the otherwise isolated, random, and socially insignificant I-experiences could be comprehended and agreed by other members as rational, faithful, and true representation of the socially significant experiences of a community. Put another way, the primary interaction between Nonresponsive Abnormal Discourse and normal discourse is characterized by a focus on knowledge, on knowing what is experience, what its meaning is, how it is formed, how it is perceived and apprehended by others, how it influences one's and others' life, how it is represented in words by different people to different audiences, and how it unites or separates people in different social contexts. For students to interact with texts in normal discourse is for students to find the common ground— linguistic, rhetorical, cultural, and ideological—to communicate with people in the mainstream culture and discourse. For students like Lena, Jimmy, and Maury, the primary interaction perhaps offers the sole opportunity for them to step outside the confinement of their previous environment, to put their experiences in perspective, to make connections between their personal experiences and the mainstream culture and discourse, and to articulate their otherwise insignificant experiences as we-experiences.[46] In a sense, for students who speak Nonresponsive Abnormal Discourse, the primary interaction is both the seeking of freedom and the desire for constraints, an inquiry into new territories so that old existences can obtain new meanings.[47]

To interact with normal discourse means to interact with the dominant ideology. As Therborn paraphrases Althusser, "ideology operates as discourse, addressing or...interpellating human beings as subjects" (in Berlin 1988, 479). Ideology, which addresses three questions: "What exists? What is good? What is possible?" is "transmitted through language practices that are always the center of conflict and contest" (478). Since answers to these questions involve choices that are "always based on discursive practices that are interpretations, not mere transcriptions of some external, verifiable certainty," students' interaction with normal discourse inevitably involves conflicts of values and beliefs, risks and pains (478). With its power as the dominant discourse, normal discourse can easily silence students who speak Nonresponsive Abnormal

Discourse through numerous ways: academic standards, institutional rules, teacher authority, discourse conventions, moral judgment, to name but a few. When students are brought into the contact zone of different cultures, different audiences, different discourses, different ideologies, different experiences, different utterances, what can ensure that the institutional power normal discourse has over Nonresponsive Abnormal Discourse will not become oppressive and exclusive?

I imagine that the secondary interaction between Responsive Abnormal Discourse and Nonresponsive Abnormal Discourse may well function as a critical and empowering force in the classroom. How will the secondary interaction work in relation to the primary interaction in order to be empowering? Kurt Spellmeyer's discussion in "Foucault and the Freshman Writer" of the tension between Institution and Inclination as motivation for writing seems to have outlined an answer to the question. Drawing on Foucault's notion of "games of truth," Spellmeyer contends that the "voice of Institution" in a discourse conflicts with the individual Inclination and that the tension between constraint and desire makes writing possible. Spellmeyer explains that, since discourse is never a system free from contradictions, discourse constraints inherent in various systems of exclusion and regulation—basic cultural presuppositions, institutional conventions, practices intrinsic to discourse itself—provide writers with "spaces" to fit their own motives and desires into the discourse. By entering the "games of truth," by repeatedly seeking an "outside" to the existing rules, by testing and examining the contradiction and anomaly of the voice of Institution, writers are able to find their freedom of expression. Thus, in Foucault's and Spellmeyer's view, "it is not membership but marginality that enables [the writer] to challenge the prevailing configuration of knowledge, and so to refashion self and knowledge together" (Spellmeyer 1989, 722). Discourse constraints, when becoming a point for "intrusion from the outside," become enabling. Spellmeyer makes his point clear with an example:

> Like the fieldworker in Jogiakarta, student-writers unfamiliar with the discourse of, say, historical inquiry or political theory can never "go native," no matter how earnestly they try to silence their voices from the past, because this persistent murmur will become audible and coherent—will become a part of their conscious life—only after they have listened to other, unaccustomed voices. We can understand Javanese culture in terms of

our culture, and we can understand ours within the problematic created by our encounter with the Javanese, but we cannot understand either without the other, without, that is, an inside and an outside, a tension between constraint and desire. (722)

Noting that weak student-writers are always subject to the constraints of Institution and seldom dare to break any rules, Spellmeyer argues that, to empower students, we should not ask students to merely imitate sample texts because imitation is only a mechanical reproduction of knowledge. We should recognize that empowerment within discourse is a special form of intrusiveness, a strategic act of resistance to the totalizing force of convention. Spellmeyer urges that teaching should allow students to commit the "knowledge-transforming violence" through trial and error in the game of truth, for the reason that

> Only through a willingness to make room for themselves in the game, only by overcoming their regard for the "rules" and the "truth," can writers undertake the knowledge-transforming violence that distinguishes the empowered from the powerless. (1989, 719)

Spellmeyer's insight into the need for an outside force—the individual's desire—to turn the institutional constraints embodied in discourse into enabling power is invaluable, but he does not specify how students can make room for themselves in the game when confronted with the hegemonic power of the dominant discourse. Since, as I have argued earlier, the outsiders' desire for freedom and justice does not neccessarily lead to the knowledge-transforming violence that distinguishes the empowered from the powerless, the Inclination that Spellmeyer deems important in writing has to be something more tangible and more powerful than the individual's desire. I offer Responsive Abnormal Discourse and its interaction with Nonresponsive Abnormal Discourse as Inclination, a discourse in which the individual's desire resides. As an outside force that intrudes into the dominance of normal discourse in the primary interaction, Responsive Abnormal Discourse and the secondary interaction aim to strengthen students' Nonresponsive Abnormal Discourse and aid them to perform the knowledge-transforming violence in thinking and writing.

How does the secondary interaction work to create the desirable tension between Institution and Inclination? How can the secondary interaction help turn the authority of normal discourse into enabling constraints?

With its hermeneutic hope for "agreement, or, at least, exciting and fruitful disagreement" and its view of inquiry as "routine conversation," Abnormal Discourse plays the hermeneutic role of seeing "the relations between various discourses as those of strands in a possible conversation, a conversation which presupposes no disciplinary matrix which unites the speakers, but where the hope of agreement is never lost so long as the conversation lasts" (Rorty 1979, 318). Thus, when Responsive Abnormal Discourse interacts with Nonresponsive Abnormal Discourse, the goal of the interaction is not to seek new common ground or new territories but to keep the conversation going, to achieve mutual understanding among people speaking different discourses, and to learn to communicate better and to live together harmoniously, a goal that is quite different from the epistemological goal of the primary interaction. Because of its interest in continuing the conversation rather than finding the truth, the secondary interaction creates a *societas* side by side with the *universitas* that is created by the primary interaction in the classroom. If in the primary interaction the teacher and students are "united by mutual interests in achieving a common end"—in an institutional setting and under institutional constraints—in the secondary interaction they are united in the *societas*—"persons whose paths through life have fallen together, united by civility rather than by a common goal, much less by a common ground" (318). In other words, they become individuals with diverse desires and varied needs trying to make connections with one another through civility.

In processes of reading and writing, the primary interaction aims at familiarizing students speaking Nonresponsive Abnormal Discourse with normal discourse so that they can break away from the shackles of their old stabilized social audience and their home discourse. The knowledge of the institutional constraints of normal discourse, in this case, becomes the "outside force" that intrudes into students' fixed belief systems and discourses to bring them into a larger intellectual world. The secondary interaction, on the other hand, keeps a watchful eye of normal discourse's authority lest it becomes silencing, for Responsive Abnormal Discourse knows well how the institutional constraints can intimidate and oppress those from the underprivileged communities. Because Responsive Abnormal Discourse is capable of seeing through the hidden ideologies of normal discourse as well as its biases and interests, it interacts with Nonresponsive Abnormal Discourse to resist the normal discourse's claim of neutrality, scientificity, and disinterestedness. If students encounter conflicts and confrontations and pains and struggles in the primary interaction, the secondary interaction will reassure them that confrontations and pains are just part of the conversation that hopes for agreement and that enjoys exciting and fruitful disagreement for the sake of full humanity. If students are humiliated or intimidated by normal discourse in the primary interaction, the secondary interaction will make them see how their Nonresponsive Abnormal Discourse is just an alternative among many alternatives, how its unique perspective enables them to see possibilities for new wonders in normal discourse, and how normal discourse has its own limitations and contradictions. In short, unlike the systematic, purposeful, and epistemological primary interaction that insists that students come out of their old world and old discourse system by learning the new discourse, the secondary interaction, with its understanding of individuals' desires and its respect for humanity, offers a leeway for those students who cannot continue in the primary interaction. Urging the students to keep engaging in the conversation, reminding students of the possibilities of finding new wonders in conversing, the secondary interaction also serves as an outside force that intrudes into the primary interaction so that students who speak Nonresponsive Abnormal Discourse will not be excluded from their conversation with the dominant culture, and so that they can learn to articulate their experiences as we-experiences and to produce their own Responsive Abnormal Discourse.

I want to emphasize that the secondary interaction functions in different ways on different occasions. In teaching reading, the secondary interaction between Responsive Abnormal Discourse and Nonresponsive Abnormal Discourse is usually subordinated to the primary interaction. For example, when students are introduced to argumentative writing, their interaction with sample texts of argument should then become the major concern of the writing class. What is an argument? What is a good or bad argument? How is an argument formulated? What are strategies often used in argumentative writing? These are a few of the general questions that students are expected to answer in their interaction with argumentative writing. In their interaction with specific texts, the questions they bring to reading become more specific: What is the author's major claim? What are subclaims? What is the evidence that the author uses to support the major claim? Are the data the author chooses to use reliable? Does the author rely too much on emotional appeal? Does the author's ethical appeal influence our view of the author's credibility? Is the author's logic convincing? How does the author organize his or her material? For what purpose? All these questions constitute part of the students' meaningful interaction with the texts at hand, and possibilities of answering them intelligently depend not only on whether students know concepts such as claim, assumption, evidence, warrant; strategies such as ethical, emotional, and logical appeal; differences between deduction and induction or between facts and interpretation of facts; but also on whether they know how individual arguments are formed for different purposes and in different ways, the means of argument being employed successfully or unsuccessfully. When students read individual argumentative texts, their interaction with the rules and conventions of argumentative writing is contextualized, and processes of how various elements and strategies of argument can be used to serve different purposes are unfolded before their eyes as they try to figure out whether a certain author's argument is convincing or not, their judgment very often being based merely on their intuition and personal experiences.[48] The interaction between students and texts aims to lead students out of their old mind-set by giving them a new vocabulary of talking about argumentative writing and by demonstrating to them how this new vocabulary can be used to help them articulate their judgment more specifically and objectively. Thus, the primary interaction between students' Nonresponsive Abnormal Discourse and normal discourse requires that the teacher speak as the knower of normal discourse, calling students' attention to important features that otherwise would have escaped speakers of Nonresponsive Abnormal Discourse.

The secondary interaction at this time lurks only in the background. The teacher speaking Responsive Abnormal Discourse is aware that underlying all these objective criteria for a good argument is the arbitrariness of selecting these criteria as criteria as well as the opacity of language that tends to distort any human observation, no matter how objectively it is intended and performed. So the teacher's Responsive Abnormal Discourse interacts indirectly with Nonresponsive Abnormal Discourse to bridge the gap between the latter and normal discourse. The teacher, observing students' difficulties in reading the texts on logic and syllogism and whatever else through the eye of a Responsive Abnormal Discourse speaker, tries to identify the roots and nature of the difficulties and to smooth the primary interaction by playing the role of translator between the two discourses. Furthermore, since the teacher speaking Responsive Abnormal Discourse has experienced the constraints of normal discourse and the breaking away from them as well, the secondary interaction functions to show students how interacting with the rules and conventions of argumentative writing can help them express themselves better instead of restricting their thoughts and ideas.[49]

In teaching writing, the secondary interaction becomes more prominent in relation to the primary interaction. While students are still expected to apply the norms and conventions of argument in their writing, their own thoughts and experiences, beliefs and values, perspectives and purposes become more important in their writing. When the teacher reads and evaluates students' writing, the voice of Responsive Abnormal Discourse will be much more enabling and encouraging than the voice of normal discourse. For, while the voice of normal discourse may tend to prescribe what constitutes good writing, the voice of Responsive Abnormal Discourse will be interested in knowing what the students speaking Nonresponsive Abnormal Discourse want to say, to whom they are saying it, why they put it the way they do, and how their writing reflects the influence of the stabilized social audience existing in their consciousness. Thus, instead of looking in student writing for signs of deficiency, the teacher speaking Responsive Abnormal Discourse treats student writing as an alternative discourse and interacts with it not merely to correct its mistakes and change its ideas but to find ways to help students experiment with alternative ways of saying things for different purposes and to different audiences.[50] Lawson and Ryan posit that, when reading and evaluating student papers, the vast majority of teachers tend to "look at a paper in light of the writer's apparent intention and in terms of our expectations for the assignment, recognizing that our own biases influence evaluation." However, Lawson and Ryan argue, many teachers are unaware of the assumptions that reflect a "very traditional, conservative view of thought and language": that thoughts and ideas can be bracketed, analyzed, discussed, and finally written down intelligibly; that this written language can be stabilized (shared and analyzed) in conferences and in tutorials; that teachers are able to discuss, analyze, and make value judgment of student idea; that teachers can recognize how effectively students' ideas are expressed in writing; and that teachers can make quality judgments according to some objective scale and rank relative success of a sample of student texts (Lawson & Ryan

1989, xv). It is the questioning of this conservative view that makes them interested in other ways of reading student texts.[51] The main purpose of the teacher's reading, in this sense, is not only to reinforce the conventions and constraints of normal discourse but to help students find more effective ways to articulate their desires and to represent their experiences.

Using the two-level interaction among Nonresponsive Abnormal Discourse, normal discourse, and Responsive Abnormal Discourse, we will be able to create a social and academic setting in which the new social audiences that students must address provide students with constraints that will enhance their learning, an environment conducive to social and academic events that will entail meaningful and provocative verbal interaction between students and their social audience, and an "evaluative context" in which students not only re-form their consciousness as they reformulate their utterances but learn to evaluate their utterances and experiences against others' utterances and experiences (Bakhtin 1973, 87). The interaction between students' Nonresponsive Abnormal Discourse and normal discourse and the interaction between students' discourse and the teacher's Responsive Abnormal Discourse are so interrelated that they further create multiple-level interactions that provide students with more opportunities to learn about alternative perspectives and different belief systems. In the process of interacting with texts and others, students also learn to use constructively the constraints of Institution to articulate their Inclination—their dreams, motivations, and desires—and to communicate across the borders of discourses and cultures. As the secondary interaction endeavors to keep the conversation going, students will gradually make their entrance into a different world of symbols: they will learn to demarcate new discourse boundaries, make new connections, reposition themselves, reformulate their experiences, and enter the conversations of academics with their new voices and fresh perspectives.

Chapter 6

Edifying Teachers as Enabling Constraints

Since the possibility of enacting the two-level interaction in the writing class depends to a great extent on teachers' ability to speak both normal discourse and Responsive Abnormal Discourse and on teachers' willingness to break away from the certainties and privileges ensured by normal discourse and its related institutional practices, teachers who participate in the two-level interaction must assume a teacher-student relationship that is substantially different from the traditional one. Teachers must also perceive their roles in the writing class differently. I will name teachers of this kind edifying teachers, borrowing the term *edifying* from Rorty.

In this chapter, I will focus on how edifying teachers, having to speak two discourses that represent different intellectual traditions and cultures and having to play conflicting roles of cultural agents and intellectual critics in teaching, are subjected to conflicts and confrontations rather than living in a harmonious, homogeneous, comfortable, and stable world. Since Responsive Abnormal Discourse exists as a critiquing and dissenting voice of normal discourse, and since the role of intellectual critics is to deconstruct mainstream culture and open it up to other cultures rather than merely to maintain its status and power and perpetuate it, teachers cannot escape from conflicts and confrontations in their endeavor to play the dual role of cultural agents and intellectual critics and to maintain the opposing voices of normal discourse and Responsive Abnormal Discourse. However, it is the *conflicts and struggles* that teachers have to experience in teaching that make them different from the traditional teacher, the cognitivist teacher, the expressivist teacher, the social constructionist teacher, and the radical teacher. In their attempt to maintain a critical distance from normal discourse, their relationship to normal discourse changes: instead of merely maintaining the status quo of normal discourse and the established institutional practices, they try to edify the existing symbolic system so that it will be less hegemonic and exclusive. In striving to create Responsive Abnormal Discourse, they have given up the comforts and security that their familiar culture and world offer, and they turn their eyes to other cultures and discourses with a genuine interest, like an artist. They are border dwellers: in trying to fulfill their obligations as cultural agents they are bound by institutional rules and standards, yet their desire to fulfill their responsibilities as cultural workers is often at odds with the constraints of the traditional academy, which, as Edward Said describes it, serves "as an agent of closure, shutting human investigation, criticism, and effort in deference to the authority of the more-than-human, the supernatural, the other worldly" (In Henricksen 1990, 35). Thus, like students who have to face conflicts between Nonresponsive Abnormal Discourse and normal discourse and to struggle to move out of their home culture in order to communicate with people in a new culture, teachers also have to face conflicts and struggles if they choose to reposition themselves across the borders of discourses and cultures.

THE CONCEPT OF THE EDIFYING TEACHER

In *Philosophy and the Mirror of Nature*, Rorty thus describes edifying philosophers:

> They are often dubious about progress, and especially about the latest claim that such-and-such a discipline has at last made the nature of human knowledge so clear that reason will now spread throughout the rest of human activity. These writers have kept alive the suggestion that, even when we have justified true belief about everything we want to know, we may have no more than conformity to the norms of the day. They have kept alive the historicist sense that this century's "superstition" was the last century's triumph of reason, as well as the relativist sense that the latest vocabulary, borrowed from the latest scientific achievement, may not express privileged representations of essences, but be just another of the potential infinity of vocabularies in which the world can be described. (1979, 367)

Edifying teachers resemble edifying philosophers in important ways: they are dubious about claims of Truth and rationality; they are suspicious of the "norms of the day"—normal discourse—and would question its inclination to perpetuate itself; they are wary of the claimed objectivity of reason and science because they know that the opaqueness of language distorts all descriptions of the world, and they are aware of the political, social, and cultural power that makes certain representations of essences more prestigious than others, representations that are just products of one of the numerous vocabularies that people in different cultures and communities use to describe the world (367).

Edifying teachers are like edifying philosophers, who seek to maintain a peripheral position in relation to the systematic philosopher. They seek to offer "another set of terms, *without* saying that these terms are the new found accurate representations of essences" (Rorty 1979, 370). They are "conversational partners" who love the practical wisdom necessary to participate in a conversation (372). Their goal is to "prevent conversation from degenerating into inquiry, into a research program," into a search for the common ground of knowledge and universal commensuration (372). Edifying teachers are interested in hermeneutics—not as the name for a discipline, nor for a method of achieving the sort of results that epistemology failed to achieve, nor for a program of research—but as an expression of hope. The hermeneutic hope cherished by edifying teachers, as by edifying philosophers, is that through conversation, space for new wonders will be kept open, "exciting and fruitful disagreement" will be welcomed as agreement is, the willingness to "pick up the jargon of the interlocutor rather than translating it into one's own" will be valued, and inquiry will be seen as "routine conversation" to realize the full humanity of all beings (318). In a sense, edifying teachers *are* edifying philosophers who happen to teach writing in an institution. As intellectuals and scholars, they hardly differ from edifying philosophers who are antifoundationalists, creators and speakers of abnormal discourse, and participants in a hermeneutic conversation who believe in the "definite *striving* for truth over 'all of Truth'" (377).

This affinity between edifying teachers and edifying philosophers differentiates edifying teachers significantly not only from the traditional teacher but also from the cognitivist teacher, the expressivist teacher, the social constructionist teacher, and the radical teacher. First and foremost, edifying teachers do not have the complacency of "arrival" that all other types of teachers secretly or openly enjoy. Here Harvey Kail's interesting analysis of the master narrative in four textbooks provides a good example to illuminate my point. Kail's reading of these textbooks—*Rhetoric: Discovery and Change* by Richard Young, Alton Becker, and Kenneth Pike; *Forming/Thinking/Writing* by Ann Berthoff; *Teaching Composing* by William Coles; and *A Short Course in*

Writing by Kenneth Bruffee—led him to claim that revealed in the master narratives is the similar assumption of teachers as heroes who have reached the zenith of their quest and who have therefore become "magic helper," "task master," and the "'shadow presence' who guards the dangerous Threshold to Adventure" (Kail 1988, 180). In these textbooks, Kail observes, the goals of the quest may differ and means to success vary, but the writer/teacher is invariably presented as a hero figure, a "World Redeemer" (Young, Becker, and Pike), a "questing knight" (Berthoff), a "spellbound hero" (Coles), or, in the least romantic sense, "an exemplary modern figure" (Bruffee). The tale told in the four textbooks "follows the ancient pattern of heroic adventure, a pattern of separation, initiation, and return," and the writer/teacher is unfailingly the hero who returns with the "boon" of his quest and conquest (Kail 1988, 179).

If we agree with Kail that the tales told in these textbooks represent a view shared by cognitivists, expressivists, social constructionists, and radical educationists, the view is that of the teacher as one who has known the zenith of the quest. The cognitivist teacher in Young, Becker, and Pike's master narrative has reached the goal of causing "psychological change in the audience, an adjustment in the reader's interpretation of the world" and has won the "struggle for a more civilized community" (Kail 1988, 182). The radical teacher in Berthoff's quest romance has discovered that one's own natural way of making sense of the world is one's imagination; hence, he is awakened to "conceptual understanding" and has regained "the only paradise available—a knowledge of meaning" (Kail 1988, 182, 184). The expressivist teacher in Coles's adventure tale has succeeded in finding his final destination and has become "an artist of identity, shaping his vocabulary into a unique expression of self, an individual voice made out of experience and language" (Kail 1988, 184, 186). As for the social constructionist teacher in Bruffee's fable, he has also obtained his magic power by having become a member of the respectable "Community of Literate Adults" and by being able to "engage in 'normal discourse,' the proficient use of their new community's prevailing symbol system" (Kail 1988, 188). In brief, all have arrived at their final destination and returned to show students the paths to success so that students can achieve the same as their teachers have.

This is all fine, except that between the teacher and students the gap becomes unbridgeable: the teacher is the success and the knower and therefore cannot be disputed with, and the student is the outsider and the ignorant and therefore has to depend on the teacher to get to the desired destination. Further, in the process of students' struggling to go through the threshold of adventure, the "world of unfamiliar yet strangely intimate forces" that threatens and tests him or her, the "supreme ordeal at the nadir of the mythological round," and the "return to the threshold," the teacher will just give some "magical aid" without having to experience the students' struggle or share the students' pains (Kail 1988, 179). In other words, the teacher hero, now that he (Kail has claimed that all four textbooks imply that the teacher is male) has obtained the boon and the magical power—theories of how to achieve success— he does not need to sweat or struggle any more. He becomes a presence that the student has to revere and obey, but never to question or challenge, if the student wants to be led to the same destination and obtain the boon like the teacher did.[52]

Unlike those teachers who have already "arrived" at their known destination, who are comfortably positioned in the institution and mainstream culture, who now consider teaching as just beckoning students to follow them to the wonderful territory they have occupied, edifying teachers, like Rorty's edifying philosophers, do not have this feeling of being at home with their knowledge of normal discourse. They are not contented with playing merely the role of spectator and magical aid. Their eyes are always gazing beyond the known for the unknown; their attention is always directed toward questions and problems created by the status quo and norms of the day; their interest is always focused on searching for better ways of living and communicating in a changing world, and they never stop actively participating in the conversation, which, to them, is the means and end of inquiry.

Stanley Fish points out in "Anti-Foundationalism, Theory Hope, and the Teaching of Composition" that the difference between foundationalist and antifoundationalist teachers lies mainly in that the former always attempt to "ground inquiry and communication in something more firm and stable than mere belief or unexamined practice," that the "foundationalist strategy is first to identify that ground and then so to order our activities that they become anchored to it and are thereby rendered objective and principled" (1987, 65–66). Believing "what they do can be justified or explained by a set of principles that stands apart from their practice, by theory," foundationalist teachers adopt "a narrative that belongs properly to a foundationalist hero, to someone *who has just discovered a truth above the situational and now returns to implement it.*" (77; emphasis added). In contrast, Fish observes, "an anti-foundationalist hero who can only enact his heroism by refusing to take either comfort or method from his creed" insists on "situatedness." Antifoundationalist teachers believe that "questions of fact, truth, correctness, validity, and clarity can neither be posed nor answered in reference to some extracontextual, ahistorical, nonsituational reality, or rule, or law or value," and that "all of these matters are intelligible and debatable only within the precincts of the contexts or situations or paradigms or communities that give them their local and changeable shape" (67–68).

If what characterizes Fish's antifoundationalist hero is also what distinguishes edifying teachers from any other kind of teachers, then edifying teachers can obtain neither comfort from the dominant discourse they are obligated to teach nor security from any of the process theories that dominate the field. Teaching then becomes an involvement requiring their active participation rather than a game at which they are spectators. In a sense, edifying teachers have voluntarily given up their boon and their paradise for the excitement of existence: the excitement of experiencing new and challenging situations, of conversing with new and different peoples, of learning about new and diverse cultures, of experimenting with new and incommensurable methods, of creating new abnormal discourses, and of hitting upon new wonders or discovering more useful tools to cope with the world. Therefore, unlike other types of teachers who are above any conflict and struggle, the edifying teacher has to face and is willing to face necessary confrontations and pains in his or her commitment to interactive teaching. For edifying teachers, teaching becomes a process of learning to deal with new situations, new audiences, new problems, new experiences, new cultures, and new discourses. It is a process characterized by participations, interactions, conflicts, confrontations, negotiations, reconciliations, disagreements, and persuasions among teachers, students, diverse cultures, and different discourses. The edifying teacher is in the midst of all this instead of above it.

In summary, edifying teachers differ from the traditional or process-oriented teachers in three major respects:

1. When playing the role of scholar, edifying teachers do not conform to the norms of the day or the dominant culture and discourse: They reexamine basic values and assumptions that are

taken for granted by the institutional establishment and reject the claim that the dominant culture and dominant discourse possess foundational knowledge and universal truth. They struggle against their own, as well as others', desire for certainty and security. They question and challenge power and authority ensured by the institution, and they participate in the edifying project whose goal is to find "new, better, more interesting, more fruitful ways of speaking" (Rorty 1979, 360). They are antifoundationalists and speakers of abnormal discourse in their intellectual lives.

2. When playing the role of cultural agent hired by the institution to perform pedagogic acts, edifying teachers owe their loyalty to the institution, the dominant culture and discourse and are obligated to teach students normal discourse even though edifying teachers are suspicious of its hegemonic power and critical of many of its basic assumptions. The teaching of normal discourse by edifying teachers, however, is not based on the assumption that normal discourse is superior to other discourses. Nor do edifying teachers consider acculturation and accommodation or the mastery of normal discourse the ultimate goal of teaching writing. On the contrary, edifying teachers teach normal discourse as one of the many alternative discourses that will enrich students' experiences and broaden their intellectual horizon (the same reason that edifying teachers want to speak Responsive Abnormal Discourse rather than the familiar normal discourse). Consequently, edifying teachers do not avoid teaching conflicts and confrontations in the writing class. They take pains in trying to make connections among different cultures, perspectives, and discourses. They encourage students to interact with other cultures, perspectives, and discourses, and they set students a model by doing so themselves. They try in every way to make the conversation in the classroom reflective of the conversation in the real world, so that students can get a foothold in the academic community and gradually learn to participate in the conversation of academics and to eventually generate their own Responsive Abnormal Discourse.

3. Because of edifying teachers' critical distance from normal discourse and their genuine interest in other cultures, perspectives, values, and vocabularies for the production of Responsive Abnormal Discourse, their attitude toward students' Nonresponsive Abnormal Discourse differs from that of other teachers. If they demand changes in students' writing products, it is not because they deem it inferior or deficient but because they believe

that students' writing will benefit from other perspectives and discourses, as well as from an awareness of the influence of changing contexts, situations, audiences, and subjects on their own writing. The purpose of the teacher's interaction with student writing is to help them communicate their experiences, thoughts, and feelings to their audiences more effectively in written words. Besides, by acknowledging students' Nonresponsive Abnormal Discourse as a new source of experiences and inspiration for their Responsive Abnormal Discourse, by insisting on reading and responding to student writing in its specific contexts and situations instead of automatically abiding by some universal standards in grading student writing, edifying teachers are able to give up, though only partly, their authority and institutional power secured by normal discourse and its prescriptions for "good" writing. Accordingly, edifying teachers do not read student papers for mere evaluation and grading but for genuine interaction and communication. Such interaction and communication may be full of challenges and surprises, conflicts and confrontations, and struggles and pains on both sides, but their reward can also be very tantalizing. In the process of interaction and communication, the teacher may pick up some of students' Nonresponsive Abnormal Discourse vocabulary and is able to use it in his or her Responsive Abnormal Discourse; the students may have learned not only conventions, rules, and rhetorical devices of academic discourse but also how to use them in specific contexts to communicate their experiences, thoughts, and feelings to different audiences for different purposes. Perhaps the teacher may even experience changes in perspective when in constant contact with students' experiences, perspectives, and languages. Perhaps students may also feel changes in their view of the world, ways with words, and even ways of thinking and living. Most important, perhaps both the teacher and students will obtain greater satisfaction from the realization that they have communicated with new people, experienced new feelings, gone through new adventures, and succeeded in keeping the conversation going. What more can a writing teacher ask for than this?

EDIFYING TEACHERS' EDIFYING ROLES

Opposing the traditional view of teachers as gatekeepers of the academy, composition teachers and scholars have invented numerous images for the new teacher. These images invariably reflect the field's perceptions of the relationships between the teacher and students and therefore directly influence the teacher's and students' classroom behavior and teaching approaches. I will classify some of the most popular images into three types: the nurturing mother, the emancipator, and the mediator. I will discuss how edifying teachers' perceptions and practice differ from the perceptions and practice embodied in these images of writing teachers and how these differences make edifying teachers' authority more enabling and empowering than that of other teachers.

THE NURTURING MOTHER AND THE EDIFYING TEACHER

The prominently feminine feature of the discipline of composition perhaps accounts for the attraction of the image of teachers as nurturing mothers who would do anything to protect entering college students from being trapped or harmed in a new world full of challenges, risks, and evils. Shaughnessy perhaps could be regarded as a pioneer nurturing mother in the field, with her exhortation for the teacher to understand the basic writers' dilemma in college, which "both beckons and threatens them," and to "learn to see below the surface of these failures the intelligence and linguistic aptitudes of his students" when "confronted by what at first appears to be a hopeless tangle of errors" (1977, 292). Shaughnessy believes that, through the teacher's understanding and patient nurturing, underprivileged students will be successfully assimilated into the culture of academia.[53]

In a more recent article, Maxine Hairston pushes the image of nurturing mother further with accusations of radical educationists, whom she describes as "chic" (1992, 184). In "Diversity, Ideology, and Teaching Writing," Hairston projects the image of a protective mother defending her naive children's interests when she, on the one hand, denounces radical educationists for putting "dogma before diversity, politics before craft, ideology before critical thinking, and the social goals of the teacher before the educational needs of the student" and, on the other hand, insists that students "do not need to be assigned essays to read so they will have something to write about—they bring their subjects with them" (180, 186). What writing teachers should do, Hairston argues, is to "stay within our area of professional expertise" and be nurturing: "helping students to learn to write in order to learn, to explore, to communicate, to gain control over their lives" (186). For Hairston, teachers of writing have "no business getting into areas where we may have passion and conviction but no scholarly base from which to operate." Since issues such as racial discrimination, economic injustice, inequities of class and gender, and multi-cultural issues are "too complex and diverse" for either the teacher or the student in the writing class to deal with, Hairston proposes that the teacher should try to create a "low-risk environment that encourages students to take chances." In other words, the teacher should be responsible for creating an environment in which no essays will be assigned for students to read, no topics will be sug-gested by the teacher for writing assignments, and no contro-versial and political issues will be raised (190, 189).[54] Such an environment will make peaceful collaboration among students possible so that students will come to understand that "each of us sees the world through our own particular lens, one shaped by unique experiences" (190). In short, the teacher in Hairston's view will do everything to ensure that in her class nothing disturbing would happen that might distract students' attention from writing about whatever they are interested in. Although Hairston also talks about an "interactive classroom," the interaction is strictly among students—a process Hairston calls "decentering"—with the teacher simply playing the role as the guardian angel of the threshold of the heavenly haven, in which students' intellectual growth without pain and struggle is ensured by the teacher, the protective and nurturing mother.[55]

Edifying teachers, however, would question whether such nurturing mothers/teachers really have the power they think they possess to make learning and growing completely apolitical and painless. Although edifying teachers would sympathize with the nurturing teacher's desire to create a peaceful environment in which students' discourses will be encouraged, edifying teachers would at the same time wonder why the development of students' multicultural consciousness has to be restricted only to their conversation with their peers, excluding not only their interaction with the outside world and the issues that are part of students' daily existence but also their interaction with the dominant discourse and the teacher's discourse. Edifying teachers would also wonder how the nurturing mother can make sure that her students do not have goals and needs different from those she sees fit for them. For example, if the nurturing teacher indicates the desirability of a multicultural consciousness, how can she ensure that every student obeys her? The nurturing mother/teacher, after all, has to resort to some institutional power to make what she says count in the classroom. And edifying teachers know that here lies the rub—that no matter how nurturing or protective a teacher is, she has to demand students' cooperation and obedience if she wants to fulfill any pedagogic tasks at all. The power play may change its appearance, but hardly its essence—this recognition differentiates the edifying teacher who may also be nurturing from the Hairston type of nurturing mother/teacher.

As a teacher of writing, Carolyn H. Hill has no illusions about the nurturing mother/teacher. She argues that, no matter how nurturing the mother/teacher is, the asymmetrical power relationship in the classroom will not change because of the teacher's soft stance. Reflecting on her own teaching, Hill observes that she wants to play the role of the nurturing mother/teacher and rejects academic authority for the sake of students' "individual authority over their mental space." However, in practice she has been vacillating between the soft stance and the hard stance because the two seemingly opposing stances are never really separated. Hill writes,

> I imagined my position to be a caring one, opposed to the rule-ridden ones I thought so unlike mine. Like Brian, I lived my professional life and argued between those two seemingly separate poles. Hindsight shows me that my long-term teaching habit of seesawing, between the conscious, accepted position and the unconscious, unacceptable one, generated some interesting entanglements with certain students. Ostensibly I wanted to give up authority, help students to be self-starters. Covertly, the institution and I collaborated to see to it that students be quickly notified if that start did not place them in the proper arms of Standard English, focused and controlled. (1990, 78)

The point Hill tries to make is that, even though her "loyalty to the hard line of that discipline was a reluctant one," and even though she "had trouble" seeing herself "in the role of controlling authority or parent," she nonetheless demands students' academic obedience and will try every means to ensure it. The nurturing mother/teacher is after all the controlling authority in the classroom; her "unsharable power of the positions" was "a given" (77). Students in the nurturing mother/teacher's classroom will not "openly or frankly assume a give-and-take negotiation of their own perceptions and sentiments about class events," Hill maintains. For either they are allowed so much freedom in the classroom to wander away, physically and mentally, from assigned work that the pain and struggle of learning new things are reduced by the lowered expectations from the teacher, or they simply subject themselves so completely to the control, judgment, and protection of the teacher that they do not feel the need for negotiation. In either case, the nurturing teacher's control is secured, whether at the expense of giving up the teacher's obligations to the institution or at the cost of impeding the development of students' independent thinking and negotiating ability.

While Hill does not differ much from Hairston in her willingness to be a nurturing teacher, her reflections upon her vacillation between the poles of soft and hard lines nevertheless indicates her consciousness of the inescapability of the teacher's authority granted by the institution, no matter in what form this authority may appear in the classroom. And here lies the important difference between a nurturing teacher and an edifying teacher. For, in acknowledging her vacillation, Hill also acknowledges the grip of institutional authority that causes her own conflict and struggle in teaching, as she has to decide from time to time, occasion to occasion, and case to case when to resist institutional constraints on students' behalf and speak as a nurturing or protective mother and when to speak as an authoritative teacher to reinforce students' sense of responsibility for their own learning.

Furthermore, by reflecting upon the power she has over students' future and academic destiny, Hill is able to realize how easily she can force students into accommodating her own views, at worst with only occasional resistance from a few students. The question for Hill, in this case, is not so much whether she should be nurturing or demanding as how she could use the two seemingly-different-but-essentially-the-same voices to foster independent thinking in her students as well as develop their negotiating ability. In other words, Hill's teaching will focus on how to help students to be more responsible for their own academic work and to be more capable of negotiating with different voices and views; the teacher's authority—whether appearing in soft or hard form—is a means for her to achieve this goal. Instead of pretending that she rejects institutional authority because she wants to be on the side of her students, Hill, through her self-reflexivity—a prominent feature of Responsive Abnormal Discourse, acknowledges the good and bad side of institutional power and struggles to help students obtain freedom from authority, including her own authority, by actively interacting with them to show them how power and authority can be obtained through negotiations (Hill 1990, 77). In Hill's practice, the secondary interaction seldom comes to the foreground; it stays behind the primary interaction, functioning as a liberating force in teaching by alerting the teacher to the possible oppressive effects that normal discourse and the teacher's authority can have on students. Hill as an edifying teacher is nurturing sometimes, but her nurturing differs significantly from Hairston's both in goals and approaches: Instead of closing the door upon the outside world and avoiding the complicated issues students encounter daily in their lives, Hill nurtures by leading students to actively interact with one another's discourse, the dominant discourse and her own abnormal discourse. What is nurtured and developed in Hill's students is the ability to converse with diverse views and conflicting ideas, the ability to create Responsive Abnormal Discourse.

THE EMANCIPATOR AND THE EDIFYING TEACHER

The image of the teacher as emancipator has been especially favored by radical educators, feminists, and expressivists, though the descriptor, "empowering"—usually associated with "emancipators"—has been one of the most often used words in composition studies. For radical educators, the teacher is the emancipator who will liberate students from the oppression of the dominant literacy by cultivating a critical consciousness in them through interrogating and criticizing the hidden ideology of the dominant literacy. For feminist teachers, the teacher is the emancipator who will awaken women students to realize their subordinate and suppressed role in the male dominant academic culture and help them get rid of the mental shackles that the male dominant society and culture have put on them. For expressivists, the teacher as emancipator will free students from the constraints of institution, society, and discourse so as to liberate students' imagination and creativity. In short, emancipatory teachers are upfront about their political and social commitment and their criticism of and resistance against the dominant ideology and its hegemonic power. Their goal in teaching is often transformation: transforming the school system that reproduces inequality and injustice (Giroux), transforming the male university culture that excludes and suppresses women's voices, transforming the composition discipline that designates working-class students as remedial (Hurlbert and Blitz), transforming traditional institutional practices that turn students into objects rather than subjects through dialogic approach, transforming classrooms into sites of struggle for democracy (Daumer and Runzo), and so forth. In a sense, emancipatory teachers are also social fighters: they fight for their political, social, and cultural ideals, and they bring their battles into the classroom where they begin the emancipatory process with their oppressed students.

Though sharing with the emancipatory teacher the utopian goal in education, edifying teachers, however, are wary of the possible assumption underlying the emancipatory role of the teacher that the teacher is a morally superior figure. Edifying teachers, therefore, are sensitive to how the emancipatory teachers' political agenda may affect their interactions with students in reading, writing, and communicating activities in the classroom. Should students abandon their own moral values and adopt their teachers' because the teachers' values are more moral? What would happen if students did not believe in what the teacher believes in? What if students' experiences make them believe and feel otherwise?

In an engaging article titled "The Feminist Teacher of Literature: Feminist or Teacher?" Nina Baym, a feminist literary teacher, investigates the dilemma of a feminist reading of literary works in pedagogical contexts. Reflecting on three experiences of her reading of and encounter with D. H. Lawrence's *Lady Chatterley's Lover*—at age fifteen, in her early twenties, as a graduate student and later at a feminist presentation as an audience member— Baym observes how the feminist's interpretation of the book as "particularly dangerous" contradicted with the feeling of pleasure she had experienced during her earlier readings of the book. The contradictory interpretations and feelings caused Baym to think:

> She [speaker] was the teacher as rescuer, a crusader arming the defenseless innocent against the aggressive sallies of the immoral text. Her stance was, simply, that of Victorian moral realism.... What is aimed for here is both to rupture the blissful connection between reader and text, and also to obliterate the reader's memory of her previous pleasure by enforcing a new, unpleasurable interpretation. The aim is to create, through interpretation, a new kind of person. For the feminist, it is to create a new kind of woman. In saying that no woman could take pleasure from *Lady Chatterley's Lover*, the speaker was instructing her audience in womanhood. (1990, 70)

and to ask:

> But wasn't that previous, unschooled reader also a woman? Wasn't I, occupying the student position in this event, actually a plurality of women, producing a plurality of readings, no one either more right or more wrong than any other, each exactly

congruent with the moment of my life that called it forth? and, too, didn't the very intensity of the speaker's insistence that no woman could take pleasure from *Lady Chatterley's Lover* betray the real intention: to make women renounce the unenlightened pleasure they had taken from the book? That is, did not her very position call for a prior pleasure as its ground? (70)

And Baym drives her point home with the conclusion:

> Deferring to the speaker's seriousness, I decided not to ask these questions at that time. And therefore, acquiescing to the force of a presentation informing me that I had erred in enjoying *Lady Chatterley's Lover*, I became a silenced woman. (70)

Thus, her own experience of being silenced by a feminist reading of a canonical work that she as a woman had enjoyed reading (wrongly!) led Baym to think about other students like herself in the classroom:

> And this is what happens to women students all the time. The silenced, perhaps resisting—but how are we to know?—readers are after all typical. Are they more silenced, or less silenced, in the classroom of a woman teacher? Of a feminist teacher? (70–71)

Baym's reflection, as she points out, underscores "how the position of certified interpreter is a political position, constraining those who occupy it in a manner that overrides their gender" (1990, 71). In other words, the authority of position that ensures the superiority of the teacher-speaker's interpretation over students' interpretations tends to silence women's voices rather than to empower them. "No voluntary disempowerment of the teacher, per se, will be of much use," Baym remarks. However, she suggests that a teacher's awareness of the politics of interpretation will help:

> Yet, to teach a wide range of works in a variety of ways, to rethink the dominance of interpretive activity in the classroom, to understand that all interpretations are contingent and none are correct, may allow a teacher to tap into the possibilities that feminism suggests. Above all, perhaps, the teacher needs to encourage her women students to say what she does not expect them to say and perhaps would rather not hear. Otherwise, the only real reader in the class will be the teacher, whether she is feminist or not. (75)

Baym's reflections and arguments reveal the silencing effects that the teacher's moral values may have on students, no matter how emancipatory the teacher intends to be. If students are forced to accept teachers' moral values in reading and writing, what the teacher will most often hear would probably be either automatic echoes of what the teacher has said or resistant silence. What the teacher will try to enforce would be the mind-set that generates the oft heard question: "What do you want?" from the student.

Feminist and radical teachers will become edifying teachers only when they recognize that whether their abnormal discourse is liberating or oppressive depends largely upon the context and situation in which it is used and only when they become aware of the potential silencing power of any discourse bearing the status of authority. As Giroux cautions radical teachers, "we should always be mindful of our obligation not to run away from authority but to exercise it in the name of self- and social formation":

> That means always reminding ourselves that power must be exercised within a framework that allows students to inform us and to be more critical about their own voices, as well as aware of the codes and cultural representations of others outside the immediacy of their experiences. As cultural workers we must be aware of the partial nature of our own views. (1992, 157; emphasis added)

To be edifying teachers we must be aware not only of the partial nature of our own views but also the connections between our views and the diverse views that our students bring into the classroom. Otherwise, no matter how progressive our political agenda and discourse may be, they will not produce the kind of transformation that we desire in the classroom.

C. H. Knoblauch's experience of trying to apply critical pedagogy to the teaching of a group of students from the "comfortable middle of the American middle class" and from the White, mainstream suburban culture may help us understand how an edifying teacher differs from an emancipatory teacher in the classroom. In "Critical Teaching and Dominant Culture," Knoblauch observes how his liberatory intention and pedagogy became seemingly out of place in a class in which most students are hardly poor, oppressed, disenfranchised outsiders but are politically, ideologically, culturally, financially, and academically comfortable people who aspire for The Good Life that only the American dominant class and culture can offer. Within such a context, Knoblauch asks himself a series of questions about critical teaching:

> Who is to be liberated from what? Who gets to do the liberating?

Is the U.S. government an oppressor in the same sense that the South African government is? Are middle-class black persons as "outside" as underclass Hispanic? Is Elizabeth Dole an outsider? Where exactly is the inside? Is the goal to make the outsider into an insider? Is it to transform one inside into another? Is it to abolish capitalism? Does the moral commitment, and the political authority, of the critical teacher properly mandate a change in the consciousness of arguably disenfranchised students regardless of their own wishes, their own sense of what they might gain or lose from accommodating themselves to the dominant culture? (1991, 15)

Further, thinking about his students who "belong to the dominant culture, not to the margins by any definition," Knoblauch asks another series of questions about critical teaching in this particular case:

Is critical teaching anything more than an intellectual game in such circumstances? If not, what does it entail, how is it justified, what are the terms of its success in classrooms filled with literate, economically privileged, young suburbanites, whose political consciousness, in fall, 1988, at least, extended only as far as the wearing of George Bush campaign buttons to class? Are these heirs to American wealth and power in fact the oppressor (re)incarnate, already too corrupted for Freirean dialogue since they have so much to gain from not listening? Can the university really serve as a site for radical teaching? (15–16)

In addition, what is the role of the teacher in this class? Knoblauch continues his questioning:

What is the meaning of "radical teacher" for faculty in such privileged institutions—paid by the capitalist state, protected from many of the obligations as well as consequences of social action by the speculativeness of academic commitment, engaged in a seemingly trivial dramatization of utopian thought, which the university itself blandly sponsors as satisfying testimony to its own open-mindedness? (16)

And all these questions boil down to a more specific and disturbing question: Is it really plausible to perform liberatory teaching in circumstances like this where "there is a powerful self-interest, rooted in class advantage, that works actively, if not consciously, against critical reflectiveness?" After all, Knoblauch asks, "What do my students have to gain?"[56]

another" ("Peer Tutoring" 1984, 12). He offers a collaborative learning approach as a means to initiate students into academic community and to enable them to join the conversation in normal discourse. The teacher in Bruffee's collaborative learning serves as facilitator and collaborator, mediating between students' dialects and the normal discourse of the academy.

It is not hard to see that the view of teachers as mediators assumes that teachers are insiders and students are outsiders of the academic community, that the insiders' culture and language are aspired to by outsiders because of their superiority, and that the outsiders have to struggle and sweat in order to become insiders. In addition, because of the intrinsic goodness of academic discourse and the desirability of gaining entrance to the privileged academic community, the good intentions of mediating teachers are taken for granted. The teachers are there to guide students to move from their minority cultures to mainstream culture, to ease their pain and suffering as they move away from their home communities to join the new community of academics.

Progressive as is the compositionists' understanding of students' pain and struggle in their cultural transition, the image of teachers as mediators nevertheless implicitly demands students' giving up their home cultures and discourses (even though temporarily, according to Bizzell) in order to be acculturated by the dominant discourse and assimilated into mainstream culture. The notion of acculturation and assimilation itself "poses problems," Terry Dean argues in "Multicultural Classrooms, Monocultural Teachers," for it assumes that all minorities are willing to go through the transition, despite the pain caused by alienation from the values and relationships of the home culture and the risks of losing their distinctive qualities in struggling to join the White, dominant culture. Dean cites social and anthropological studies to support his view that cultural transition does not occur in a vacuum and that "cultural conflict affects the preschool child, the university undergraduate, the graduate student, and the faculty member as well" (1989, 26). What the teacher should do, Dean suggests, is to turn acculturation and assimilation into a process of cultural interaction so that teachers, in helping students make cultural transitions, "learn from them how to make transitions ourselves" (37). For Dean, the teacher stops being a mere mediator; like students, the teacher is also subject to changes and transitions in the process of teaching.

Dean's view has been further elaborated by Min-Zhan Lu in a more recent article, "Conflict and Struggle: The Enemies or Preconditions of Basic Writing?" Lu questions Thomas Farrell's assumptions that basic students exist in a "residual orality" and that their "emigration from 'orality' to 'literacy' is unequivocally beneficial for everyone, since it mirrors the progression of history" (Lu 1992, 894). She also argues that Bruffee's collaborative learning is based on similar assumptions that school culture is more desirable than students' home cultures and that academic discourse is superior to students' home discourses. Lu takes issue with Farrell's and Bruffee's implicit argument that "discourse communities" are "discrete and autonomous entities rather than interactive cultural forces." Lu insists that such a position reveals an intention to protect the autonomy of the literate community from the threat open admissions students seem to pose to the university (1992, 895). For Lu, in their attempt to persuade students to "willingly move into the 'literate community,'" both Farrell and Bruffee erred in ignoring the "positive use of conflict and struggle" in teaching the "process of repositioning" (910).

Edifying teachers perhaps will find in the image of the teacher as the cultural mediator a perception that is close to their own, as edifying teachers are also cultural workers interested in conversing with different cultures and communities. In the classroom, as edifying teachers have the obligation to teach normal discourse, they may very well play the role of the mediator to make the cultural transition easier. However, edifying teachers perhaps will not assume that normal discourse is a superior discourse to other discourses and that the academic community is a more literate community than other communities, even though academic discourse and academic community enjoy more power and prestige in this country than minority dialects and minority communities. From these premises, edifying teachers will play their mediating role differently: instead of beckoning students to join them from the zenith of their quest—the academic community—edifying teachers will actively interact with students in reading and writing activities. They will switch between normal discourse and Responsive Abnormal Discourse as they try to engage students in the conversation of the academic community, so that students can experience communicating with people from another culture and another community, starting with the teacher. They will make efforts to learn more about students' home cultures and discourses, not only for the sake of helping students to master academic discourse faster, but also for their own intellectual goal of producing Responsive Abnormal Discourse.[58]

Teachers who do not speak Responsive Abnormal Discourse can hardly become good mediators between students' home cultures and mainstream culture or between students' home discourses and academic discourse. The stories told by Linda Brodkey in "On the Subject of Class and Gender in 'The Literacy Letters'" serve to illustrate this point. Brodkey analyzed a group of letters—correspondences between six White middle-class teachers (four women and two men) and six White working-class women enrolled in an Adult Basic Education course—to study "the ways discourses construct our teaching" (1989, 126). Brodkey's findings are enlightening: the seven-letter exchange between Don and Dora was marked by the teacher Don's "extended and humorous anecdotes that portray him as a man at odds with himself at work, school, and home" and by the student Dora's "consolation by letting him know how amusing she and the other women in her class find his stories" (131). This pattern of Don as the narrator and Dora as the faithful audience lasted for several weeks until Dora reversed the pattern and took the role of the narrator of a tragedy and wrote to Don the following letter:

> I don't have must to siad this week a good frineds husband was kill satday at 3:15 the man who kill him is a good man he would give you the shirt off his back it is really self-defense but anyway I see police academy three it was funny but not is good as the first two. (131)

As Brodkey points out, even as Dora is representing the stark reality in her letter as a narrator, she fulfillls her task as a student and dutifully answers the teacher's questions—"but anyway I see police academy three it was funny but not is good as the first two" (132).

According to Brodkey, Dora's shift from audience to narrator and then back to audience again indicates her desire to critique a teacher's exclusive right to initiate topics as well as her hesitation to make such a shift, hence her remark about the movie—an offer to "return to the already established subject positions of teacher/narrator and student/audience" (1989, 133). However, Don obviously failed to recognize both the meaning of the life event that Dora told him about and the student's struggle and hesitation to change from the audience to the narrator. Don's response, which suggests that he is "nonplussed" and also indifferent, alienated Dora and brought their correspondence close to its end. In her next and last letter to Don, she made this remark, among others:

> I wouldn't want to see you living in Kensington with the rest of us
> bums. ha ha. (133)

She never returned Don's next letter.

What Brodkey sees in this seven-letter correspondence is an educational discursive practice that implicitly assigns all the discursive power and control to the teacher. The teacher Don, unaware of the "tension over the control of subject positions" and assuming the "transcendent" nature of the educational discursive practice, inadvertently "contributes rather than alleviates class antagonism" when he fails to recognize and acknowledge the student Dora's desire to "narrate herself as a subject unified in relation to the violence that visited her working-class neighborhood" (1989, 133).

Brodkey's stories highlight the importance of the secondary interaction in teaching: Unless teachers speak Responsive Abnormal Discourse, they will not be able to recognize the discursive hegemony of teachers over students in various ways—through classism, racism, and sexism, and in developmental terms—as cognitive deficits, emotional or intellectual immaturity, ignorance, and cultural illiteracy. Unless teachers are conscious of the discursive hegemony of normal discourse and make efforts to resist it through Responsive Abnormal Discourse, students will not be encouraged to take the subject position as the narrator when interacting with the teacher. Unless teachers speak Responsive Abnormal Discourse and are genuinely interested in what students have to say, the asymmetrical relationships in educational discursive practice between its knowing subjects, teachers, and its unknowing subjects, students, will not be changed. The teachers observed by Brodkey perhaps have good intentions, but their failure to admit class concerns into the correspondences inevitably distance and alienate themselves from their students (1989, 139).[59] Insensitive to the tension caused by class, race, and gender differences, they prove to be unable to mediate successfully between different cultures and different discourses as they may wish.

EDIFYING TEACHERS AS ENABLING CONSTRAINTS

In theory, to participate in the two-level interaction among normal discourse, Responsive Abnormal Discourse, and Nonresponsive Abnormal Discourse, edifying teachers will often switch between the roles of cultural agent and antifoundationalist intellectual, between normal discourse and Responsive Abnormal Discourse, and between the voice of the authority and the voice of a conversational partner in the writing classroom. However, when to switch roles, discourses, and voices is contingent upon tasks, purposes, situations, contexts, audiences, students, and students' cultures, discourses, and experiences in a writing class. For this reason, edifying teachers not only need to know all the existing normalized theories and pedagogies in their discipline, but they also need to critique and investigate the implications of these theories and pedagogies to create Responsive Abnormal Discourse. Edifying teachers do not have a stabilized agenda or pedagogy to abide by, for an exhaustive and systematic description of how edifying teachers act or should act in teaching is, on the one hand, quite an impossible task and, on the other hand, an attempt to normalize their Responsive Abnormal Discourse. The edifying teachers' reluctance to form a well-defined pedagogy perhaps caused Thomas Kent to resort to a "rhetoric of paralogy" to describe their classroom practices.[60] Nevertheless, through comparing edifying teachers with other kinds of teachers in teaching practice, I have attempted to provide glimpses of edifying teachers at work. Conscious of the asymmetrical power relations in the classroom, edifying teachers gingerly guard against the tendency of normalizing their own discourse in teaching writing. Switching between Responsive Abnormal Discourse and normal discourse, between different roles and voices, they are more capable of creating a more democratic learning environment than other types of teachers, an environment in which students' discourses, cultures, consciousness, and experiences are *artfully edified* through the two-level interaction in various reading, writing, and collaborative activities rather than drastically transformed.

In *Beyond the Culture Wars*, Gerald Graff cites the common joke among English professors that when people meet them at parties, all they can think to say is, "Oh, you teach English? I guess I better watch my grammar." The joke, for Graff, reflects society's persistent view of the English professor as an old fashioned "grammatical pedant." Quite contrary to this old image of the English professor as one who makes his living by poring over students' grammar mistakes is the even less flattering new image of the English professor as "urban guerilla" who is more interested in politics than academics (1992, 36, 33). As Graff sees it, both images indicate society's misunderstanding of the profession of teaching English, but the misunderstanding is caused mainly by the discipline's indifference to its public image and its disdain to clarify its concerns to outsiders. The laughable jokes about the English professors, therefore, underscore a serious problem: "the poor quality of communication between the academic humanities and the outside world," the "poor quality of communication between academic humanists themselves and between sectors of the university in general," and the poor quality of communication between the professor and students (36). Graff traces the roots of this poor quality of communication not just to the profession's "notorious proclivity for jargon" but to "a deeper source in institutional practices that isolate teachers from one another and prevent conflicting views from entering into clarifying dialogues" (36). Two institutional practices Graff criticizes are the "pluralist cafeteria counter curriculum," which "leaves it up to students to connect what their teachers do not," and the "separatist" curriculum, with each subject and course being an island with little regular connection to other subjects and courses" (13). Both curriculums, Graff argues, expose students to "a great clash of values, philosophies, and pedagogical methods among their various professors," but deny students "a view of the *interactions and interrelations* that give each subject meaning" (12; emphasis added). Graff explains,

> They [students] are exposed to the *results* of their professors' conflicts but not to the process of discussion and debate they need to see in order to become something more than passive spectators to their education. Students are expected to join an intellectual community that they see only in disconnected glimpses. This is what has passed for "traditional" education, but a curriculum that screens students from the controversies between texts and ideas serves the traditional goals of education as poorly as it serves those of reformers. (12)

Graff proposes to change this institutional practice, a change that brings him to the camp of edifying teachers: he teaches conflicts when teaching literary texts, he exposes students to various ways of interpreting texts and to various critical ideas focused on a specific text, he uses canonical texts and minority texts for comparative reading and study, he invites his colleagues to debate with him among his students, trying to involve the students in the debate at the same time. In short, Graff's approach to the teaching of literature provides wonderful examples of how conflicts can be used to create a context in which the authority of traditional ways of interpretation are challenged to open space for students to read, write, think, and communicate critically. Though Graff in his book does not directly address the teacher's authority, his teaching nevertheless shows how the authority of the canon and of the teacher's voice can be made less oppressive and more empowering by the teacher's willingness to face the challenges to his or her own assumptions and values posed by noncanonical texts and voices of the others.

Edifying teachers' questioning of traditional institutional practices and their attempt to change them in order to make their authority more enabling make teaching an involvement and a struggle for teachers, for whenever there is questioning there is conflict and confrontation; whenever there is change, pain and struggle are inevitable. For example, edifying teachers espousing deconstruction would like to change traditional ways of reading student papers because, as Bruce Lawson and Susan Sterr Ryan point out, the assumptions underlying the traditional practice reveal a very conservative view of thought and language (1989, xv).[61] The change, however, can be complex and baffling at times, as Randall Knoper's article demonstrates. In "Deconstruction, Process, Writing," Knoper argues that the notions oriented from the process theories oppose a deconstructionist view of writing, for deconstruction insists that "there are no clear divisions between 'free writing' and premeditated control of an audience, and play among parts of a text and between texts goes on despite efforts to stop it" (1989, 133). According to Knoper,

> Most of the advice given to students under the authority of the ideal of "reader-based prose" would be called immediately into question by a poststructuralist writing. The basic maxims for saving readers from difficulty, for easing their passage through a text, for avoiding excessive demands on short-term memory— that a writer "orient" readers by providing a telling title and using headings, guide them by quickly presenting an overarching thesis, use topic sentences to subordinate paragraphs to the thesis and to encapsulate units of meaning, provide periodic summaries that divide the argument into graspable stages—all aspire to a hierarchy and control that a poststructuralist perspective would consider delusory (because of the insecurity of pretensions to immobilize meaning) or unfortunate (because of the reductions such limits try to enforce, the dodges involved in their coherence, the manipulations and prescriptions enacted through their clarity). (133–34)

In other words, a deconstructive pedagogy offers a quite different view of the conventions that process theories deem important. A deconstructive pedagogy would not refuse such markers and devices, but it would treat them always as "parts of the general textual economy—not outside of it, not transcendent, not as external controls that would arrest 'the concatenation of writing'" (134). As Knoper explains it, "Title and themes become pieces in the play of meaning, not the rules of the game. A deconstructive pedagogy would promote a writing interested in, aware of, and ready to exploit such 'gambols of language'" (134).

Knoper contrasts writing practices based on process theories and on deconstruction and argues that the former, emphasizing the writer's control of the text, denies the notion that the writer is also "written" by language:

> Hand-in-hand with the processes that are thought to bring writing to reader-based ideals are processes thought to bring writers to control of their texts—to self-assertion, and ownership, and masterfully autonomous shaping. The "empowerment of students" is an idea attractive enough (to us all) to make even crusading poststructuralists drop their notions that the writing "I" is always in process, always modifying and modified, continuously dislocated, knocked about by the repercussions of language. (1989, 134)

The latter, on the contrary, would "throw into question the 'consciousness of ideal mastery'" and treat writing as happening rather than "empowerment" or "disenfranchisement":

> Deconstruction "in the general sense," on the other hand, "puts into question the grounds of the critic's power."...But perhaps the real point is that, just as we need general theory that both respects the autonomous and purposive subject and acknowledges its divisions, constitution, and dissemination, so we need to face writing—including student writing—unbridled by the impulse to take sides on simple oppositions between empowerment and disenfranchisement, authority and uncertainty. This would entail, now, being much more ready to take language (I am again quoting *Dissemination*) as "a force whose effects are hard to master, a dynamics that constantly surprises the one who tries to manipulate it as master and as subject" (135).

Such a deconstructive view of writing, according to Knoper, will "loosen" the teacher's authority when responding to student writing:

> To extend deconstruction into student writing would mean taking student texts as never finished—in the sense of a smooth surface, a clinched argument, or a rounded discussion—but instead

encouraging the rough edge that signals troubles, vexing compli-
cations, contradictions, allowing the insecure articulations that
hover around an undecidability. The pretense of certainty a
thesis has, the security of a conclusion, the assertion of mastery
over a text would give way. (136–37)

Knoper is advocating changing the traditional practice of
writing and reading student papers. And his argument for favoring
"thinking-writing," the kind of writing Derrida creates, is eloquent:
"If embedded in our best writing is an education about writing
itself—its figurative, rhetorical, shifting capacities, its provisional
place in the interweavings of other writings—then we are right to
share this education with our students" (1989, 138). However,
with Knoper's call for change comes the tension: when students
are not mature enough in writing and thinking to produce the
kind of writing that is "carefully attentive and wise to its scat-
terings of meaning" and that "displays a careful estimate of the
tenuousness of its positions and of the writer's limited control over
text, language, and signification," how can the teacher help
students to get a sense of "good" writing except by offering some
rubrics and strategies (137)?

To this question Elaine O. Lees has much to offer. Reporting
her experiment with a hermeneutical approach in teaching writing,
specifically editing, Lees exemplifies a teacher's struggle to apply
deconstruction to teaching so as to make theories, conventions,
and rules enabling rather than confining. For example, the first
theory Lees deconstructs is the notion of outsider/insider. Quoting
Fish, that an outsider is not "*absolutely* outside" but "outside in
relation to a set of assumptions," Lees argues that "[p]edagogies
that clarify how communities distinguish outsiders from insiders
simultaneously rationalize exclusions" (1989, 153, 159). "It is not
self-evident that examining the politics of discourse communities
will encourage a student—especially one who feels the lack of an
acceptable public voice—to write," Lees's teaching experience and
insight leads her to ponder (159). And she is unequivocal that the
denial of the substantiality of the boundary between the outside
and inside is important for both Black and White students. The
reason is simple, according to Lees. "A student must regard
himself as *already* entitled to participate in the dialogue of the university—well before he has mastered the community's rule book"
(156).

For Lees, teaching certainly does not begin with the community's rule book. Teaching for her begins with activities

characterized by what Donald Davidson calls "passing theory" and what Rorty calls a "hermeneutic guessing"—with interactions between the teacher and students:[62]

> By themselves, teachers cannot locate the patch of common ground, the point of shared agreement, where a student's growth as an editor can begin. The student must participate in this process. (Lees 1989, 159)

And the teacher's responsibility is to "prompt" students, through reading their papers and interpreting the issue of errors, to "begin reinterpreting [their] position in the academy" (156). As Lees sees it, errors, rules, and conventions are still the teacher's concerns, but they are approached in a different way. For example, teachers still provide students with basic information on the nature of reading, but the purpose is not merely to prescribe rules but to reassure students that their ability to read and write will improve as they become aware of different ways of reading a text. Teachers can also talk about politics of error—why certain errors are considered less tolerable in the academic world—so that student writers will benefit from recognizing these errors as they approach the common "rule book" (156). Further, explicit instruction in the politics of error is also a way to "empower [students] to make informed decisions about where to focus their efforts" (157).

Lees's teaching will be approved by the edifying teacher, for Lees, speaking Responsive Abnormal Discourse, is able to challenge the established binary of insider/outsider and change the established pedagogic practice of leading outsiders into academic community. Having broken the theoretical boundary of "inside" and "outside," Lees is able to listen to students' Nonresponsive Abnormal Discourse and help them constructively cope with the constraints of rules, words, and communities to form their own voices. In the end, students are still faced with the same task of joining the academic community, but the community in Lees' eyes is no longer the paradise inhabited only by comfortable middle-class teachers but a conglomerate culture characterized by communicating teachers and students:

> The intriguing prospect for a developing writer may be, in the end, the possibility that someone will listen, that someone will hear what he or she has to say. A need to emerge, not simply to fit in, produces writing: a need to seem someone worth listening to, someone memorable—someone who appears...to "express himself," to "have some freedom in the way he wrote his works."

Although the issue here, too, is community, it is community on a different scale.

As a result, the work that confronts the student editor is neither so difficult nor so simple a task as breaking and mastering "the society's" code. Though writers and their medium are constituted and sustained by community, those whose work is valued as their communities evolve are valued for reasons other than their adherence to convention. A teacher's task in teaching editing is to keep both sides of this constraint in view, and to assert—even before a student sees such affiliation as desirable— that the student already belongs to a group who gain (and give) something by wrestling with the written word (1989, 161).

And needless to say, only edifying teachers, who are willing to give up the security of the academic community, the prestige of normal discourse, the certainty of the foundational knowledge for the sake of continuing the conversation and producing abnormal discourse, will be able to take such a risky step as debunking the protective boundary between "insider" and "outsider" so that their students can learn to break their silence into words.

CONCLUSION, OR A NEW BEGINNING

As I am thinking about ending my description of the edifying teacher, I recall the first time I walked into a classroom in this country as a teacher of English, or as a teaching assistant, to be more accurate, and looked right into twenty-five pairs of questioning American eyes. "Are you the teacher?" Marian Yee said that sometimes one of her students—"a wise-mouthed student or just an unwitting one"—would actually "snap it out like the sudden, sharp burst of gum" upon seeing her, a Chinese woman, walking into the classroom and claiming the platform on the first day of school (1991, 24). None of my students uttered a word, but I could hear the unasked question in their minds: "Are you the teacher?" Although by then I had already been a teacher of English for more than ten years, it was in another country. "What entitles me to teach these young people who speak English as their mother tongue?" I asked myself. In the quiet classroom I heard my own voice, and I judged it as if it were from a stranger: The tone was uncertain, indicating a lack of confidence? The words came out in staccatos, betraying the speaker's nervousness? The accent was conspicuously foreign, perhaps baffling the listeners? I was expecting someone to stand up and walk out of the classroom; I expected someone to snicker or make a joke to break the dominance of the strange voice. But nothing happened. Toward the end of the class period, I was reassured: "These *American* students have granted me their consent to be *my* students; what can I do to be worthy of their trust?"

Now that I have taught writing for more than five years in this country, I look back to that very first day and to the other first days of school and wonder: What makes my students give their consent to my authority so readily? What makes them trust that I could teach them something about writing in English? What makes them willing to tolerate my foreign accent not for just a couple of hours but for weeks and weeks? There could be several possible answers: They must trust the institution that has hired me and therefore extend their trust to me; perhaps they have trusted their own intuition that I would be good to them and they are, therefore, willing to ignore the differences between them and me; they may have thought that being a foreigner and a teaching assistant I would be less authoritative and demanding; or they may simply care very little about how much they can learn as long as they can get a decent grade out of the compulsory writing courses. In any case, the initial consent of the students is not hard to obtain: they will take a look at me and my syllabus and either decide to stay or simply disappear forever after the first day of class. If they accept me as their teacher, it is not me that they trust; it is the institutional position of the teacher that they trust. Perhaps to some students the teacher and the institution are the same.

To sustain and strengthen students' confidence and trust, however, is a much more demanding and complicated task for the teacher. When I talk with students about their writing and explain why a certain paper needs revision, when I am confronted with a student complaining about the grade I put on his or her paper and have to go through the academic standards with him or her, when I am troubled by some students' nonchalance in accomplishing a certain task, when I have to persuade some students to listen to others rather than being absorbed only in their own opinions, when I agonize over some student papers for not knowing what to do to help them improve, I find myself experiencing as much pain and struggle, if not more, as my students. There are always individual students who will come along and challenge my beliefs, values, and pedagogic practices. There are always special situations, circumstances, and cases that call for more than just theories to cope with. There are always new questions, new experiences, new uses of languages emerging from student writing that force me to reflect upon my own assumptions about teaching, living, and language. I have never experienced any sense of arrival, of being the insider of the academic community, or of being able to rise above my students' struggle in learning to read and write better. I am always struggling along with them.

Perhaps that is why the written exchanges between Carole Deletiner and her students on the subject of pain and struggle touched me deeply, for Deletiner as a graduate student (like I was) was being honest with her students. Instead of assuming an impersonal authority in the classroom, Deletiner turned herself into one of the conversational participants in the classroom, taking the risk of baring her inner world to the students for the sake of changing the traditional pedagogical practice—communication that has no genuine communicative value. Though others have raised their voices criticizing Deletiner for having ignored teaching academic discourse, I admire her for her courage as an edifying teacher who genuinely values conversation and has shown her students the value of words by example.[63]

As I read our field, more stories about teachers struggling in the classroom have caught my attention. One of them is unusual: a story about Scott Lankford as "an openly gay instructor" being "bashed" by a student's writing, how he dealt with the paper, and how the paper became a topic of interest and dispute for two years at the Conference on College Composition and Communication (CCCC) (Richard Miller 1994, 391). We hear the story from Richard Miller: In a writing assignment, a student of Lankford's wrote about a drunken trip he and his friends made to "San Fagcisco" to study "the lowest class...the queers and the bums." What makes the story unusual is that the student writer not only recounts how they harassed a bum, asking him if he was a "fag" but also narrates how they urinated on a homeless person and, in a frenzy, began to "kick the homeless person, stopping after "30 seconds of non-stop blows to the body," at which point the writer says he "thought the guy was dead" (392).

Miller explains that the debate over the paper focuses on several issues: First, should the teacher who reads the paper be morally and legally responsible for what the student said he had done—harassing and killing a homeless person? Second, since the student's paper also reveals a strong bias against differences—that is, the teacher's "gay culture"—should the teacher confront the student's bias when commenting on his paper? And third, on a more general level, how should teachers deal with "unsolicited oppositional discourse" like this, discourse that marks the "fault lines in the contact zone" in the classroom (Richard Miller 1994, 399)? These questions, though raised around one specific paper, have involved some of the most important issues in composition studies: How should teachers read student papers, read them for content, for form, or for both? Should teachers make moral judgments about student writing? Should teachers use their authority to make students agree with them? How should teachers deal with students' discursive resistance when it threatens the teacher's values and beliefs or invades the teacher's private sphere? How should teachers treat conflicts and confrontations in the writing classroom? I believe that edifying teachers will answer these questions quite differently from the traditional teacher and other process-teachers.

It is time for a conclusion. However, I am still hearing voices arguing with others and with themselves: I still hear Giroux insisting that schools and teachers "need to gain a vision of why they're doing what they're doing," that teachers as intellectuals must remember that the "battle to extend democratic possibilities has to be fought in education at a very primal level," and that teachers' authority should be exercised to "establish conditions in which a central tension lies at the heart of how we teach," a method that "encourages self-reflection, learning from others, and refiguring forms of cultural practice" (1992, 154, 156–57). For Giroux, schools are first and foremost "democratic public spheres" in which the "very notions of knowledge, values, testing, evaluation, ethics all ultimately relate to social criticism and its role in democratic struggle" (154, 156). For Giroux, teachers' political role and pedagogic role can never be separated, even in the classroom.

I detect a conflicting note in Derrida's voice, the conflict between a radical deconstructive master speaking an abnormal discourse and a traditional professor who does not conceal his reverence for tradition. Derrida frankly tells his interviewer, Gary Olson, that his way of teaching is "traditional and even conservative," and he freely admits that he does not think that there is a model for teaching and an alternative between a conservative and a progressive teaching. Through "very academic, very quiet and conservative ways of teaching, something nonconservative and disturbing arises," the founding father of deconstruction observes. Is he suggesting that the content is more important than the form in teaching (130–31)? Teaching should start from tradition, Derrida concurs with Rorty:

> I call my students in France back to the most traditional ways of reading before trying to deconstruct texts; you have to understand according to the most traditional norms what an author meant to say, and so on. So I don't start with disorder; I start with the tradition. If you're not trained in the tradition, then deconstruction means nothing. It's simply nothing. (Olson 1991, 132)

Derrida warns that "if deconstruction is only a pretense to ignore minimal requirements or knowledge of the tradition, it could be a bad thing," for "there's no deconstruction without the memory of the tradition." For Derrida, the responsibility of the teacher is to help students "*read* what are considered the great texts in our tradition," and to prepare them for a deconstructive practice that requires as its ground "a minimal culture and minimal knowledge of the basic foundations of the canon" (131). As I listen, I wonder if I really have grasped what he means by "a minimal culture and minimal knowledge"—how much is minimal? and how minimal is enough for students to start a deconstructive practice?

I notice that Fish's voice is similarly puzzling. Well esteemed for his antitheory position, Fish nevertheless holds on to the much criticized traditional performance model in his teaching without feeling guilty. He tells his interviewer Olson,

> For me the classroom is still what she [Jane Tompkins] has formally renounced: a performance occasion. And I enjoy the performances; I enjoy orchestrating the class in ways that involve students in the performances, but no one is under any illusion that this is a participatory (or any other kind) of democracy in a class of mine. (Olson 1994, 47)

Is Fish, like Derrida, trying to send the same message that what method we use in teaching does not matter much as long as we have something important to teach? Or is he simply dismissing his own antitheory theory in practice?

J. Hillis Miller sounds more straightforward. He insists that a professor's political concerns should always go "by way of the ethical" and that questions of the ethics of reading are always associated with teachers' role as cultural agents in the academic institution. As a professor, Miller is reluctant to evade the ethical questions:

> What ethical responsibility, if any, do I have to students when I'm teaching? What's my ethical responsibility to the text? What about the institution I teach for? The institution hired me; don't I have certain responsibilities to it? (Olson 1994, 139)

These questions, Miller says, help him separate his role as a scholar from his role as a teacher, roles that are very different in nature to him.

As I am listening to these voices and other voices agreeing, disagreeing, arguing, persuading, explaining, preaching, and positing, as I am re-viewing the composition discipline's struggle to adapt teaching writing to the postmodern world, as I am rethinking the various perspectives, theories, and pedagogies advanced by composition teachers and scholars in the past decades, Rorty's "hermeneutic hope" has become more apprehensible: "The hope is not a hope for the discovery of antecedently existing common ground, but *simply* hope for agreement, or, at least, exciting and fruitful disagreement" (1979, 318). The voices, as Hubert L. Dreyfus sums it all up, indicate that life is going on behind the walls of the institution:

> The social sciences, on the other hand, are at their best in the perpetual revolution and conflict of interpretations which inevitably arise when they are trying to account for all human behavior, even the pervasive background of cultural interpretation which makes action meaningful. For them, normal science would show that the disciplines involved had become conformist, complacent, and ultimately sterile. (1985, 240–41).

Dreyfus has explained well why the voices of Rorty, Derrida, Fish, Miller, and Giroux must be heard, no matter how diverse and conflicting they are. For the same reason that these masters' voices are important, many other voices—voices of cognitivist teachers, expressivist teachers, social constructionist teachers, radical teachers, edifying teachers—should also be heard if we want the life of the discipline of composition to continue. Perhaps that is why edifying teachers deem it so important for students' voices to be heard, too, behind the walls of the classroom. And it is precisely for the same reason that I have argued that teachers need to speak Responsive Abnormal Discourse and normal discourse and to confront the institutional constraints they are working within and with rather than ignoring them. Teachers need to strive to make their authority enabling and constructive rather than evading its existence. Teachers need to enact the two-level interaction in the writing classroom rather than believing that a certain discourse, a certain theory, or a certain pedagogy is intrinsically better than others. Most important, teachers need to play the significant role in the writing class as students' conversational partners, showing them the art of communicating with others, keeping spaces open for new voices and new wonders, and endeavoring to live up to the promise of the humanities as a life-giving force in the changing world.

Notes

1. Between 1960 and 1980, American colleges and universities saw an increase in enrollment of 8.5 million students. Of the total enrollment of 12 million by 1980, minorities represented 17 percent and women students slightly outnumbered male students (Kerr, *Great Transformation* 1991, xiv). By 1990, 13 million students were enrolled in institutions of higher learning. In fact, 32.5 percent of all White 18- to 24-year olds, 25.4 percent of all African-American 18- to 24-year olds, and 15.8 percent of all Hispanic 18- to 24-year olds were enrolled in college (Hourigan, *Beyond Gender*, 1992, 185).

2. See Carolyn Ericksen Hill's wonderfully engaging discussion and criticism of the expressivist position as represented by Ken Macrorie, Peter Elbow, William Coles, Jr., and John Schultz in *Writing from the Margin* (1990, 101–39). See also Lester Faigley's analysis of the ideologies of the self hidden in expressivists' argument for "authentic voices," "private minds," and "confessional writing" in *Fragments of Rationality* (1992, 111–31).

3. Berlin's criticism of the hidden dominant ideology of cognitivism in *Rhetoric and Reality* (1987, 159–65) and "Rhetoric and Ideology" has been one of the most influential views in the field. Caroline Ericksen Hill's analysis of the assumptions underlying cognitivists' sole concern with the "cognitive mind" and their interest in computer-stimulated writing leads her to conclude that, from the cognitivist stance, the writing process becomes "primarily calculative because known and programmable (and therefore teachable, as teaching is defined by its control over 'knowns')." Hill questions this mechanistic view of writing and of the teaching of writing because it strips the mind of "its force and its nonformalizable properties," and of the "mutable context in which it operates" (*Writing from the Margins*, 1990, 184). See also Anthony R. Petrosky's "Review of *Problem-Solving Strategies for Writing*, by Linda Flower" (1983); John Clifford's "Review of *Cognitive Processes in Writing*" (1988); Lester Faigley's "Competing Theories of

Processes" (1986); David Bartholomae's "Inventing the University" (1988); and Patricia Bizzell's "Composing Processes" (1986) for criticism of cognitivism.

4. See Kurt Spellmeyer's response to the preexisting criticism of cognitivism and his own critical analysis of Flower and Hayes' process theory in "Being Philosophical about Composition." Spellmeyer argues that "while Flower and Hayes celebrate the writer's ability to solve problems, they also deny the trustworthiness, and indeed the relevance, of the writer's own self-understanding" (1993, 21). This view helps to support my argument that cognitivists' process approach does not ensure the change of the traditional teacher's authority.

5. The recent criticism of social constructionism has been articulated by Jeffrey Bineham in "The Cartesian Anxiety in Epistemic Rhetoric" (1990), Joseph Petraglia in "Interrupting the Conversation" (1991), Stuart Greene in "Toward a Dialectical Theory of Composing" (1990), and Thomas Kent in "On the Very Idea of a Discourse Community" (1991). Kent argues that social constructionist position assumes a conceptual scheme that is based on Kantian epistemology and the Cartesian split of "in here" and "out there." He also argues that the concept of "discourse community" suggests that language and conventions are codifiable and systemizable, and that the suggestion can easily lead to assigning all power and authority to a discourse community and its discourse, hence the danger of relativism and solipsism.

6. As the title indicates, "Knowledge, Social Relations, and Authority in Collaborative Practices of the 1930s and the 1950s" (1993), Mara Holt in this article examines the use of collaborative learning in the two different historical periods and comes to the conclusion that collaborative learning can be employed for quite different purposes. The student-centered form, according to Holt, can be used to emphasize a "hierarchical notion of authority" and to maintain the teacher's established authority, as indicated by the assumptions underlying the collaborative learning practices in the 1950s. Holt's historical study provides a useful perspective of different collaborative models proposed by expressivists, social constructionists, radical pedagogues, and even antifoundationalists in the field.

7. It is important to point out that antifoundationalists like Rorty, Fish, Bleich, and Kent are also advocates of a "dialogic" or "conversational model" in education. Their conversational model, however, is characterized by its "denial of absolute standards by which rival claims may be negotiated" and is therefore "relativistic," according to Bruce Henricksen (1990, 34). Since, as Henricksen points out, a "dialogical model may seem to reduce the university to something like a perpetual motion machine for empty signifiers" (35), many radical compositionists have attempted to avoid relativism by introducing a moral goal into the dialogic model. Perhaps that accounts for the popularity of Freire's liberatory pedagogy among radical pedagogues such as Bizzell, Richard Ohmann, Michael Holzman, Jane Tompkins, and others.

8. Cognitivists' emphasis on scientific research and discourse, expressivists' preference for private discourse, social constructionists' favor of academic discourse, radical educationists' espousal of critical consciousness and emancipatory discourse—all reveal the assumption that authority of expertise is benign and that the teacher's possession of this authority will suffice in teaching.

9. The term reproduction theorists is used by Aronowitz and Giroux to refer to those who view education mainly as a process of reproducing the economic, cultural, and ideological hegemony of the dominant class. Aronowitz and Giroux include French social theorist Louis Althusser, French cultural critic Pierre Bourdieu, Italian Marxist theorist Antonio Gramsci, and others in the group.

10. See Aronowitz and Giroux for a detailed critique of reproduction theories.

11. For example, the curricula are usually developed for the purpose of equipping different groups of students with the knowledge and skills they will need to perform productively in the workplace. And the policy of extensive remedial programs is formulated to control the distribution of labor force. Both indicate that schools are "distribution agencies" responsible for maintaining the structure of labor division in society (Aronowitz and Giroux, *Education Under Siege*, 1985, 93).

12. Bourdieu and Passeron insist on distinguishing "pedagogic communication" from other forms of communication. Pedagogic

communication depends on a power relation that does not usually exist in "a normal definition of communication" for its own "specifically symbolic effect" (*Reproduction in Education*, 1977, 7). Freire's dialogue between the educator and educatees would probably be considered anti-intuitive by Bourdieu and Passeron.

13. Mao's determination to change the old educational system resulted in a nationwide Educational Revolution in 1958, which was preluded by his Blooming and Contending Campaign in 1956 to enlist support from the nonparty intelligentsia and by his Anti-Rightist Campaign in 1957 to punish intellectuals for having disappointed him with their criticisms of the Chinese Communist Party. Like the Cultural Revolution, the Educational Revolution was targeted at the academic institution and intellectuals. During these campaigns and revolutions, thousands and thousands of intellectuals were branded as "enemies of socialism" and condemned as "counterrevolutionaries" and sent to engage in physical labor, mostly in the countryside (Meisner, *Mao's China*, 1977).

14. After the Cultural Revolution, restricted by the factory rules, Tang Li was only able to go to college to major in textile industry. She was still Number One in all the English classes she took in college, she told me.

15. See Faigley's discussion of personal writing in *Fragments of Rationality* (1992, 119–30). Faigley concurs with Foucault that personal narratives are "institutional confession" because "its production is thoroughly imbued with relations of power" (130).

16. Weber locates personal authority in "traditional" and "charismatic" forms. In cases of personal authority, such as the ancient monarch or modern dictator, "obedience is owed to the *person*" rather than to authority validated by logic and dictated by law (Mortensen and Kirsch, "On Authority," 1993, 560).

17. In another article, "Classroom Authority and Critical Pedagogy," Bizzell makes the same point: what differentiates coercion from authority is that the former is "power exercised by A over B for A's best interests and without B's consent" whereas the latter is "exercised by A over B instrumentally in the sense that sometimes B must do what A requires without seeing how B's best interests will be served thereby" (1991, 849; 851). Bizzell empha-

sizes authority as a "two-stage process" constituting 1. persuasion, through which the teacher tries to get students' consent to obey her; and 2. authority, by wielding which the teacher can insist "that she controls the classroom agenda" (851). Implicit in this "two-stage process" is the same idea that once the teacher has persuaded students that he or she is serving their best interests, the students should then rely on the teacher for all decisions in the class.

18. A good example is Lad Tobin's recounting of the conflict between him and several resisting students in a writing class. Tobin confesses that the students' disruptive behavior made him want to use his institutional authority, i.e., grades, to punish them. Reflecting on this experience, Tobin remarks how the teacher can oppress students not only ideologically but also psychologically with his or her authority when compelled by his or her desire for revenge.

19. In their wonderfully written book, *The Western Intellectual Tradition*, J. Bronowski and Bruce Mazlish characterize this tradition as growing out of "the movement and the conflict of ideas" (1960, xii). The conflict of ideas, according to Bronowski and Mazlish, gives a community its character:

> In a community the conflict of ideas has a special force: established ideas held rigidly for social reasons or for reasons of interest are at odds with new ideas, and the character of the community derives from the struggle and balance between these. (xii)

The legitimacy of "reasoned dissent" in the Western society is what allows the teacher to oppose and resist the dominant culture and ideology.

20. Paul Willis, in his *Learning to Labor* (1981), demonstrates how the "counterculture" of the "lads"—a group of working class male students—in an English secondary school leads to their ultimate exclusion from any possibility of pursuing an emancipatory relationship between knowledge and dissent. John Ogbu's research into the relationship between minority cultures and school performances of minority students also reveals that the more resistant and hostile a minority is toward the dominant culture, the more likely its children are to fail in school.

21. In *The Postmodern Condition: A Report on Knowledge*, Jean-François Lyotard defines postmodern as "incredulity toward metanarratives," an incredulity that is "undoubtedly a product of progress in sciences" and that is presupposed by that progress. (1984, xxiv). Lyotard believes that in a postmodern society there are many "different language games—a heterogeneity of elements. They only give rise to institutions in patches—local determinism" (xxiv). As a result, "postmodern knowledge is not simply a tool of the authorities; it refines our sensitivity to differences and reinforces our ability to tolerate the incommensurable" (xxv). In the "Foreword" to Lyotard's work, Fredric Jameson defines post-modernism as "a rich and creative movement, of the greatest aesthetic play and delight" that are characterized by two important features: first, the "falling away of the protopolitical vocation and the terrorist stance of the older modernism" and, second, "the eclipse of all of the affect" that marked high modernism, "a commitment to surface and to the *superficial* in all the senses of the word" (xviii). For a better understanding of postmodernism, see also Jameson's *Postmodernism, or, The Cultural Logic of Late Capitalism*, 1990.

22. It should be pointed out that the notion of academic discourse is so widely accepted in the field of composition that almost all schools of thought directly or indirectly claim it as the major goal of teaching first-year English. For example, Mike Rose, a cognitivist, does not deny that teaching academic discourse is an important way of helping underprivileged students to change their lives on the boundaries. Peter Elbow, an influential expressivist, admits that he admires "what's *in* academic discourse" even though he does not want to teach academic discourse to his students ("Reflections," 1991). On the other hand, social construc-tionists such as David Bartholomae and Anthony Petrosky prefer to teach academic discourse through teaching literature and auto-biography (Bartholomae, *Facts*, 1986), an approach not unlike the expressivists' approach advocated by Donald Murray and others. Furthermore, even radicals like Bizzell have, at times, longed for a comparatively stable content for the writing courses for fear of "pedagogical bad faith" ("Beyond Anti-Foundationism," 1988).

23. Radical composition scholars who are influenced by Marxian, feminist, deconstructionist, and cultural theories have critiqued the social constructionists' emphasis on disciplinary

conventions and community consensus and have argued for the teaching of oppositional discourses in the writing class. Patricia Harkin and John Schilb's *Contending with Words* (1991), a collection of essays written by radical scholars, provides a whole array of arguments for using oppositional discourses to contend for power with the dominant discourse and the dominant culture. *Cultural Studies in the English Classroom* (1992), a collection of essays edited by Berlin and Michael J. Vivion, also advocate changing the traditional curricula of English and composition studies to accommodate marginal texts.

24. Thomas Kent's critique of social constructionism in "On the Very Idea of a Discourse Community" (1991) and his theory of paralogy and hermeneutic teaching in "Externalism" (1992), "Beyond System" (1989), and "Paralogic Hermeneutics" (fall 1989) are representative of the antifoundationalist stance in composition studies.

25. In *Reorientations: Critical Theories and Pedagogy*, edited by Henricksen and Morgan, both Barbara C. Ewell and Reed Way Dasenbrock raise questions about opening the canon to include the literatures of women, blacks, Hispanics, and third-world writers. For Dasenbrock, the tendency to cast out classics and to institutionalize texts written by marginalized groups threatens to create a new canon, even a new hierarchy ("What to Teach," 1990). From a feminist perspective, Ewell argues that such a quandary can be resolved only by teachers' reorientation in pedagogical practice, a reorientation that dialogizes the canon and the student's experience through the diversity of women's voices and interests ("Empowering Others," 1990).

26. In the introduction to a recently published collection of her articles written over the past years, reflecting upon her stance on academic discourse, Bizzell remarks that she is "alarmed" to hear that she is regarded as "advocating the imposition of academic discourse on all students at all costs with total disregard for whatever knowledge they might bring to school from other discourse community" (*Academic Discourse*, 1992, 27). Bizzell defends her stance by saying that she did not try to name academic discourse as "a totally unified entity with impermeable boundaries" and that, although she advocates teaching academic discourse, she tries to "find ways of doing it that were not quite so

dominating as the notion of 'inculcation' might imply" (27). However, one of the ways that Bizzell resorts to—that is, that the teacher should uphold the Marxian values and beliefs in teaching— does little in making "symbolic imposition" less dominating in the classroom.

27. Elaboration of the "situatedness" and contingency of rhetoric can also be found in Rorty's "The Contingency of Language" and in Fish's "Anti-Foundationalism, Theory Hope, and the Teaching of Composition" (1987).

28. In his interview with Olson, Rorty agrees that normal discourse should be taught in schools. He sees "abnormal discourse as a gift of God rather than anything anybody gets educated for or into" and, therefore, is impossible to be taught. But after this remark, Rorty emphasizes that "education should aim at fixing it so the students can see that the normal discourse...is itself a historical contingency surrounded by other historical contingencies" (234). In other words, Rorty does not see the teaching of normal discourse as merely teaching its norms and conventions. Normal discourse has to be taught in specific historical contexts and in relation to other alternatives so that it plants the seed of abnormal discourse for later blossom.

29. Rorty cites these as examples of new cognitive feats: the rediscovery of Aristotle, Galilean mechanics, the development of self-conscious historiography in the nineteenth century, Darwinian biology, mathematical logic (*Philosophy*, 1979, 366).

30. The metalevel rule that Rorty refers to is "the rule that one may suggest changing the rules only because one has noticed that the old ones do not fit the subject matter, that they are not adequate to reality, that they impede the solution of the eternal problems" (*Philosophy*, 1979, 370). Edifying philosophers are abnormal at this metalevel, whereas revolutionary systematic philosophers such as Husserl and Russell are not (369).

31. John Schilb resists Rorty's distinction between normal and abnormal discourse for "our own theoretical or administrative convenience" ("On Personally Constructing," 1991, 240). Evidently, Schilb only sees the inconvenience of the dichotomy and ignores its potential power to illuminate how the authority of discourse

can be made enabling and liberating by abnormal discourse. Also, Schilb errs just as Bruffee does in oversimplifying the relationship between normal and abnormal discourse by calling it a dichotomy.

32. Whether Rorty's interpretation of Heidegger is accurate or not is a controversial issue. See John D. Caputo's criticism of Rorty's appropriation of Heidegger's thought in "The Thought of Being and the Conversation of Mankind: The Case of Heidegger and Rorty" (1985).

33. Mina Shaughnessy's monumental work in the field, *Errors and Expectations*, provides a most detailed examination of the "abnormality" of basic writers' essays. After analyzing errors in about 4,000 basic writers' essays, Shaughnessy ventures a new view of students' errors: "that basic writers write the way they do, not because they are slow or non-verbal, indifferent to or incapable of academic excellence, but because they are beginners and must, like all beginners, learn by making mistakes" (1977, 5). In other words, their writing is the product of their ignorance of the conventions of academic discourse.

34. Peter McLaren remarks that "Giroux refuses to discriminate between his responsibility as a public intellectual and his role as a university professor" (*Teachers*, 1988, xviii).

35. See Richard Ohmann's viewpoint in "On Speculacy" (1987, 240). Ohmann argues that the acquisition of speculacy—a kind of literacy that "grounds thinking that is abstract, individualized, probalistic, game-theoretic, monetarist, supply-sided, masculine, and quantum-mechanical—depends on "the contexts within which people learned and practices speculacy" (240). J. Elspeth Stuckey's persistent argument in *The Violence of Literacy* (1991) is that intellectuals and teachers, including Giroux and Freire, are unable to escape from their middle-class ideology and values and beliefs in their progressive discourse.

36. In fact, many studies have shown that students from underprivileged groups aspire to learn standard English and are willing to embrace the dominant ideologies. For cxample, as early as 1977, Mina Shaughnessy observed that students' errors in writing did not result from their resistance or negligence but from their trying to express their thoughts in a new discourse. Shaughnessy,

therefore, proposed the well-known notion of "intelligence of errors," errors that are signs of students' grappling with language and thoughts, as well as a process of mastering the new discourse.

37. In "Reflections on Academic Discourse" (1991), one of the features of academic discourse that Elbow dismisses as "aids to authority" is academics' use of footnotes, quotations, citations, and names of important figures in their writing. Giroux's writing is certainly "guilty" of all the features that Elbow objects to in academic discourse.

38. *Education under Siege* by Aronowitz and Giroux (1985) provides a detailed discussion of theories of reproduction. A major analysis of all the three discourses can be found in Richard Johnson's "What Is Cultural Studies Anyway?" (1984).

39. Perhaps few teachers of writing would deny that there are conspicuous differences between student writing and academic writing of professionals. However, different interpretations of the differences reveal teacher's attitude toward student writing and the teaching of writing. Mike Rose, for example, problematizes the political implications of the term "remediation" in "The Language of Exclusion" (1985). He argues that the term not only implies the linguistic, moral, and mental inferiority of students from nonmainstream cultures (and therefore justifies treating them as people suffering from diseases) but also suggests a denial of the existence of other cultures and literacies besides mainstream culture and school literacy. Today, Rose's view is widely accepted in the field, as is the concept of "multiple literacies" first proposed by Sylvia Scribner and Michael Cole in *The Psychology of Literacy* (1981).

40. Whether the book, *Marxism and the Philosophy of Language* (1973), was written by Bakhtin or V. N. Volosinov is a controversial issue. Since in composition studies Bakhtin is generally acknowledged as the author, I deem it more convenient to follow the established practice in the field.

41. Graff cites President George Bush as representing the old American tradition when the latter declared that "class conflict is 'for European democracies...it isn't for the United States of America. We are not going to be divided by class'" (*Beyond Culture Wars*, 5). While Graff views Americans' avoidance of conflict as a

cultural legacy belonging uniquely to America, Stuckey nonetheless sees it as Americans' lack of political consciousness
resulting from their gullible acceptance of the dominant ideology—
that is, everybody in America belongs to the middle class. See
Robert C. Smith and Richard Seltzer's study of race, class, and
culture.

42. For Kuhn, "disciplinary matrix" refers to "the body of
elements to which most practitioners of a specific scientific discipline are committed" (Shank and Vampola, "Negating Positivism,"
36). For Kuhn, "the disciplinary matrix provides the framework in
terms of which scientists in a given field speak about their field,
think about their field, and see the world. The possession of this
common language or dialect marks off—in part—one group of spe-
cialists from another, which by comparison seems to 'talk funny.'"
(37). The closest term in composition studies correspondent to
Kuhn's disciplinary matrix is perhaps "academic discourse."

43. Bakhtin claims that the "experiential, expressible element
and its outward objectification are created...out of one and the
same material," and that "there is no such thing as experience
outside of embodiment in signs." Furthermore, the expression
does not depend on experience for organization but organizes
experience (*Marxism*, 1973, 85). Bakhtin's view is close to the
social constructionists' argument that language is not a mere
mirror of the mind and the real world but is constitutive of both.

44. Bakhtin also distinguishes between the "individualistic
self-experience" and the "I-experience." The former is "fully
differentiated and structured," belonging to the "we-experience."
Bakhtin thus describes it,

> Individualism is a special ideological form of the "we-experience"
> of the bourgeois class (there is also an analogous type of indi-
> vidualistic self-experience for the feudal aristocratic class). The
> individualistic type of experience derives from a steadfast and
> confident social orientation. Individualistic confidence in oneself,
> one's sense of personal value, is drawn not from within, not from
> the depths of one's personality, but from the outside world. It is
> the ideological interpretation of one's social recognizance and
> tenability by rights, and of the objective security and tenability
> provided by the whole social order, of one's individual livelihood.
> (*Marxism*, 1973, 89)

45. It is important to note that Graff's argument for focusing on teaching students how to read is based on his acceptance of conflicts in the academy as legitimate and important. This premise makes his argument all the more different from the conservatives' argument for emphasizing teaching reading in the humanities, a point I will discuss later in this chapter.

46. Mike Rose's *Lives on the Boundary* (1989) can be read as a minority student's struggle to turn the I-experience into the we-experience. Rose's recounting of his encountering and grappling with literary texts and standard English speaks most eloquently of the need for academic outsiders to interact with academic texts in order to make their experiences comprehensible to the large audiences in the mainstream culture. See John Trimbur's 1993 article, "Articulation Theory and the Problem of Determination: A Reading of *Lives on the Boundary*," for an interesting analysis of the conflicting ideologies in Rose's narrative.

47. If students can only tell stories about their personal experiences without being able to explain what these experiences mean to them and to others, the experiences they write about are only the random and nonstructured I-experience in the Bakhtinian sense. In fact, much criticism of expressivism is directed towards its emphasis of private writing as writing for exorcism to get rid of thoughts or feeling—a kind of writing that seems to encourage students to ignore social milieu, as well as discourse that shapes their personal experiences and even feelings (see Elbow, "Closing My Eyes as I Speak: An Argument for Ignoring Audience," 1987).

48. I have experienced more than once the shock of seeing my students come up with absolutely opposite conclusions when asked to evaluate two articles expressing opposite views on the same subject (usually one article is substantially inferior to the other in quality for the purpose of contrast). As I found out each time, most students based their judgment merely on which author's view they favor rather than on the criteria that I expected them to use in their evaluative reading.

49. In *The Social Uses of Writing: Politics and Pedagogy* (1990), Thomas Fox proposes the idea of "an interactive classroom." Fox's discussion of the interaction between the radical teacher and students through social issues provides a good example to illustrate how the secondary interaction works in the classroom.

50. With remarkable perspicuity and refreshing insight Bruce Lawson et al. explore issues concerning reading student papers in their collection of essays, *Encountering Student Texts* (1989).

51. These essays not only reveal differences between reading canonical texts and student texts but also inquire into the influence of trends and periods of academic thoughts on the teacher's interpretive stances and ways of responding to student writing. The essays, characterized by the teachers' willingness to reflect on the assumptions underlying their own reading of student papers, provide good examples of how the interaction between Responsive Abnormal Discourse and Nonresponsive Abnormal Discourse can help turn the constraints of normal discourse into enabling elements.

52. In "Beyond System: The Rhetoric of Paralogy," Thomas Kent argues that current process theories of discourse production generally follow three epistemological approaches: the Kantian approach which understands discourse production to be generated from innate mental categories that constitute human consciousness (expressivism); the neopositivist approach which understands discourse production to be an empirical phenomenon that can be tested and measured (cognitivism); and the social-semiotic approach which understands discourse production to be a communal activity that is socially and historically determined (social constructionism). In other words, all these theories in composition studies belong, in one way or the other, to systematic philosophy, with the assumption that discourse production may be codified in a logical/systematic manner (1989, 495).

53. In both "Redefining the Legacy of Mina Shaughnessy" (1991) and "Conflict and Struggle" (1992), Min-Zhan Lu criticizes Shaughnessy for assuming the innocence of the dominant language in her pedagogy and for her uncritical adoption of the notion of assimilation in teaching writing. However, neither Lu or any others in the field would deny Shaughnessy's unique contribution to composition teaching in a period when universities underwent drastic changes and when teachers had to face a diverse and confusing student population. Besides, Shaughnessy's insight into error patterns and their causes, as well as her suggestion of an interactive approach to correcting errors in student writing, is still invaluable to teachers of writing today.

54. Linda Brodkey's first-year composition writing program on issues of gender and race at the University of Texas at Austin in 1990 has attracted much attention in the discipline of composition. Hairston accuses it of having "enforced conformity" and "severely" limited "freedom of expression for both students and instructors" and hails its compulsory revision ordered by the administration (Hairston "Diversity" 1992, 189). In contrast, John Clifford, a professor at the University of North Carolina at Wilmington, sees the dean's postponement of the program until the fall of 1991 as a direct response to "pressure from professors in other disciplines who were upset for the usual reasons: We should teach writing and not something else, certainly not something controversial or political" and to a campaign by the "conservative National Association of Scholars." For Clifford, criticism of the program as an "encroachment on academic freedom, as leftist indoctrination that would unfairly blame white males for many of the injustices in America" was made through "distortion and hyperbole," indicating other disciplines' lack of understanding of the scholarship in composition studies (Clifford "Neopragmatic Scene" 1991, 102).

55. Elizabeth Daumer and Sandra Runzo also suggest a mother/teacher model and advocate transforming the traditional classroom into a supportive context within which women's texts constitute what the mother teaches. Susan C. Jarratt criticizes the nurturing model for its tendency to ignore differences and conflicts of gender, race, and class among students and teachers in the composition classroom ("Feminism and Composition" 1991, 111–13).

56. Similar questions have been raised by other compositionists friendly to critical pedagogy, too. For example, Blitz and Hurlbert dwell on the questions at a more general level in "An Uncomfortable State of Mind." Discussing the goal of teaching for critical consciousness espoused by radical pedagogues, they, like Knoblauch, see a paradox in the two conflicting roles the radical teachers have to play: the role as "agents of an institution whose design is more and more visibly to uphold 'characteristics of excellence' as defined by, for example, the Middle States Association" and the radical teachers' commitment to encouraging critical consciousness and action, a "potentially dangerous and endangering role of teaching people to challenge an institution's 'mission'" ("Uncomfortable" 1991, 43). In addition, they question

the end of teaching for critical consciousness: to make students "cynical" or "ironic" or "melancholic" and resistant of authority? Are English teachers powerful enough to challenge and change political and economic realities for the disenfranchised students? If not, what is the relevance of critical consciousness in the teaching of reading and writing? Blitz and Hurlbert resolve that teachers should become "counter-educators" who are capable of "criticizing and restructuring" "the ways in which knowledge is organized and distributed, the ways in which students and teachers are managed, the ways in which educational institutions and corporate powers tend to each other's interests." In other words, for Blitz and Hurlbert, teaching writing should involve teaching "the lives of teachers and students in all their contradictions, confusions, discomforts and comforts, and connections and disconnections to something typically called the 'social whole.'" Different from Knoblauch's view that literary texts provide ample opportunities for developing students' critical thinking, Blitz and Hurlbert believe that it is the lives of teachers and students that "constitute the most pressing *subject*-matters" in a writing classroom (45).

57. That cultural differences can affect learning has been most eloquently supported by Heath's ten-year research reported in *Ways with Words* (1983). Heath's study has revealed how differences in ways of using language in the natural language environment of working-class Black and White children can interfere with their success in schools designed primarily for children from middle-class mainstream culture. Ogbu's study of Chicano and Black children in California schools and Susan Urmston Philips's study of native American children in a school system in Oregon also underscore the interrelationship between minority students' cultural experiences and school performance.

58. In her influential work, *Ways with Words*, Shirley Brice Heath suggests that teachers' willingness to know students's home culture is an important way to help students succeed in mainstream schools. She says, "Unless the boundaries between classrooms and communities can be broken, and the flow of cultural patterns between them encouraged, the schools will continue to legitimate and reproduce communities of townspeople who control and limit the potential progress of other communities who themselves remain untouched by other values and ways of life" (1983, 369). Ever since Heath's research, ethnography as a research

method, as well as the idea of knowing students' home cultures, has been popular in composition studies. However, instead of agreeing that teachers who belong to mainstream culture should make a reverse transition from the mainstream culture to students' home cultures, I believe that teachers should be genuinely interested in students' home cultures for two main reasons: to obtain knowledge of different perspectives so as to teach better, and to gain diverse experiences for generating Responsive Abnormal Discourse. In a sense, these two purposes correspond with the purposes of first-year composition: to open students' eyes to multiple perspectives and to enable them to generate Responsive Abnormal Discourse. And this is why I argue that teaching is also struggle for teachers.

59. Brodkey accentuates her point about class concerns in writing with the observation: "To the credit of the teachers who participated in this study, none took the usual recourse of justifying their discursive control by focusing on errors in spelling, grammar, and mechanics that are indubitably there and that make reading the literacy letters as difficult as reading Lacan, Derrida, Foucault, or Althusser. Yet the teachers frenetically protected educational discourse from class, and in their respective rcfusals to admit class concerns into the letters, they first distanced and then alienated themselves from their correspondents" ("Class and Gender," 1989, 139). Brodkey's remark also makes me wonder whether the student correspondents would have appreciated their teachers more if the teachers had actually taken the trouble to point out some of the most persistent grammar errors in the students' letters.

60. Influenced by pragmatism and antifoundationalism, Kent offers "paralogic rhetoric" derived from the Sophistic tradition as an alternative to "systemic rhetoric" based on the "Platonic-Aristotelian rhetorical tradition" ("Paralogic Hermeneutics" 1989, 25). Kent obviously intends that his "paralogic rhetoric" be the abnormal discourse in composition studies. However, in ignoring the relations of paralogic rhetoric to systemic rhetoric, Kent has missed a key point in the theories of Rorty, Derrida, and Donald Davidson—the inseparability of abnormal discourse from normal discourse (Rorty), the dependence of deconstruction upon tradition (Derrida, "Jacques Derrida on Rhetoric," 1991), and the inevitable connection between conventions and creativity (Davidson, in Dasenbrock, "Response," 1994, 37).

61. Lawson and Ryan observe that the vast majority of teachers "look at a paper in light of the writer's apparent intention and in terms of our expectations for the assignment, recognizing that our own biases influence evaluation." Such a practice, they argue, reveal that teachers "take for granted the notion that thoughts and ideas can be bracketed, analyzed, discussed, and finally written down intelligibly," that "written language can be stabilized" and ideas waiting to be expressed, and that teachers can make "quality judgments which conform to some sort of objective scale" and rank 'relative' success of a sample of student texts ("Introduction," 1989, xv). How should such a practice be changed if teachers consider it nonconstructive and disempowering?

62. See Kent's discussion of Davidson's "passing theory" in "Beyond the System" and Rorty's discussion of hermeneutic guessing in "The Contingency of Language" (1986).

63. See the debate over Deletiner's article in *College English* 55.6 (1993): "Comment & Response" 666–73. Evidently, Deletiner also teaches "academic discourse" in first-year English classes.

Works Cited

Arendt, Hannah. "What Is Authority?" *Authority*. Ed. Carl J. Friedrich. Cambridge, MA: Harvard University Press, 1958.

Aronowitz, Stanley, and Henry A. Giroux. *Education Under Siege: The Conservative, Liberal, and Radical Debate over Schooling*. South Hadley, MA: Bergin, 1985.

Ashton-Jones, Evelyn. "Collaboration, Conversation, and the Politics of Gender." *Feminine Principles and Women's Experience in American Composition and Rhetoric*. Ed. Louise Wetherbee Phelps and Janet Emig. University of Pittsburgh Press, 1995. 5–26.

Bakhtin, Mikhail (or V.N.Volosinov). *Marxism and the Philosophy of Language*. Trans. Ladislav Matejka and I.R. Titunik. New York: Seminar, 1973.

Ball, Stephen, ed. *Foucault and Education: Disciplines and Knowledge*. London: Routledge, 1990.

Bartholomae, David. "Inventing the University." *Perspectives in Literacy*. Ed. Eugene R. Kintgen, Barry M. Kroll, and Mike Rose. Carbondale: Southern Illinois University Press, 1988. 273–85.

Bartholomae, David, and Anthony Petrosky. *Facts, Counterfacts, and Artifacts: Theory and Method for a Reading and Writing Course*. Portsmouth, NH: Boynton/Cook, 1986.

Baym, Nina. "The Feminist Teacher of Literature: Feminist or Teacher?" *Gender in the Classroom: Power and Pedagogy*. Ed. Susan L. Gabriel and Isaiah Smithson. Urbana, IL: University of Illinois Press, 1990. 60–77.

Bechtel, Judith. "Why Teaching Writing Always Brings Up Questions of Equity." Caywood and Overing. 179–83.

Berlin, James A. "Contemporary Composition: The Major Pedagogical Theories." *College English* 44 (1982): 765–77.

———. "Rhetoric and Ideology in the Writing Class." *College English* 50 (1988): 477–94.

———. *Rhetoric and Reality: Writing Instruction in American Colleges, 1900–1985.* Carbondale: Southern Illinois University Press, 1987.

Berlin, James A., and Michael J. Vivion. *Cultural Studies in the English Classroom.* Portsmouth, NH: Boynton/Cook, 1992.

Berthoff, Ann E. "From Problem-solving to a Theory of Imagination." *College English* 33 (1972): 636–49.

Bineham, Jeffrey. "The Cartesian Anxiety in Epistemic Rhetoric." *Philosophy and Rhetoric* 23.1 (1990): 43–62.

Bizzell, Patricia. "Composing Processes: An Overview." *The Teaching of Writing.* Eighty-fifth Yearbook of the National Society for the Study of Education, Part 2. Ed. Anthony R. Petrosky and David Bartholomae. Chicago: National Society for the Study of Education, 1986. 49–70.

———. "Foundationalism and Anti-Foundationalism in Composition Studies." *PRE/TEXT* 7.1-2 (1986): 37–56.

———. "What Happens When Basic Writers Come to College?" *College Composition and Communication* 37 (1986): 294–301.

———. "Arguing about Literacy." *College English* 50 (1988): 141–53.

———. "Beyond Anti-Foundationalism to Rhetorical Authority: Problems Defining 'Cultural Literacy.'" *College English* 52 (1988): 661–75.

———. "Classroom Authority and Critical Pedagogy." *American Literary History* 3 (1991): 847–63.

———. "Power, Authority, and Critical Pedagogy." *Journal of Basic Writing* 10.2 (1991): 54–70.

———. *Academic Discourse and Critical Consciousness.* Pittsburgh: University of Pittsburgh Press, 1992.

———. "Marxist Ideas in Compostion Studies." *Contending with Words.* Ed. Patricia Harkin and John Schilb. New York: MLA, 1991. 52–68.

Bleich, David. *The Double Perspective: Language, Literacy and Social Relations.* New York: Oxford University Press, 1988.

Blitz, Michael, and C. Mark Hurlbert. "An Uncomfortable State of Mind." *Composition and Resistance.* Ed. C. Mark Hurlbert and Michael Blitz. Portsmouth, NH: Boynton/Cook, 1991. 43–46.

Bloom, Allan. *The Closing of the American Mind.* New York: Simon and Schuster, 1987.

Bourdieu, Pierre, and Jean-Claude Passeron. *Reproduction in Education, Society and Culture.* Trans. Richard Nice and Tom Bottommore. London: Sage, 1977.

Brodkey, Linda. "On the Subject of Class and Gender in 'The Literacy of Letters.'" *College English* 51 (1989): 125–41.

Bronowski, J., and Bruce Mazlish. *The Western Intellectual Tradition.* New York: Harper and Row, 1960.

Bruffee, Kenneth. "The Way Out." *College English* 33 (1972): 457–70.

———. "Collaborative Learning and the 'Conversation of Mankind.'" *College English* 46 (1984): 635–52.

———. "Peer Tutoring and the 'Conversation of Mankind.'" *Writing Centers: Theory and Administration.* Ed. Gary A. Olson. Urbana, IL: National Council of Teachers of English (NCTE), 1984.

———. "Social Construction, Language, and the Authority of Knowledge: A Bibliography." *College English* 48 (1988): 773–90.

Bryden, David P. "It Ain't What They Teach, It's the Way That They Teach It." *The Public Interest* 103 (spring 1991): 38–53.

Bullock, Richard, and John Trimbur, eds. *The Politics of Writing Instruction: Postsecondary*, gen. ed. Charles Schuster. Portsmouth, NH: Boynton/Cook, 1991.

Caputo, John D. "The Thought of Being and the Conversation of Mankind: The Case of Heidegger and Rorty." *Hermeneutics and Praxis*. Ed. Robert Hollinger. Notre Dame, IN: University of Notre Dame Press, 1985. 248–71.

Carino, Peter. "Deconstruction for Cultural Critique: Teaching Raymond Carver's 'What We Talk About When We Talk About Love." *Cultural Studies in the English Classroom*. Ed. James A. Berlin and Michael J. Vivion. Portsmouth, NH: Boynton/Cook, 1992. 283–95.

Caywood, Cynthia L., and Gillian Overing. *Teaching Writing: Pedagogy, Gender, and Equity*. Albany, NY: State University of New York Press, 1987.

Cixous, Hélène. "The Laugh of the Medusa." *New French Feminisms*. Ed. Elaine Marks and Isabelle de Courtivron. Amherst, MA: University of Massachusetts Press, 1980. 245–6.

Clifford, John. "Review of *Cognitive Processes in Writing*." Ed. Lee W. Gregg and Erwin R. Steinberg. *College Composition and Communication* 39 (1988): 99–101.

———. "The Neopragmatic Scene of Theory and Practice in Composition." *Rhetoric Review* 10.1 (1991): 100–07.

Connolly, William E. "Modern Authority and Ambiguity." *Authority Revisited*. Ed. J. Roland Pennock and John W. Chapman. New York: New York University Press, 1987. 9–27.

Cooper, Marilyn M. "Unhappy Consciousness in First-Year English: How to Figure Things Out for Yourself." *Writing as Social Action*. Ed. Marilyn M. Cooper and Michael Holzman. Portsmouth, NH: Boynton/Cook, 1989. 28–60.

———. "Why Are We Talking about Discourse Communities?" Cooper and Holzman 202–20.

Cooper, Marilyn M., and Michael Holzman. *Writing as Social Action.* Portsmouth, NH: Boyton/Cook, 1989.

Crowley, Sharon. *A Teacher's Introduction to Deconstruction.* Urbana: NCTE, 1989.

Dasenbrock, Reed Way. "The Myths of the Subjective and of the Subject in Composition Studies." *Journal of Advanced Composition* 13 (1993): 21–32.

———. "A Response to 'Language Philosophy, Writing, and Reading: A Conversation with Donald Davidson.'" *Philosophy, Rhetoric, Literary Criticism.* Ed. Gary A. Olson. Carbondale: Southern Illinois University Press, 1994. 35–40.

———. "What to Teach When the Canon Closes Down: Toward a New Essentialism." *Reorientations.* Ed. Bruce Henricksen and Thais E. Morgan. Urbana, IL: University of Illinois Press, 1990. 63–76.

Daumer, Elizabeth, and Sandra Runzo. "Transforming the Composition Classroom." Caywood and Overing 45–62.

Davenport, Doris. "Dismantling White/Male Supremacy." *Social Issues in the English Classroom.* Ed. C. Mark Hurlbert and Samuel Totten. Urbana, IL: NCTE, 1992. 59–75.

Davis, Robert Con. "A Manifesto for Oppositional Pedagogy: Freire, Bourdieu, Merod, and Graff." *Reorinetations.* Ed. Bruce Henricksen and Thais E. Morgan. Urbana, IL: University of Illinois Press, 1990. 248–67.

Dean, Terry. "Multicultural Classrooms, Monocultural Teacher." *College Composition and Communication* 40 (1989): 23–27.

Deletiner, Carole. "Crossing Lines." *College English* (1992): 809–17.

Derrida Jacques. *Of Grammatology.* Trans. Gayatri Spivack. Baltimore, MD: Johns Hopkins University Press, 1976.

———. "Jacques Derrida on Rhetoric and Composition: A Conversation." *(Inter)views.* Ed. Gary A. Olson and Irene Gale. Carbondale, IL: Southern Illinois University Press, 1991. 119–41.

Donahue, Patricia, and Ellen Quandahl. *Reclaiming Pedagogy: The Rhetoric of the Classroom.* Carbondale: Southern Illinois University Press, 1989.

Dreyfus, Hubert L. "Holism and Hermeneutics." Hollinger 227–47.

Elbow, Peter. *Writing without Teachers.* New York: Oxford, 1973.

———. *Writing with Power: Techniques for Mastering the Writing Process.* New York: Oxford University Press, 1981.

———. "Closing My Eyes as I speak: An Argument for Ignoring Audience." *College English* 49 (1987): 50–69.

———. "Reflections on Academic Discourse: How It Relates to Freshmen and Colleagues." *College English* 53 (1991): 135–55.

Ellsworth, E. "Why Doesn't This Feel Empowering? Working through the Repressive Myths of Critical Pedagogy." *Harvard Educational Review* 59 (1989): 297–342.

Emig, Janet. *The Composing Process of Twelfth Graders.* Research Report no. 13. Urbana, IL: NCTE, 1971.

Enos, Theresa, ed. *A Sourcebook for Basic Writing Teachers.* New York: Random, 1987.

Ewell, Barbara C. "Empowering Otherness: Feminist Criticism and the Academy." *Reorientations.* Ed. Bruce Henricksen and Thais E. Morgan. Urbana, IL: University of Illinois Press, 1990. 43–62.

Faigley, Lester. "Competing Theories of Process: A Critique and a Proposal." College English 48 (1986): 527–42.

———. *Fragments of Rationality: Postmodernity and the Subject of Composition.* Pittsburgh, PA: University of Pittsburgh Press, 1992.

Fish, Stanley. *Is There a Text in this Class?* Cambridge, MA: Harvard University Press, 1980.

———. "Anti-Foundationalism, Theory Hope, and the Teaching of Composition." *The Current in Criticism: Essays on the Present and Future of Literary Theory*. Ed. Clayton Koelb and Virgil Lokke. West Lafayette, IN: Purdue University Press, 1987. 65–79.

———. "Fish Tales: A Conversation with 'The Contemporary Sophist.'" *Philosophy, Rhetoric, Literacy Criticism: Interviews*. Olson. Carbondale: Southern Illinois University Press, 1994. 43–67.

Flower, Linda. *Problem-Solving Strategies for Writing*. 2nd ed. San Diego: Harcourt, 1985.

Flower, Linda, and John Hayes. "A Cognitive Process Theory of Writing." *College Composition and Communication* 32 (1981): 365–87.

Fox, Thomas J. *The Social Uses of Writing: Politics and Pedagogy*. Norwood, NJ: Ablex, 1990.

Freire, Paulo. *Pedagogy of the Oppressed*. Trans. Myra Bergman Ramos. New York: Continuum, 1970.

———. *Education for Critical Consciousness*. New York: Seabury, 1973.

Gabriel, Susan L., and Isaiah Smithson, eds. *Gender in the Classroom: Power and Pedagogy*. Urbana, IL: University of Illinois Press, 1990.

Gale, Fredric G. *Political Literacy: Rhetoric, Ideology, and the Possibility of Justice*. Albany, NY: State University of New York Press, 1994.

Geertz, Clifford. *Local Knowledge: Further Essays in Interpretive Anthropology*. New York: Basic Books, 1983.

Giroux, Henry A. *Schooling and the Struggle for Public Life: Critical Pedagogy in the Modern Age*. Minneapolis: University of Minnesota Press, 1988.

———. *Teachers as Intellectuals: Toward a Critical Pedagogy of Learning*. Granby, MA: Bergin and Garvey, 1988.

————. "Reading Texts, Literacy, and Textual Authority." *Journal of Education* 172.1 (1990): 84–103.

————. *Border Crossings: Cultural Workers and the Politics of Education.* New York: Routledge, 1992.

————. "Textual Authority and the Role of Teachers as Public Intellectuals." *Social Issues in the English Classroom.* Ed. C. Mark Hurlbert and Samuel Totten. Urbana, IL: NCTE, 1992. 304–21.

Goodson, Ivor, and Ian Dowbiggin. "Docile Bodies: Commonalities in the History of Psychiatry and Schooling." *Foucault and Education.* Ed. Stephen Ball. London: Routledge, 1990. 105–29.

Graff, Gerald. *Beyond the Culture Wars: How Teaching the Conflicts Can Revitalize American Education.* New York: W. W. Norton, 1992.

Greene, Stuart. "Toward a Dialectical Theory of Composing." *Rhetoric Review* 9.1 (1990): 149–72.

Hairston, Maxine. "The Winds of Change: Thomas Kuhn and the Revolution in the Teaching of Writing." *College Composition and Communication* 33 (1982): 76–88.

————. "Diversity, Ideology, and Teaching Writing." *College Composition and Communication* 43 (1992): 179–93.

Harkin, Patricia, and John Schilb, eds. *Contending with Words: Composition and Rhetoric in a Postmodern Age.* New York: MLA, 1991.

Heath, Shirley Brice. *Ways with Words: Language, Life, and Work in Communities and Classrooms.* Cambridge, Eng.: Cambridge University Press, 1983.

Henricksen, Bruce. "Teaching against the Grain." *Reorientations.* Ed. Henricksen and Morgan. Urbana, IL: University of Illinois Press, 1990. 28–42.

Henricksen, Bruce, and Thais E. Morgan, eds. *Reorientations: Critical Theories & Pedagogies.* Urbana, IL: University of Illinois Press, 1990.

Hill, Carolyn Ericksen. *Writing from the Margin: Power and Struggle for Teachers of Composition.* New York: Oxford University Press, 1990.

Hollinger, Robert, ed. *Hermeneutics and Praxis.* Notre Dame, IN: University of Notre Dame Press, 1985.

Holt, Mara. "Knowledge, Social Relations, and Authority in Collaborative Practices of the 1930s and the 1950s." *College Composition and Communication* 44 (1993): 538–55.

Holzman, Michael. "A Post-Freirean Model for Adult Literacy Education." *College English* 50 (1988): 177–89.

———. "Observations on Literacy: Gender, Race, and Class." *The Politics of Writing Instruction: Postsecondary.* Ed. Richard Bullock and John Trimbur. Portsmouth, NH: Boynton, 1991. 297–305.

———. "The Social Context of Literacy Education." *Writing as Social Action.* Ed. Marilyn M. Cooper and Michael Holzman. Portsmouth, NH: Boynton/Cook, 1989. 133–39.

hooks, bell. *Yearning: Race, Gender, and Cultural Politics.* Boston: South End, 1990.

Hourigan, Maureen. *Beyond Gender: The Influence of Class and Culture on Students' Writing.* Ph.D. diss., University of South Florida, 1992.

Hurlbert, C. Mark. "This Desire for Change." *Composition and Resistance.* Ed. C. Mark Hurlbert and Michael Blitz. Portsmouth, NH: Boynton/Cook, 1991. 139–44.

Hurlbert, C. Mark, and Michael Blitz. "Rumors of Change: The Classroom, *Our* Classrooms, and *Big* Business." *Social Issues in the English Classroom.* Ed. C. Mark Hurlbert and Samuel Totton. Urbana, IL: NCTE, 1992. 269–82.

Hurlbert, C. Mark, and Michael Blitz, eds. *Composition and Resistance.* Portsmouth, NH: Boynton/Cook, 1991.

Hurlbert, C. Mark, and Samuel Totten, eds. *Social Issues in the English Classroom.* Urbana, IL: NCTE, 1992.

Jameson, Fredric. "Foreword." *The Postmodern Condition.* Jean-François Lyotard. Trans. Geoff Bennington and Brian Massumi. Minneapolis: University of Minnesota Press, 1984. vii–xxi.

———. *Postmodernism, or, The Cultural Logic of Late Capitalism.* Durkham: Duke University Press, 1990.

Jarratt, Susan C. "Feminism and Composition: The Case for Conflict." *Contending with Words.* Ed. Patricia Harkin and John Schilb. New York: MLA, 1991. 105–23.

Johnson, Richard. "What Is Cultural Studies Anyway?" Mimeo. Birmingham, Eng.: Centre for Contemporary Cultural Studies, 1984.

Kail, Harvey. "Narratives of Knowledge: Story and Pedagogy in Four Composition Texts." *Rhetoric Review* 6 (1988): 179–89.

Kent, Thomas. "Beyond System: The Rhetoric of Paralogy." *College English* 51 (1989): 492–507.

———. "Paralogic Hermeneutics and the Possibilities of Rhetoric." *Rhetoric Review* 8 (fall 1989): 24–42.

———. "On the Very Idea of a Discourse Community." *College Composition and Communication* 42 (1991): 425–45.

———. "Externalism and the Production of Discourse." *Journal of Advanced Composition* 12 (1992): 57–89.

Kerr, Clark. *The Great Transformation in Higher Education, 1960–1980.* Frontiers in Education Series. Albany, NY: State University of New York Press, 1988.

Kintgen, Eugene R., Barry M. Kroll, and Mike Rose, eds. *Perspectives in Literacy.* Carbondale: Southern Illinois University Press, 1988.

Klaus, Carl. "Public Opinion and Professional Belief." *College Composition and Communication* 26 (1976): 335–39.

Knoblauch, C. H. "Critical Teaching and Dominant Culture." *Composition and Resistance*. Ed. C. Mark Hurlbert and Michael Blitz. Portsmouth, NH: Boynton/Cook, 1991. 12–21.

———. "Some Observations on Freire's Pedagogy of the Oppressed." *Journal of Advanced Composition* 8 (1988): 50–54.

Knoper, Randall. "Deconstruction, Process, Writing." *Reclaiming Pedagogy*. Ed. Patricia Donahue and Ellen Quandahl. Carbondale: Southern Illinois University Press, 1989. 128–43.

Lawson, Bruce, and Susan Sterr Ryan. "Introduction: Interpretive Issues in Student Writing." Lawson, Bruce, Susan Sterr Ryan, and W. Ross Winterowd. *Encountering Student Texts*. Urbana, IL: NCTE, 1989. vii–xvii.

Lawson, Bruce, Susan Sterr Ryan, and W. Ross Winterowd. *Encountering Student Texts*. Urbana, IL: NCTE, 1989.

Lees, Elaine O. "The Exceptable Way of the Society: Stanley Fish's Theory of Reading and the Task of the Teacher of Editing." Donahue and Quandahl 144–63.

Lindemann, Erika. "Freshman Composition: No Place for Literature." *College English* 55 (1993): 311–16.

Lortie, Dan C. *Schoolteacher: A Sociological Study*. Chicago: Chicago University Press, 1975.

Lu, Min-Zhan. "Redefining the Legacy of Mina Shaughnessy: A Critique of the Politics of Linguistic Innocence." *Journal of Basic Writing* 10 (1991): 26–40.

———. "Conflict and Struggle: The Enemies or Preconditions of Basic Writing?" *College English* 54 (1992): 887–913.

———. "Symposium on Basic Writing, Conflict and Struggle, and the Legacy of Mina Shaughnessy." *College English* 55 (1993): 894–903.

Lutz, William D. "Making Freshman English a Happening." *College Composition and Communication* 22 (1971): 35–38.

Lyotard, Jean-François. *The Postmodern Condition: A Report on Knowledge*. Trans. Geoff Bennington and Brian Massumi. Minneapolis: University of Minnesota Press, 1984.

Martin, L., H. Gutman, and P. Hutton, eds. *Technologies of the Self*. London: Tavistock, 1988.

McKoski, Nancy. "A Postmodern Critique of the Modern Projects of Fredric Jameson and Patricia Bizzell." *Journal of Advanced Composition* 13 (1993): 329–44.

McLaren, Peter. "Foreword: Critical Theory and the Meaning of Hope." *Teachers as Intellectuals*. Henry Giroux. Granby, MA: Bergin and Garvey, 1988. ix–xxi.

Meisner, Maurice. *Mao's China and After: A History of the People's Republic*. New York: Free, 1977.

Middendorf, Marilyn. "Bakhtin and the Dialogic Writing Class." *Journal of Basic Writing* 11 (1992): 34–46.

Miller, J. Hillis. "Rhetoric, Cultural Studies, and the Future of Critical Theory: A Conversation with J. Hillis Miller." *Philosophy, Rhetoric, Literary Criticism: (Inter)views*. Gary A. Olson. Carbondale: Southern Illinois University Press, 1994. 115–43.

———. "Nietzsche in Basel: Writing Reading." *Journal of Advanced Composition* 13 (1993): 311–28.

Miller, Richard E. "Fault Lines in the Contact Zone." *College English* 56 (1994): 389–408.

Morgan, Thais E. "Reorientations." *Reorientations*. Ed. Bruce Henricksen and Thais E. Morgan. Urbana, IL: University of Illinois Press, 1990. 3–27.

Mortensen, Peter, and Gesa E. Kirsch. "On Authority in the Study of Writing." *College Composition and Communication* 44 (1993): 556–72.

Murray, Donald. *A Writer Teaches Writing*. Boston: Houghton, 1968.

Neel, Jasper. "Learning about Learning about Deconstruction: An Epi(tryingtobe)gone." *Philosophy, Rhetoric, Literary Criticism: (Inter)views.* Gary A. Olson. Carbondale: Southern Illinois University Press, 1994. 152–58.

North, Stephen M. "Rhetoric, Responsibility, and the 'Language of the Left.'" *Composition and Resistance.* Ed. C. Mark Hurlbert and Michael Blitz. Portsmouth, NH: Boynton/Cook, 1991. 127–36.

———. *The Making of Knowledge in Composition: Portrait of an Emerging Field.* Upper Montclair, NJ: Boynton, 1987.

Ogbu, John U. "Cultural Diversity and School Experience." *Literacy as Praxis.* Ed. Catherine Walsh. Norwood, NJ: Ablex, 1991. 25–50.

———. *The Next Generation: An Ethnography of Education in an Urban Neighborhood.* New York: Academic, 1974.

Ohmann, Richard. "Literacy, Technology, and Monopoly Capital." *The Politics of Letters.* Richard Ohmann. Middletown, Conn.: Westleyan University Press, 1987. 215–29.

———. "On Speculacy." *The Politics of Letters.* Richard Ohmann. Middletown, Conn.: Westleyan University Press, 1987. 236–40.

Olson, Gary A. *Philosophy, Rhetoric, Literary Criticism: (Inter)views.* Carbondale: Southern Illinois University Press, 1994.

Olson, Gary A., and Irene Gale. *(Inter)views: Cross-Disciplinary Perspectives on Rhetoric and Literacy.* Carbondale, IL: Southern Illinois University Press, 1991.

Paine, Charles. "Relativisim, Radical Pedagogy, and the Ideology of Paralysis." *College English* 51 (1989): 557–70.

Petraglia, Joseph. "Interrupting the Conversation: The Constructionist Dialogue in Composition." *Journal of Advanced Composition* 11 (1991): 37–55.

Petrosky, Anthony R. "Review of *Problem-Solving Strategies for Writing,* by Linda Flower." *College Composition and Communication* 34 (1983): 233–35.

Philips, Susan Urmston. *The Invisible Culture: Communication in Classroom and Community on the Warm Springs Indian Reservation.* New York: Longman, 1983.

Reid, Louann, and Jeff Golub. "An Interactive Approach to Composition Instruction." *Composition and Resistance.* Ed. C. Mark Hurlbert and Michael Blitz. Portsmouth, NH: Boynton/Cook, 1991. 82–91.

Rorty, Richard. *Philosophy and the Mirror of Nature.* Princeton, NJ: Princeton University Press, 1979.

———. "The Contingency of Language." *London Review of Books* April 17, 1986: 3–6.

Rose, Mike. "The Language of Exclusion." *College English* 47 (1985): 341–59.

———. *Lives on the Boundary: The Struggles and Achievements of America's Underprepared.* New York: Penguin, 1989.

———. "Remedial Writing Courses: A Critique and a Proposal." *A Sourcebook for Basic Writing Teachers.* Ed. Theresa Enos. New York: Random, 1987. 104–24.

Schilb, John. "On Personally Constructing 'Social Construction': A Response to Richard Rorty." *(Inter)views: Cross-Disciplinary Perspectives on Rhetoric and Literacy.* Carbondale, IL: Southern Illinois University Press, 1991. 238–40.

Scribner, Sylvia, and Michael Cole. *The Psychology of Literacy.* Cambridge, MA: Harvard University Press, 1981.

Seitz, James. "Roland Barthes, Reading, and Roleplay: Composition's Misguided Rejection of Fragmentary Texts." *College English* 53 (1991): 815–25.

Shank, Michael H., and David Vampola. "Negating Positivism: Language and the Practice of Science." *The Philosophy of Discourse.* vol. 1. Ed. Chip Sills and George H. Jensen. Portsmouth, NH: Boynton, 1992.

Shaughnessy, Mina P. *Errors and Expectations: A Guide for the Teacher of Basic Writing*. New York: Oxford University Press, 1977.

Sheils, Merrill. "Why Johnny Can't Write." *Newsweek* 8 December 1975: 58–65.

Shor, Ira. *Critical Teaching and Everyday Life*. Boston: South End, 1980.

———. *Culture Wars: School and Society in the Conservative Restoration, 1969–1984*. Boston: Routledge, 1986.

———, ed. *Freire for the Classroom: A Sourcebook for Liberatory Teaching*. Portsmouth, NH: Boynton/Cook, 1987.

Shor, Ira, and Paulo Freire. *A Pedagogy for Liberation: Dialogues on Transforming Education*. Massachusetts: Bergin, 1987.

———. "What Is the 'Dialogic Method' of Teaching?" *Journal of Education* 169.3 (1987): 11–31.

Simon, John. *Paradise Lost*. New York: Penguin, 1980.

Simon, R. "Empowerment as a Pedagogy of Possibility." *Language Arts* 64 (1987): 370–81.

Sledd, Andrew, and James Sledd. "A Comment on 'Beyond Anti-Foundationalism to Rhetorical Authority.'" *College English* 53 (1991): 717–21.

Smith, Louise Z. *Audits of Meaning*. Portsmouth, NH: Boynton, 1988.

Smith, Robert C., and Richard Seltzer. *Race, Class, and Culture: A Study in Afro-American Mass Opinion*. Albany, NY: State University of New York Press, 1992.

Smith III, Robert E. "Reconsidering Richard Rorty." *College English* 54 (1992): 138–58.

Snook, I. A., ed. *Concepts of Indoctrination: Philosophical Essays*. London: Routledge, 1972.

Spellmeyer, Kurt. "Foucault and the Freshman Writer: Considering the Self in Discourse." *College English* 51 (1989): 715–29.

———. "Being Philosophical about Composition: Hermeneutics and the Teaching of Writing." *Into the Field: Sites of Composition Studies.* Ed. Anne Ruggles Gere. New York: MLA, 1993.

———. "Knowledge against 'Knowledge': Freshman English, Public Discourse, and the Social Imagination." *Composition and Resistance.* Ed. C. Mark Hurlbert and Michael Blitz. Portsmouth, NH: Boynton/Cook, 1991. 70–80.

Stewart, Donald C. "Collaborative Learning and Composition: Boon or Bane?" *Rhetoric Review* 7.1 (1988): 58–83.

Stuckey, J. Elspeth. *The Violence of Literacy.* Portsmouth, NH: Boynton: 1991.

Tate, Gary. "A Place for Literature in Freshman Composition." *College English* 55 (1993): 317–21.

Tebo-Messina, Margaret. "Authority and Models of the Writing Workshop: All Collaborative Learning Is Not Equal." *Writing-Instructor* 8.2 (1989): 86–92.

Tobin, Lad. "Reading Students, Reading Ourselves: Revising the Teacher's Role in the Writing Class." *College English* 53 (1991): 333–48.

Tompkins, Jane. "A Short Course in Post-Structuralism." *College English* (1988): 733–47.

———. "Pedagogy of the Distressed." *College English* 52 (1990): 653–60.

Totten, Samuel. "Educating for the Development of Social Consciousness and Social Responsibility." *Social Issues in the English Classroom.* Ed. C. Mark Hurlbert and Samuel Totten. Urbana, IL: NCTE, 1992. 9–55.

Trimbur, John. "Articulation Theory and the Problem of Determination: A Reading of *Lives on the Boundary.*" *Journal of Advanced Composition* 13 (1993): 33–50.

Tuman, Myron C. "Class, Codes, and Composition: Basil Bernstein and the Critique of Pedagogy." *College Composition and Communication* 39 (1988): 51.

Villanueva, Victor. "Considerations for American Freirestas." *The Politics of Writing Instruction: Postsecondary.* Ed. Richard Bullock and John Trimbur. Portsmouth, NH: Boynton/Cook, 1991. 247–62.

Walsh, Catherine, ed. *Literacy as Praxis: Culture, Language, and Literacy.* Norwood, NJ: Ablex, 1991.

Willis, Paul. *Learning to Labor.* New York: Columbia University Press, 1981.

Wood, Robert G. "The Dialectic Suppression of Feminist Thought in Radical Pedagogy." *Journal of Advanced Composition* 13 (1993): 79–95.

Yee, Marian. "Are You the Teacher?" *Composition and Resistance.* Ed. C. Mark Hurlbert and Michael Blitz. Portsmouth, NH: Boynton/Cook, 1991. 24–42.

Zeiger, William. "The Exploratory Essay: Enfranchising the Spirit of Inquiry in College Composition." *College English* 47 (1985): 454–66.

Index

abnormal discourse, viii, 4, 65,
68–72, 73, 166n.28, 166n.31
(*see also* Responsive Abnormal
Discourse; Nonresponsive
Abnormal Discourse)
academic discourse, 20–22, 74–75,
141–143, 164n.22, 165n.26,
168n.37, 175n.63; community,
vii, 2, 31; as passport, 22, 30;
change of, 72–73
academic audience, 102
academic freedom, 172n.54
academic institution: authority of,
41–42, 43–45; autonomy of, 36,
39, 46; dual role of, 36; relations
with dominant groups, 39–46
agents: students as, 31 (*see also*
Subjects)
antidialogue, 24–25
antifoundationalist: criticism, 61;
teacher, 127–128; theory, 62–63;
stance, 161n.7; 165n.24
Arendt, Hannah, 33
Aronowitz, Stanley, and Henry A.
Giroux, 34–37, 49, 50–51, 86
Ashton-Jones, Evelyn, 66
attitudes toward student writing.
See student writing
assimilation, 171n.53
audience. *See* academic audience;
stabilized social audience
authority: assumptions about, 34;
classroom, vii, 133–134;
162n.17; institutional (*See*
Institutional Authority); of expertise, 46–49, 161n.18; pedagogic,
8, 45; personal, 8, 49–55,
162n.47; scholarly, 8; teacher's
(*See* teacher's authority)

authoritarian: institutional setting,
15 (*see also* Classroom)
autonomous minorities, 104
autonomy of academic institution.
See academic institution

Back-to-Basics movement, 42–44
banking concept of education, 24
Bakhtin, Mikhile, 99–100,
108–110, 122, 169nn.43, 44
Bartholomae, David, 141
Baym, Nina, 136–138
Bechtel, Judith, 27–28
Berlin, James, 13, 15, 16, 17, 18,
28, 29, 115
Berthoff, Ann E., 125–126
Bizzell, Patricia, 4, 51–53, 61–62,
87–88, 141
Bloom, Allan, 112–114
Bourdieu, Pierre, and Jean-Claude
Passeron, 3, 8–12, 37–39, 48,
53, 76–77, 81
Brodkey, Linda, 144–145
Bryden, David P., 111–113
Bruffee, Kenneth, 4, 18, 19–22,
30–31, 64–65, 101–102,
125–126, 141–142

Canon, the, 2; battle over, 60; new,
165n.25; reading, 111–114
Caputo, John D., 58–59
Carino, Peter, 73
Cixous, Hélène, 78–79
class, 168n.41
classless society, 8
classroom: American, 26; interactive, 128, 132, 134, 170n.49;

insiders, 30, 142, 150
institutional confession. *See*
  Expressivist; Personal Writing
institutional authority, 29–30, 34,
  39, 46–47, 53–55, 151–153,
  163n.18
interaction: dialectic, 18; two-level,
  140; with Great Works, 111–114;
  with dominant ideology,
  115–116
interactive classroom. *See*
  Classroom
interdependence of institution and
  teaching, 37–46
interpretive community, 30
involuntary minorities, 105

juridical authority, 38

Kail, Harvey, 125–127
Kent, Thomas, 146
Knoblauch, C. H., 25–26, 138–140
Knoper, Randall, 148–150
knowledge: as social constructs,
  18; as linguistic entities, 18; cre-
  ation of, 18–19; impart, 20;
  teacher's, 2, 19
knowledgeable peers. *See*
  Community of Knowledgeable
  Peers
Kuhn, Thomas, 68–69

Lady Chatterly's Lover, 136–137
Lawson, Bruce, and Susan Sterr
  Ryan, 121–122, 148
learning, 114; active, 115–116;
  epistemological goal of, 115;
  liberatory, viii. *See also* Radical
  Pedagogy
Lees, Elaine O., 150–152
legitimacy crisis, 39–46
legitimacy of teacher's authority, 9,
  38–39, 48
Lindemann, Erika, 60

literacy, 30, 167n.35; letters,
  144; crisis in America, 42–46;
  crisis in China, 40–42
Lortie, Dan C., 86
Lu, Min-Zhan, 142-143
Lutz, William D., 15

marginal works, 32, 106
Marxian: theories, 73; values, 62
master narrative, 125–127
matrix: disciplinary, 169n.42; of
  thought, 19
McKoski, Nancy, 62
Miller, J. Hillis, 3, 60, 80–82,
  156–157
Miller, Richard E., 154
minorities: autonomous, 104;
  immigrant, 104–105; involuntary, 105; and school performance, 105–106; texts of, 106
mode: authoritarian-individualist, 19; dialectic, 32
monologue of the teacher, 10 (*see
  also* Teacher's Discourse)
Mortensen, Peter, and Gesa E.
  Kirsch, 48–50
Murray, Donald, 17

needs of the student, 21 (*see also*
  Student Writing)
neutrality of knowledge, 28
new paradigm, the, 12–13
Nietzsche, 80–81
Nonresponsive Abnormal
  Discourse, 5, 58, 80, 86, 88,
  107, 118
normal discourse, 4, 21, 64; definition, viii, 68–72; in teaching,
  129, 143, 166nn.28, 31
normal science, 68
nurturing teacher, 131–132;
  172n.55 (*see also* Teacher)
Neel, Jasper, 61